STUDENT SUCCESS

■ ■ ■

Douglas College

Editors: Amy Modahl and Jillian Hull

Second Edition

KENDALL/HUNT PUBLISHING COMPANY
4050 Westmark Drive   Dubuque, Iowa 52002

Copyright © 2002, 2004 by Douglas College

ISBN 0-7575-1179-1

Kendall/Hunt Publishing Company has the exclusive rights to reproduce this work,
to prepare derivative works from this work, to publicly distribute this work,
to publicly perform this work and to publicly display this work.

All rights reserved. No part of this publication may be reproduced,
stored in a retrieval system, or transmitted, in any form or by any
means, electronic, mechanical, photocopying, recording, or otherwise,
without the prior written permission of Kendall/Hunt Publishing Company.

Printed in the United States of America
10 9 8 7 6 5 4 3 2 1

CONTENTS

Chapter 1 ■ College Orientation   1

Chapter 2 ■ Time Management   13

Chapter 3 ■ Learning Styles/Instructional Styles   47

Chapter 4 ■ Remembering to Concentrate   69

Chapter 5 ■ Active Listening and Note Taking Skills   87

Chapter 6 ■ Reading and Note Taking   109

Chapter 7 ■ Critical Thinking and Analysis   123

Chapter 8 ■ Writing a Research Paper   161

Chapter 9 ■ Preparing for and Taking Tests   207

Chapter 10 ■ Teamwork   239

Chapter 11 ■ Communication   245

Chapter 12 ■ Identifying and Dealing with Stress   257

Chapter 13 ■ Managing Your Finances   283

Chapter 14 ■ Planning for a Career   293

CHAPTER 1
College Orientation

What Does It Mean to Have a College Education?

When asked what college means to them, students say such things as it's:

" . . . a means to a better job."
" . . . something to do instead of working."
" . . . my parents' dream for me."
" . . . something that comes after high school."
" . . . a place to learn."
" . . . a place to be irresponsible and have fun."

While a college experience may be any or all of the above for a student, a college education is not a product nor a "thing" one gets; it is a process one participates in. A college education:

- is an exposure to a life and a way of looking at the world through many new and different lenses.
- can provide a better understanding of the world in which we live and increase our ability for meaningful interactions within our environments.
- expands and deepens an increasing awareness of our creativity.
- provides an opportunity to grow in compassion and understanding of other people, to gain a new appreciation of differences, and a new sense of responsibility for our life.
- helps develop effective problem solving skills and strategies that equip us for various employment, cultural, and interpersonal opportunities.

The comedian Woody Allen is reported to have said that 80 percent of success in life simply comes from "showing up." Unfortunately "showing up" is not enough to guarantee success in college. It's what a student chooses "to do" after "showing up" that makes the difference. The college furnishes the environment and the opportunities for success. The task for every student is to decide whether or not to take advantage of those opportunities. Attending class, completing assignments, interacting with professors, passing tests, and being involved in extracurricular activities are important parts of the next

---

From *Your Utah State Experience: Strategies for Success, Fourth Edition* by Utah State University Academic Support Services. © 1998 by Utah State University Academic Support Services. Used by permission of Kendall/Hunt Publishing Company.

four years. Equally important are the decisions made, the goals set, and the relationships formed. In sum, your college experience depends on what you choose to do now that you have shown up.

> *"Now, here, you see, it takes all the running you can do to keep in the same place. If you want to get somewhere else, you must run twice as fast as that."*
>
> Lewis Carroll
> *Through the Looking-Glass*

Realizing that the first year is a challenging time, the college provides a wealth of resources to help its new students with the transition. Read carefully and think about the transition and what it means to you. Catalogs outline the campus offices, clubs, and opportunities for students. Find out what offices, services, policies and clubs your college offers by completing Exercise 1: Campus Treasure Hunt.

New students are encouraged to join clubs and participate in campus activities. Campus involvement is a way of making connections with the larger student body. A word of caution: balance in life is an important ingredient of success. A careful examination of personal goals and use of time gives one a fairly good idea of how to balance the time between studies, work, and extracurricular activities.

What Is Expected of New Students?

> *"The freedom from work, from restraint, from accountability, wondrous in its inception, became banal and counterfeit. Without rules there was no way to say no, and worse, no way to say yes."*
>
> Thomas Farber

In a college community, each student has the freedom to choose to participate or not participate in extracurricular activities, courses, or meetings. Many students find this personal freedom liberating, but it's important to note where personal freedom ends and interests of the larger college community begin. Students are expected to assume responsibility for their own education and behaviour. Among these expectations are the following:

Classroom Conduct

Appropriate classroom conduct is expected of all students. Students should arrive at class on time and be prepared with the necessary books, notes, paper, and writing supplies. Coming prepared to class also means having completed assigned readings, reviewed notes, and prepared questions.

Working on homework from another course, reading the campus newspaper during class, carrying on side conversations, and chattering during a lecture are not appropriate.

Cultivating Relationships with Faculty Is Important

Develop the interpersonal skills that promote interaction with instructors. The first step is to find out what they expect of students and what students can expect from them. This information is usually found in the course syllabus and/or is discussed on the first day of class. Generally speaking, most professors expect students to:

- *Attend class regularly.* You lose when you skip a class. If you must miss a class arrange for another student to keep notes for you (don't expect instructors to give you theirs). Make sure you get any assignments that were announced.

- *Accept responsibility.* Don't make excuses; accept responsibility for your own learning.
- *Submit high quality work in both content and form.* Do the best you can in quality and neatness. Students who have difficulty writing papers should seek a tutor. Some instructors only accept typed papers, and students without personal computers should take advantage of the campus computer labs.
- *Turn assignments in on time.* Late assignments suggest a lack of enthusiasm and commitment. Habitually handing assignments in late is a bad habit that employers are less forgiving of.
- *Arrive on time and be attentive in class.* Late arrivals are a distraction to the entire class. If you must be late, find the nearest convenient seat and quickly and quietly sit down.
- *Participate in class discussions.* Participation in class is valued by some instructors and not encouraged by others. Follow the preferences for each instructor.
- *Meet with your instructors outside of class.* A good way to get to know your teacher is to prepare some questions based on previous classes, readings and your own reflections that you can ask the professor before, after class, or in his/her office.

Academic Honesty

The faculty and staff expect students and faculty alike to maintain the highest standards of academic honesty. Dishonesty includes but is not limited to:

- Stealing a copy of the exam ahead of time
- Copying from someone else's paper
- Sending or receiving signals during an exam
- Using unauthorized notes during an exam
- Taking an exam for another student
- Letting another student take an exam for you
- Handing in a paper that you have not written

Plagiarism is a specific form of cheating in which a student fails to give proper credit for written work that belongs to someone else. It is trying to pass off the work of others as one's own. Students falsely assume that they will not be caught; however, instructors are very adept at identifying work that has been incorrectly documented or "borrowed" from another source without proper citation. Knowingly representing the words or ideas of another as your own in any academic exercise or activity carries with it serious consequences.

Elements of Success

Success in all of its forms and varieties is a goal of every student who enrolls at the college. However, wanting to succeed and doing what is necessary to succeed are two very different things. This section details suggestions and ideas about how to bridge the gap between desiring and actually achieving success. We encourage you to read and make use of the ideas presented because they are only as helpful as you make them. There are no quick fixes, no easy answers.

> *"Two roads diverged in a wood and I took the one less traveled by, and that has made all the difference."*
>
> *Robert Frost*
> *The Road Not Taken*

The first step in succeeding at something is realizing that wanting to succeed is just the starting place. Additional factors in any successful college experience include: (1) attitude about school and life; (2) prior academic experience and ability; (3) ability to effectively manage time and to discipline oneself; (4) ability to relate to and get along with others; and, (5) the learning environment.

Attitude

Attitude is a combination of thoughts and feelings. Much of a student's attitude about college is determined by how and why s/he chose to be here and how s/he feel about that choice. Some students find themselves in college but are not aware how they arrived at the decision to attend. Do you want to be here? Are you in school because someone said you had to come? Enrolling in college because someone else said you should may motivate you to enroll, but won't necessarily enable you to succeed. In order to succeed, you need to have your own reasons for attending; you need to "own" the decision to come to school.

There are many different (but no right) reasons for attending college. Some students pursue a degree in order to get a good job or to advance into a higher position in their current job. Others come to school for social reasons—high school was fun, so college will be even more fun! Some would rather go to school than work full-time. Others find it an easy way to move away from home and have their parents or others pay for it! Some students decide on a college education because they love learning and see college as an opportunity to pursue that love.

The reasons for choosing to go to college are as limitless as the persons attending. Reasons for attending also change over time as events and circumstances unfold. Be reflective, visit with yourself from time to time about why you are here. Are those reasons being fulfilled? What are you doing to fulfill them?

The thing to remember is that when the days are long and the nights are short your attitude about school will determine how hard you are willing to work to make it work!

Experience and Ability

Prior academic experience and ability play an important role in your success. Students who arrive at the college with a strong academic background have an advantage. New ideas are more quickly assimilated when they can be associated with prior knowledge. Don't rest on your laurels—professors expect a lot.

This is not to say that a lack of prior strong academic experience prohibits success, but it will take greater commitment and hard work to catch on in some of your classes. It is also a fairly common experience for "average" high school students to "catch fire" in the stimulating environment of college.

Prior academic experience includes a knowledge of basic learning and life skills. Do you know how to study, how to manage time, how to set goals, and how to communicate effectively? Many students come to college unaware of the need for these skills. They register for classes, buy their books, attend the first day of class, and begin to "study." They are quickly disillusioned with the college and their own abilities as the old habits that worked in high school don't seem to be working now and the work piles higher and higher and the probability of success sinks lower and lower.

Success is not a matter of studying more or studying harder, it is a matter of studying smarter. An average student in high school will probably need to work harder and smarter to be an average student in college. College is definitely more difficult than high school, and success in high school does not necessarily ensure success in college. Taking the time to learn some study strategies that are applicable in all of your classes is time well spent.

1: COLLEGE ORIENTATION

Your experience introduces some basic college level study strategies on: listening and note-taking, how to read a textbook, test-taking, and memory. In addition, it explores some of the life skills appropriate and necessary for success. We challenge you to examine and reflect on your values and your goals and the strategies you need to develop as school begins. Principles and strategies that are helpful in learning how to successfully juggle the demands of college, work, family, friends, and extracurricular activities are described herein. Discover how learning takes place and how you can best structure your own learning experiences to promote success.

Experiences are dynamic. Periodically take the time to stop and reflect on yours. What's going right? Wrong? What can you do to sustain or alter the experiences you are having?

Self-Discipline

Self-discipline and effective time management are vital keys to success. Students who are self-disciplined are better able to handle the increased freedom that comes with college. One of the first things that is discovered about college life is that in many classes attendance is not required. Unfortunately, some students interpret this to mean that attendance is not important. Nothing can be farther from the truth. Skipping class is a poor strategy for achieving success. Having decided to enroll and having paid the tuition, deciding not to attend class is counterproductive and costly!

Self-discipline includes taking care of yourself physically, mentally, and emotionally. Many of these issues, including ways to enhance and improve existing strategies for self-discipline and effective time management are discussed in later chapters.

Interpersonal Skills

Another very important part of success at any college is the ability to relate to and get along with other people. This includes roommates, friends, other students, faculty, and family. Although satisfactory progress towards a degree is measured in grades, the sense of well-being and accomplishment may well be measured by the ability to make friends, relate to classmates, and interact with faculty.

Having significant people who support you in your decision to attend college is a big help in your success. These are the people who remind you of your commitment and encourage you to continue on with your plans when you are tired and discouraged. They are the same people who share in your accomplishments and your success. These people comprise an important part of your support network. Although they cannot make you succeed, they can remind you of your goals and even help lighten some of the burden you carry. Recognize their support. "Good strokes for good folks" goes a long way to ensuring their continued support.

Environment

Finally, success in college is determined by the learning environment which includes defining and setting up an area for studying. By following a few basic suggestions a supportive study environment can be created. Study in the same place at the same time and use a signal to tell roommates and yourself that you are studying.

The System

Understanding the language and system of a college can be an important part of your student success. As a new student, you already know how to register for classes. Likely you noticed when registering that there is a vocabulary specific to your college or the system of colleges and universities in your province. One goal of this course is to help familiarize students with the college system and language. To help meet this goal, your college registrar will present about the terminology of grading and transferring to other institutions. To start understanding the college language and system, begin by learning about GPA. First, what is GPA? and why is it important to you as a student? To investigate this topic and the ins and outs of grading at your college, complete Exercise 2: Grade Point Average.

In summary, a successful college student is one who is making satisfactory progress towards his or her personal and educational goals. The rate of progress (time it takes and the qualitative measurement of that progress (grades received) are determined by individual circumstances. Understanding the factors that impact on that success—attitude, prior academic experience, self-discipline, relations with others, and working/studying environment—helps to bridge the gap between wanting success and achieving success.

Reflect

1. In this chapter you learned that "appropriate classroom conduct is important." Do you agree or disagree with that statement? Why?

2. Your college calculates your GPA for you each semester and publishes it in your transcript. Considering this, why do you need to know how to calculate GPA?

3. This chapter listed a few of the elements that can lead to success for college students. What can you add to this list? What pointers can you offer your fellow college students?

Name: _____ Date: _____

■ Exercise 1: Campus Treasure Hunt

Get to know the services and facilities on your campus and familiarize yourself with campus policies by completing the treasure hunt below. The answers can be found by hunting the campus on foot and by searching the college website.

1. Are campus child care services free for students? What number should you call to get more information?
2. The Faculty of Health Sciences at your college offers services at a reduced price. What dental services do they offer?
3. Your college also has a Vision Centre. Does the vision centre offer reduced rates for students?
4. Where is the office for the Centre of Sport, Recreation, and Wellness?
5. Name four recreation and wellness activities that are offered this semester at your college.
6. What number do you call to make an appointment with an academic advisor?
7. Does your college have a centre for students with disabilities?
8. What kinds of counselling services are offered at your college? What number can you call to make an appointment?
9. What campus office provides information on bursaries, scholarships, and grants?
10. How can you become a member of the student newspaper at your college?
11. What free services are offered at your student's union building?
12. What hours is your campus library open on Saturdays? On Sundays?
13. What are the library's hours Monday to Friday?
14. Can you renew your library materials on-line?
15. Name two guides or tutorials provided on your library's web site.
16. What is one other service or facility on campus you think other students should know about?
17. Name two good locations to study on campus?

Refer to the college policies published on the college website to answer the following questions:

18. How does your college define disruptive/inappropriate behaviour?
19. Give one example of a disruptive behaviour covered in the policy.
20. How does your college define violence?
21. Who should you inform if you observe a violent act or are the victim of a violent act on campus?

According to the Academic Dishonesty policy:

22. How does your college define plagiarism?
23. What is one thing an instructor should do to encourage academic honesty?
24. What is one thing you can do to avoid academic dishonesty?
25. Name three possible consequences of an act of academic dishonesty.

Name: _____ Date: _____

■ Exercise 2: Grade Point Average

Getting to know GPA

1. What is GPA?
2. Why is GPA important to you as a student?
3. List three things that can prevent you from getting the grades you want.
4. List three things that you can do to help yourself achieve the grades you want.
5. What is Term GPA? How is it calculated?
6. What is Cumulative GPA? How is it calculated?
7. Douglas College calculates your cumulative GPA on your grade report. Why should you have to know how to calculate GPA?

The True and the False of GPA

1. A "W" on your transcript is equal to an "F" in your Grade Point Average.
2. To drop a course and receive a "W" all you have to do is tell your teacher you are dropping.
3. Your teacher will tell you when the last date to withdraw is.
4. If you repeat a course at Douglas College, the best grade you receive will be the only grade calculated into your GPA.
5. A "UN" is better than an "F".

Calculate Grade Point Average

Directions: Joe Student just finished his second semester at Douglas College. Help Joe figure out his *term GPA* from his first semester. Then calculate his *cumulative GPA* for his first year in school. Find the Grade Points for each letter by searching the Douglas College website.

Calculate GPA for Joe's first term: *Term GPA*

1. In column D, fill in the Grade Points that correspond to the letter grade Joe Student received.
2. For each course, multiply the Credits (column C) by the Grade Points (column D). Write your results for each row in column E.
3. At the bottom of column C, write the total number of credits Joe Student took in his first semester.
4. Add the sums you recorded in column E.
5. Divide the total for column E by the amount of credits Joe took this semester (column C total).

\	\	\	\	\
\multicolumn{5}{c}{**Table 1: Joe's first semester**}
A	**B**	**C**	**D**	**E**
Course	Letter Grade	Credits	1. Grade Points	2. Credits x Grade Points
History 120	C −	(3 cr.)	1.67	5.01
French 101	B	(3 cr.)	3.00	9.00
Biology 100	F	(5 cr.)	0	0
STSU 100	B	(3 cr.)	3.00	9.00
	3. **Total for column C:**	14	4. **Total for column E:**	23.01
Term GPA 5. **Divide** Total for column E by Total for column C:				1.64

What should Joe have done differently to achieve a better GPA?

What might Joe do to bring up his GPA?

Calculate GPA for Joe's first year: *Cumulative GPA*

1. In column D, fill in the Grade Points that correspond to the letter grade Joe Student received.
2. For each course, multiply the Credits (column C) by the Grade Points (column D). Write your results for each row in column E.
3. At the bottom of column C, write the total number of credits Joe Student took in first and second semesters.
4. In column E, add the sums you recorded in each row to the to Joe's first semester column E total.
5. Divide the total in column E by the total in column C.

\multicolumn{5}{c	}{**Table 2: Joe's Second Semester**}
A	**B**	**C**	**D**	**E**
Course	Letter Grade	Credits	1. Grade Points	2. Credits x Grade Points
English 130	B –	(3 cr.)	2.67	8.11
French 102	A	(3 cr.)	4.00	12.00
Biology 100	B	(5 cr.)	3.00	15.00
Math 110	W	(3 cr.)		
3. **Total for column C, include semesters 1 & 2:**		11	4. **Total for column E, include both semesters:**	35.21
Cumulative GPA 5. **Divide** Total for column E by Total for column C:				3.18

What did Joe do to bring up his second term GPA?

Now that you have looked at the results of Joe's first two semesters in college, what advice can you give him before he starts his third semester?

11

Douglas College Grade Information on the Web

Directions Search the Douglas College website to find answers to the questions below.

For this semester . . .

1. What is the last day you can drop a course and have no record of the course on your transcript (without receiving a "W" on your record)?
2. Will you get any refund if you drop on the above day?
3. What is the last date you can withdraw from a course and still receive a "W" on your transcript?
4. Will you get any refund if you drop on the above day?
5. Where at on the college campus can you go for help with your homework or when you feel stressed by school and life?

Part 2: Search the BC Transfer Guide at http://www.bccat.bc.ca/.

8. Does *Douglas College Math 110* transfer to SFU?
9. Does *Douglas College English 130* transfer to UBC?
10. Does *Douglas College English 124* transfer to University of Victoria?

CHAPTER 2
Time Management

It's a sad but true fact that much of your success or failure in college (and probably the factor that you can control the most) depends directly on how you manage your time. Even though it is such an important factor to master, it is probable that most of us have developed our "time management plan" simply by habit and not by devising a workable action plan. Have you ever stopped to consider that time is one thing in life that can never be saved? It can only be spent and, unfortunately, too many of us have developed the skill of wasting time to a fine art! We may value many things and possessions in life, yet if we had all the money in the world we could not buy one hour. Maybe we should examine this valuable commodity a little more closely!

Before continuing this chapter, complete Exercise 1 to uncover where you currently spend your time.

■ New Outlook on Time[1]

You have probably already noticed that the way you use your time in college is much different from the way you used it in high school. In college, you are expected to be much more responsible for your own scheduling. For example:

1. In college, many courses do not meet daily. It is essential to keep track of class times, assignments and due dates.

2. Many college instructors do not take attendance. If you miss class, you will have a vague awareness that your grades will suffer, but attendance is up to you.

3. Usually "homework" is not turned in on a class-by-class basis, but assignments are more long-term. They require more sophisticated scheduling to be completed on time. The same is true for studying for tests—preparation is a more long-term project.

4. College work is demanding. You need to plan to study two hours outside of class for every hour in class. So if you're carrying 15 credit hours, your total time commitment is 45 hours—the equivalent of a full time job.

5. Your parents are less likely to keep tabs on your assignments; and your friends are more likely to come up with tempting activities to distract you from your studies.

---
[1]From *Practical Approaches for Building Study Skills and Vocabulary, Second Edition* by Funk et al. © 1996 by Kendall/Hunt Publishing Company. Used by permission.

Time Management Strategies[2]

Effective time management will be your most important study strategy. To new college students facing academic, social, and personal demands, there never seems to be enough time. The academic environment presents new opportunities and challenges that appear to demand more time than you may think you have. You can't create more time, but you can become more skilled at how you manage time. Time management involves setting goals, planning, flexibility, commitment, and managing procrastination.

GOAL SETTING. Managing time and setting goals go hand-in-hand. Using your time wisely helps you to achieve what you want, when you want. Knowing what your goals are for college and your future career help guide decisions regarding the use of your time.

There are several types of goals:

- *Short-range or immediate:* Goals you want to achieve tomorrow, next week, or within the semester. (Attend class each week, find a study partner for each class, or locate the free math tutor services.)
- *Mid-range:* Goals you want to achieve within two to three years. (Complete all the general education requirements.)
- *Long-range:* Goals you want to achieve within five years. (Obtain a degree in biology.)

Establishing goals can be difficult. The following guidelines will help you:

- Goals must be related to your **values.** You will find it very difficult to pursue a goal that is not directly linked to something that is important and meaningful for you. For example, if the goal is to pursue a career in social work, but you do not value interpersonal relationships, it will be difficult to succeed in accomplishing it.
- Goals are **specific and concrete**. A goal must state exactly what you are going to do. It can't be some vague, hopeful wish. A goal to stop procrastinating sounds nice, but it is not specific. A specific goal would state, "I will write a study plan by the end of the first week of class so that I can finish my paper for English by the tenth week of the semester."
- Goals are **measurable.** Progress toward completion of the goal needs to be evaluated. ("I must select my paper topic by the fourth week of class to finish my paper by mid-term. When my paper is typed and bound by the day before it is due, I will have completed my goal.")
- Goals are **realistic**. Your goal must be attainable, taking into consideration personal resources and abilities. (If you have not taken an algebra class in high school, it is not realistic to register for Math 301, before taking Math 201 or Math 101.)
- Goals are **time framed.** Always set a beginning and end date for your goal.
- Goals are **written.** Committing a goal to writing makes it more concrete. It encourages you to be committed to completing it. A goal written on a piece of paper tacked to your bulletin board or written in your daily planner is difficult to ignore.

---

[2]From *Your Utah State Experience: Strategies for Success, Fourth Edition* by Utah State University Academic Support Services. © 1998 by Utah State University Academic Support Services. Used by permission of Kendall/Hunt Publishing Company.

- **Goals are shared.** Telling someone else of your goals establishes accountability. You will be less likely to procrastinate or waiver in your commitment to attaining the goal. Be sure to tell someone who will support you in your efforts to complete your goal.
- **Goals need to be flexible.** There are many factors that can affect attaining a goal. Rarely is a goal followed through to completion without any problems. Temporary setbacks that will interrupt progress are common. These interruptions do not have to keep you from reaching the goal. Instead, reexamine your plan, revise or make a new one. You may discover that the original time frame is unrealistic. Changing the goal may be necessary. (You may have reassessed what is important to you). This is okay, as long as the revisions are a way to ensure success versus avoiding doing something you really don't want to do. Establish short-range, mid-range, and long-range goals by completing Exercise 2: Goal Setting. Make your goals realistic and applicable to your academic life and professional life.

PLANNING. Your goals indicate where you want to go. Creating an action plan tells you how to get there. The saying, "If you don't know where you are going, you may end up somewhere else," is a good reminder of what happens without planning. Using these planning tools, write down specifically what you will do, and when and where you will do it. It is through a plan that "time management" becomes tangible and visible. It is no longer a "wish" or a "hope." Plans put you in charge of your time.

Making A Study Schedule

In this class, we will focus more on developing plans to meet short-range academic goals; for example, to finish a research paper, you will need to break down such a large assignment into manageable tasks that take small chunks of time to complete. The same can be done for any assignment, test, or studying you need to do.

Quantity

Each semester you will be bombarded with a wealth of information to process and remember. If you don't keep up with studying, reading, and attending class, you can get lost and find yourself unable to catch up when test time comes. For each hour spent in a class, you should plan to study two hours for that class. That adds up to 24 hours of studying in a week for a student taking 12 credits. When making a study schedule, make room in your schedule to devote 2 hours to every class hour. Making a schedule will help you review how you have spread out your time. Have you devoted hours to too many areas?

Learning

Even letting a week pass without devoting time to a class means you have double the work to do the next week to catch up. Because the human mind remembers better when it is exposed to the same information at least seven times, you should split up your study and review times to cover the same material multiple times.

Below is an example of how you might cover the same material seven times:

1. Read and make notes on assigned reading material.

2. At the end of your reading notes, summarize what you learned in your own words. Record any confusion or question you have so you can inquire in class.

3. Before class, take ten or fifteen minutes to review your reading notes and summary.

4. During class lecture, take notes and consider how the reading assignment and lecture material relate and build on each other. Ask any questions that arose from the reading assignment.

5. After class, within 24 hours, fill in your Cornell Notes (covered in the Note-taking chapter). Mark any gaps you need to investigate in your text or discuss with another student.

6. Within two to three days after class, meet with a classmate and compare notes. In your own words, discuss the reading and class lecture.

7. Within a week after class, make consolidation notes at the end of your class notes.

Repetition ZAP

Notice in the example above how the material was read then reviewed three times before class and three times after class. Each time you review material, ZAP, you are one step closer to putting it into your long-term memory. Think of each review time as a ZAP.

Multi-Sensory Review

Variety is the spice of life and is also what keeps studying productive. Don't plan to review a reading assignment three times by simply reading and rereading. Try to use as many of your senses as possible, so that you can store new information in many parts of the brain. For example, if a reading contains a lot of new vocabulary, put the vocabulary onto note cards. Your second review session could then be spent memorizing new vocabulary from the note cards. You could even turn the cards into a game, put the definitions on one set of cards and the vocabulary words on another set of cards. Lay the cards out on a table and play a matching game. This activity will keep your mind and body active. While you are making decisions about which cards match, moving the cards around will keep you awake and attuned. Also, connect with a study partner or study group in each of your classes. Working together makes studying an active, motivating experience.

Each chapter of this text introduces ideas for study tools. Some examples include:

- Learning Styles chapter: Creating study tools that cross visual, aural, and kinaesthetic learning styles.
- Critical Thinking chapter: Enhancing problem solving skills and integrating problem solving into study sessions.
- Reading and Note-taking chapter: Using the SQ3R reading method as a way to organize a study session.
- Memory chapter: Building study tools that develop memory and recall.

Non-Negotiables vs. Negotiables

What do you absolutely have to do in your week? Your answers to that question are the things that are non-negotiable in your schedule. For example, for many students, time at work is non-negotiable, because missing work might mean getting fired. Missing class doesn't lead to getting fired, but it affects your performance as a student. Missing class only results in having to study more or in knowing less; therefore, class time should also be non-negotiable. What other things are non-negotiable in your schedule?

Negotiables are difficult to define for many students. If you find yourself trying to pack too much work, school, exercise, time with friends and family, and entertainment into your schedule you are going to become run down before the semester gets rolling. Deciding what is negotiable in your life will help you to relax and recognise when an activity can wait until later or be passed over altogether. What is negotiable in your schedule? Maybe you spend every weekend hanging out with friends. Or your family has many demands on your time and you want to please them. Being in school means making some changes to how you spend your time. You may have to compromise with your friends and only spend one day of the weekend with them. Maybe you can turn some of your family time into study time. If you have children, you might try getting the kids to work on their homework while you do yours.

One mistake many people make is defining all time with friends and family and entertainment as negotiable. It is important to balance your life to avoid the stress of feeling like you have no free time or enjoyment. Make sure to include some exercise, time with friends and family, and entertainment in your non-negotiables. Completing the scheduling assignment will allow you to see where you spend your time now and what activities you might consider non-negotiable.

FLEXIBILITY AND COMMITMENT. Students need to allow for changes in schedules and plans. There are students who feel that writing their schedules is too rigid, that a written plan does not allow them to relax and enjoy life. But, in order to achieve a goal, there must be a basic commitment to accomplish what you set out to do. Yes, there should be flexibility and time to relax, but with the dedication to return to the plan. Often students use procrastination as an example of incorporating flexibility into their planning. You need to be honest with yourself and ask if procrastinating will detract from your commitment to accomplishing your goal. For many, procrastination is a barrier to accomplishing their goals. It is important to identify the reasons for planning.

Nine Easy Time Management Tips

1. Ask yourself: "What's the best possible use of my time RIGHT NOW?"

2. Schedule time for relaxation and enjoyable activities.

3. Don't be afraid to ask for help if things get stressful (delegate tasks, reduce work load, ask for extended deadlines, talk to a counselor).

4. Take advantage of "waiting time" (carry a book, your calendar, note paper, balance your checkbook, plan your weekly meals).

5. Try getting up a half hour earlier. Commit to using that time productively (exercise, cook and freeze a meal, wash a load of clothes, re-read today's assignment).

6. Find a way to get a feeling of accomplishment when you finish a task (cross it off, and reward yourself).

7. Identify the "very first step." Often all it takes to get us motivated and rolling on a plan is to define the very first action one has to take to put the plan in motion. Take the "very first step" and the others will follow more easily.

8. Break each assignment into three manageable tasks.

9. Keep a clear vision of your most important goal. Learn to daydream, seeing yourself and your life as it will be when that goal is attained.

Procrastination. Before your brain has a chance to tell you, "Sleeping is good," get a grip on your priorities. What's urgent? NAME IT! Look at your study schedule, if it applies, or ask yourself what the very first step is in the direction of that goal or "urgency."

What does your study schedule tell you you're supposed to be doing right now? For example, you have a term paper in the works. You have to finish the research today if you're going to meet the deadline. But you stayed up late last night and at 9:00 a.m., your stationary body wants to stay that way. What's the first step? If you can tell yourself, "If I get up and get in the shower," you will usually find that's enough to get you "in motion."

Maybe your problem is really *avoidance*? Your reluctance to get going on the research paper may stem from the notion that a) you chose the wrong topic and there's not enough research to support it, or b) the subject is too difficult and you feel you may not be able to tackle the paper successfully, or c) a myriad of other self-defeating thoughts. There are many reasons why we procrastinate based on the desire to avoid something unpleasant. For instance:

1. Fear of failure, or not doing as well as we'd like
2. Fear of not being able to handle success
3. Desire to avoid particular people, relationships or situations
4. Desire to avoid an unpleasant task, like doing dishes or figuring taxes
5. Feeling overwhelmed by the size or scope of a task
6. Perfectionism—"If I can't make it perfect, why even start?"
7. Fear of someone else's judgement of your work

To handle *avoidance* type procrastination, you need to break down your dreaded task into its parts or steps, then tackle the very first step without worrying about the others. Another essential way to overcome avoidance is to deal with the emotional issues and mental attitudes that are getting in your way. It's easy for someone else to tell you to "feel confident"; but only you can get to the bottom of this! In the chart below are some suggestions to help you.

Overcoming Distractions: Sara's Demolished Study Plan[3]

Sara had planned to study Saturday afternoon, and had made detailed plans for how she would use her time to finish assignments for math, physics, literature, and music history. She needed to be finished studying by 5:00 p.m. since she had a date Saturday evening and she wanted enough time to look really hot. She planned to begin studying at 1:00, right after lunch.

Sara jumped into the car and ran down to Wendy's to get some chili for lunch. While there, she ran into her high school friend, Laura, whom she hadn't seen in a couple of months. They spent some time catching up—a lot of time, actually—and Sara didn't leave the restaurant until 1:30. On the way home she noticed she was nearly out of gas. She stopped at the gas station, and also checked out the mini-mart for some study-break snacks.

---

[3]From *The Community College: A New Beginning, Second Edition* by Aguilar et al. © 1998 by Kendall/Hunt Publishing Company. Used by permission.

> ## Procrastination Hints
>
> 1. Break the big tasks down into small steps. Schedule them, using your scheduling tools. Especially use your to-do list; it's motivating to see tasks checked off.
>
> 2. Find "step one" and start there without contemplating the rest of the project yet.
>
> 3. Set a time limit: "I'll work on step one (or two or ten) for 15 minutes." Sometimes you'll get involved and keep going.
>
> 4. Find a buddy to whom you'll agree to be accountable. Share your plan for tackling the project and ask him to check up on you.
>
> 5. Suppose you missed something in class and the assignment doesn't make sense. You'll need to find a fellow student or ask the instructor for clarification. That, of course, would be your step one.
>
> 6. Establishing a study space. The trick is to train your mind that "When we sit here, it's time to study." Have all your materials ready, too, so you don't waste time looking for them.
>
> 7. Use positive self-talk. Remember Stuart Smalley on "Saturday Night Live"? "I'm good enough, I'm smart enough, and gosh darn it, people like me!" It was silly when "Stuart" did it, but actually the concept does work. Try to replace a negative thought with a positive one. Instead of, "I'll never get all this work done!", think, "I know I can at least read the chapter; I'll do that first."
>
> 8. It helps to hold out a carrot for yourself—something you will find really rewarding that you'll do for yourself after, say, reading three chapters or writing a rough draft.

By the time Sara got home it was nearly 2:00. Sara had wanted to save some bucks while at community college, so she was still living at home. Sometimes her parents didn't realize that college studying was more time consuming than high school had been, and asked her to help out at home more often than Sara would like. Today, for instance, she arrived home and her mom asked her to please "keep an eye" on her little brother, age 10, so Mom could go shopping. Sara shoved a video into the VCR and told her brother to stay out of trouble while she studied.

Fifteen minutes into the literature reading assignment, the phone rang. It was the guy Sara was going out with that night, calling to ask if she'd rather see a movie or go to a dance club. They talked for a while, maybe twenty minutes, but after they hung up, Sara found it difficult to concentrate. She was really looking forward to the date.

After trying for a while to keep reading, Sara finally got up and went down to the kitchen for a soft drink. There she found the mess left after her brother had fixed himself a snack.

By the time Sara cleaned up the mess, got her drink, and got back to work, it was past 3:30. She decided to switch to working on math problems. About half an hour later, the doorbell rang. Sara grudgingly plodded downstairs, opened the door, and there stood her best friend Kim, jumping up and down, thrusting her hand under Sara's nose—she was wearing an engagement ring! Naturally, Sara had to hear every detail of the proposal, and the ring selection . . . and it was more than an hour later when Kim left.

Sara's 5:00 deadline had come and gone, and she still had not finished a single assignment. Now she had a choice to make: finish at least one assignment, skip her shower and not look as great as she'd hoped; or give up and try again tomorrow . . .

Obviously, Sara faced a lot of external distractions which sabotaged her studying plans. We think of distractions as "things" (or people) that tend to pull us off course, but there are also internal distractions that may plague us. For example, Sara faced that type

> **Suggestions for Avoiding Distractions**
>
> 1. Close your door. Unplug your phone. Simply be unavailable.
> 2. Avoid the temptation to "finish one more errand," "make one more phone call," anything that takes up time you've already scheduled for studying.
> 3. Schedule your breaks and be specific about what you're going to do on your break. Just saying, "take a break" invites prolonged malingering.
> 4. Pile a whole bunch of junk on your bed so it's a real pain to try to get in it. Remember, we're trying to avoid temptation.
> 5. Identify people, places, and things that tend to tempt you and waste your time. Don't answer Carla's knock at your door. Don't go to the college cafeteria to study.
> 6. Get enough sleep. Eat right. Exercise.

of distraction when she was unable to maintain her concentration after the call from her date. Look at this list of possible distractions and see how many are best avoided simply by adjusting personal habits or attitudes:

1. Physical: hunger, thirst, fatigue, illness
2. Mental: daydreaming, personal problems, worrying, stress, thinking about other activities, or someplace you'd rather be
3. Environment: uncomfortable room/chair, wrong lighting, too hot or too cold, noise (phones, people, music, TV)
4. Other: negative attitude about assignment, course, or instructor; other people wanting your attention

The chart above offers some suggestions to avoid being distracted. You also have to plan ways to handle distractions when they occur and get yourself back on target.

Summary

Time management is an essential part of a successful college career. Large assignments and tests can easily become overwhelming without regular study and review. Avoid procrastination by breaking assignments into manageable chunks. Record tasks, due dates, and study blocks in a study schedule and semester calendar. With a little planning you will know when your homework is finished and when you have free time. Remember, scheduling is not only about getting homework done, it's about fun. Don't leave enjoyable activities out of your schedule; instead, work to make a balance between school, work, family, friends, and entertainment. Also, leave blanks in your schedule that allow you to catch up or relax. Think of each task in your schedule as building to the end of a course and each course as building to a greater goal that is unique to you. By focusing on that goal, be it "finish school," "gain knowledge" or "get a job," you will give meaning to your hard work and effort.

Special Time Management Situations

Some students have more challenges than average, because of their lifestyles or circumstances. Here are some brief tips to help meet those extra time-management challenges:

1. Part-time students with full-time jobs:

You need to pay particular attention to the concept of dividing your time into blocks or chunks, and be certain to schedule in time for unexpected emergencies at work or at home. Your health and rest are of utmost importance; be especially careful of overextending yourself so that you are unable to get enough sleep. You probably need to decide which is your top priority—school or work—and if necessary, adjust the time frame of your goal to take fewer classes at a time. If you take more than one class at a time, ask your advisor to help you choose classes that are "balanced." For example, don't take Chemistry and Calculus in the same semester.

2. Moms (or Dads) going to school and raising kids and running a home:

Time management skills are essential for parents who have a never-ending list of commitments: household chores, shopping, cooking, taking the kids to school and activities, listening to problems, drying tears, and so on. That list didn't begin to mention your own school commitments. Say, do you get to have a life, too? There is so much stress in this situation, sometimes you will be tempted to think it isn't worth it. Two hints for parents: First, get a very firm grip on your goals. Why seek that degree? What improvements will it make in your life and the lives of your loved ones? If you can see this clearly, it will make all the difference when things look bleakest. Second, everybody has to have a schedule, not just you. The scheduling tools include activities of each family member, and you can then remind and encourage each other. Also, try to find a friend at school who is in the same situation. That support can be crucial for both of you.

3. Students with health problems:

Once again, your health must be your top priority, even if it means slowing down the achievement of your goals by taking fewer classes at once. Whether you have a chronic illness or a disability, you need to schedule in time for rest, physical therapy, proper nutrition, visits to the doctor, etc. before you schedule your class and study time. Be realistic about what you can handle. If you become ill during the semester, don't just stop going to class. See your instructor and try to work out time to catch up, or ask for an Incomplete grade which you can finish the following semester.

4. Multiple commitments:

If part of your reason for attending college is the opportunity it affords you to play your sport or perform using your talents, you need to consider your activity and your education as equally important. If eligibility is an issue, naturally you are going to want to keep your grades up. Your best bet is to rely on the "buddy system" with a teammate or friend who is in the same situation. Hold each other accountable for maintaining a wise study and practice schedule. Obviously, not enough can be said about picking out the right person for your "buddy." The guy who thinks it won't hurt to party on school nights is probably not the "buddy" to choose.

5. Overcommitment:

Full time school and work, too many activities, etc. What's your priority? We repeat, what's your priority? Get a firm vision of where you want to be in, say, five years. If you are working full time and going to school full time, your grades are going to suffer. You are going to be tired. You are not going to have time for relaxation or social activities. The same is true if you have committed yourself to too many activities. It's great to take advantage of the opportunities college has to offer for sports, music, theater, clubs, and new friends. But to handle your goal-related responsibilities, you just have to decide which of these activities you can't live without, and pass on the rest.

6. Personal problems:

When you are in college, the rest of your life doesn't just stop. You will fall prey to personal pitfalls of all kinds: emotional, relationship-related, or financial to name a few. If you find yourself overwhelmed by a personal problem while the semester is in progress, take advantage of your school's counselors. They are there to help, they've seen it all before, and most of them are easy to talk to and have lots of ideas to help you through. There is no better wisdom than knowing when you need help and asking for it. Don't even wait until it gets out of hand—go today!

Reflect and Apply

Choose what you believe to be the three most valuable tools or hints you found in this chapter, whether from the discussions, examples, or sidebars. During the next week, find as many opportunities as you can to utilize those three ideas. At the end of the week, write a one-page essay discussing how those tools or hints helped (or didn't help) you manage your time more effectively.

BREAK DOWN OF THE WEEK
             THE DAY
             THE TASK

7 STEPS OF STUDYING

PRIORATIZE   FIND OUT WHAT'S
             IMPORTANT TO ME

Name: _____ Date: _____

Exercise 1: Time Management Pretest

Purpose: To help you find areas to improve as you handle the responsibility of scheduling your own time as a college student.

A. How much time per week do you believe you devote to the following activities?

Activity	# Hours Per Week
✓ 1. Attending class	11
✓ 2. Studying/reading/doing homework	22
✓ 3. Working at a job	24
✗ 4. Watching TV	
✓ 5. Sleeping	70
✓ 6. Personal care (bathing, hair, etc.)	7
✓ 7. Hobbies /ALONE TIME	5
✗ 8. Shopping	
✓ 9. Eating	10
✓ 10. Being with friends /GF	9
✗ 11. On the phone	
✓ 12. Other TRAVEL	10
TOTAL HRS. =	168

B. Have any of the following happened to you since you started college?

	Yes	No
1. Overslept and missed/late to class		
2. Forgot to do an assignment		
3. Chose to go out with friends and didn't complete an assignment		
4. Asked an instructor for a deadline extension		
5. Got your work schedule mixed up		
6. Missed or was late to class due to transportation problem		
7. Skipped class for no particular reason		

Name: _____ Date: _____

■ Exercise 2: Goal Setting

Short-range or immediate goals: _____
_____
_____
_____

Mid-range goals: _____
_____
_____
_____

Long-range goals: _____
_____
_____
_____

Name: _____ Date: _____

■ Exercise 3: Making a Semester Plan

Directions:

1. Fill in the blank calendars on the following four pages with days and months.

2. Gather all outlines/syllabi for all of your courses.

3. Plot the due dates for all tests, assignments and papers. Highlight these dates in a bright colour.

4. Add any other big dates you need to remember. For example, you might have an interview coming up, school registration, or scholarship or financial aid forms, etc. to turn in.

5. Now plot your "breakdown" of each of the tests, assignments and papers you listed in #4. For example, if today is January 5 and you have a 10-page research paper due on February 15, when will you plan to have the research portion completed? Plot that date. Also consider when an outline and a first and second draft will be completed. And, last but not least, plot your due dates so that you complete all work at least one day before the due date!

Name: _____ Date: _____

■ Exercise 4: Personal Schedule

Directions:

1. Analyze your answers in Exercise 1: Time Management Pretest. Plot your activities on the personal schedule. This schedule should show all of your activities for the week (24 x 7). However, be careful not to break down your schedule into overly-tight time frames. For most people, two-hour time frames work best. For study blocks, you need only put "Study." You do not have to note what course you will be studying for.

2. Highlight all of your **non-negotiable** activities.

3. For study time, ensure that you have allowed for at least two hours of study time for each hour that you are in class (e.g., 12 hours class time = 24 hours study time).

4. Analyze your schedule. Does it show a balance between school, work and leisure time?

Name: _____ Date: _____

Exercise 5: Study Schedule Details

Directions:

1. Analyze your Personal Schedule (Exercise #4). Then, using a separate piece of paper (or copies of the Study Schedule Details on the following pages), begin constructing your own, individualized Study Schedule. Follow the times you have allotted for study on your Personal Schedule. Each week, your study commitments will vary. For this assignment, look at your course syllabi and plan your activities for the second or third week of classes.

2. To decide approximately how many hours you should study for each class each week, multiply the number of hours your class meets per week by two. For example, if you have 12 hours of class time per week, you will need 24 additional hours for study.

3. Specify the particular course you will study, rather than just marking "study." Break down the tasks. For example: STSU 100—review/highlight lecture notes, pre-read/annotate Chapters 1 & 2, *Student Success*, meet with study group to discuss time management reading. Remember to vary your study activities and adopt a multi-sensory approach when devising new study strategies. Other activities might include writing summaries or consolidation notes, reading notes out loud, making up quizzes, cue cards or illustrations, meeting or talking with study groups or study partner. Schedule a minimum of three different study sessions (three *zaps*) for each class, each week.

4. For maximum effectiveness, allow 50–90 minute blocks of study for each course and try to break up study blocks to avoid excessively long study periods (e.g., schedule two, 90-minute study blocks at different times during the day rather than a long 3–4 hour block.)

5. Figure approximately 5–10 minutes for a break for each hour of study.

6. If possible, allow five minutes or more *after* each class to review material, e.g., review a lecture by highlighting or completing your notes right after class.

7. Try to schedule a review period *before* each class.

8. Allow a break of at least 20 minutes between studying and retiring for the night.

9. Once a week (Sunday evening is a good choice), schedule a recap session in for activities such as reviewing the previous week's text and lecture notes, previewing your commitments for the next week and organizing your time accordingly.

10. Review your Study Schedule Details. Have you allowed for reasonable, realistic time frames within which to complete the tasks you set for yourself?

FRIDAY	SATURDAY	SUNDAY
Study block #7 Subject: STSU 100 Time: 1300-1350 • Complete scheduling assignment. • Read over highlighting and annotating. • Read *Parental Stress in the Adolescent Years*.	Study block #8 Subject: STSU 100 Time: 2100-2150 Complete any unfinished homework and begin to review notes from the week.	Study block #9 Subject: STSU 100 Time: 1100-1150 • Continue to review and summarize notes from class. • Begin chapter exercises.
10 Minute break	10 minute break	10 minute break
Study block #7 cont. Subject: STSU 100 Time: 1400-1450 • Begin highlighting and annotating assignment. • Highlighting main ideas and the thesis and some but not all supporting facts.	Study block #7 cont. Subject: STSU 100 Time: 2200-2300 • Review all notes and text pages covered in the week by comparing them. • Make summaries of notes.	Study block #9 cont. Subject: STSU 100 Time: 1200-1250 Look ahead in course syllabus, scan, question, then begin reading assigned chapters.
10 minute break		10 minute break
Study block #7 cont. Subject: MODL 102 Time: 1500-1600 • Review vocabulary cards 3X • Make cards for new vocabulary.		Study block #9 cont. Subject: MODL 102 Time: 1300-1400 • Look ahead in course syllabus, scan, question, and read assigned chapter. • Complete chapter-end exercises

CHAPTER 3
Learning Styles/Instructional Styles

Introduction[1]

The population at any college is a diverse one. Look around you at the composition of the students in your class. They come from all ages, ethnic, national, social, cultural, and religious backgrounds. Each person is indeed a unique individual. Each student has a unique learning style. Each instructor you meet along the way will have a different teaching style. The people who will be guiding your educational experiences will also bring their personal attributes into the classroom. How will you adapt to all of this diversity?

This chapter will focus on the differences in learning styles, environmental factors and instructional styles. You will identify your learning style and determine the mode in which you learn best. Also, you will examine the different teaching techniques used in your classes and develop strategies to help you adapt your strengths, weaknesses, and learning styles to your instructors' teaching styles. These strategies will help you to be successful in college.

Learning Styles

Our brains do not all function in the same manner or on the same level. Not everyone learns in the same way. Your learning style is the way in which you gather, process, and retain information. Some people are more visually oriented, others are auditorially or kinaesthetically oriented. Others are a combination of all three. Your learning style is both your preferred way of learning and the conditions under which you find it easiest to learn. In order to work to the best of your ability, it is important to discover your individual learning style. You can analyze your own style or use a standardized inventory.

To illustrate the three different kinds of learning styles, read the stories of the following four students: Victor Visual, Annie Auditory, Kenny Kinaesthetic, and Terry Tactile.

---

[1]From *The Community College: A New Beginning*. Second Edition by Aguilar et al. © 1998 by Kendall/Hunt Publishing Company. Used by permission.

Victor

Victor Visual learns best by seeing how things are done. He has always liked to read. Ever since he was little he was always aware of his surroundings. When he was a baby he liked to look at mobiles and the interesting toys his mother placed in his crib. His mom always said she could take him anywhere; he would sit there quietly, staring at the people and things around him. When he went to school Victor loved the brightly colored posters and bulletin board displays hanging on the walls of his classroom. He learned the ABCs by staring at the alphabet posted above the board. His teachers were impressed at his ability to recognize words at an early age. In fact, learning to read sight words was no problem for Victor.

In fourth grade when the class was studying planets, he suggested to the teacher that they hang models of the planets from the ceiling. He really did not want to construct the models, but he did make sure they were labeled correctly. In the sixth grade he qualified for the pizza party by reading more books than anyone else in his class. For his birthday, when he received toys that needed to be assembled, he always read the instructions before trying to put them together.

In high school Victor did well. He read his textbooks faithfully, but he really disliked classes where the teachers just lectured without using the board or providing handouts. When the teacher asked questions about the reading assignments from the night before, Victor was the only one who raised his hand, except for Vanessa Vision. At sixteen, when Victor learned to drive, he got 100% on the written test, but it took him three times to pass the behind-the-wheel portion of the test. Even now when Victor is going to drive somewhere he has never been before, he needs a good map with landmarks. In fact, Victor prefers written instructions for everything. In computer class Victor was one of the few students who actually read the manual.

As a college student Victor continues to do well in classes where the teacher uses the overhead projector or writes on the board. In lab classes he prefers that the instructor or another student do the experiments so he can watch. At home when Victor is watching TV, he becomes really annoyed when his younger brother stands in front of the TV. If he goes to an assembly or any kind of performance, he likes to sit in full view of the stage. He gets more out of the performance if he is able to see the speaker directly.

Annie

As a baby Annie Auditory could always be soothed with a lullaby. She liked to listen to her mother talk on the phone or with friends. Her favorite toy was a stuffed teddy bear that played music. She loved to have the radio or television turned on, and by the time she was three she had memorized all the commercials. She even knew the Empire Carpet phone number. She learned the alphabet by singing the ABC song. She learned her numbers in Spanish from hearing them sung on *SESAME STREET*.

In school Annie learned best by listening closely to the teacher. She needed to have everything explained. If the teacher did not read the directions at the top of the page, Annie had a hard time getting started on her seatwork. As she got older her teachers remarked how well Annie participated in class discussions. She always knew what was going on in school because she paid attention when the announcements were read over the loudspeaker. Annie's favorite birthday present was a cassette player/recorder. She loved to listen to books on tape, and has always liked listening to music. She also loved to record her own voice and play it back.

In high school Annie used the tape recorder to help her study. She made audio study guides and read her textbook onto a tape so she could listen to it again. She understood the chapters better if she could hear them. She enjoyed getting her friends together to study for an exam by discussing the material for the test. She became proficient in foreign language classes because she was able to pick up the inflections and the accents. When Annie started to drive, her instructor usually had to tell her where to turn and when to stop. Even now when Annie gets lost, she needs to stop and ask someone to tell her the directions. Giving her a map would not do her any good.

Annie enjoys lecture classes in college; she hates long reading assignments. She did well in Music Appreciation, but had difficulty with her Introduction to the Visual Arts course. If it were not for the Visual Arts course, Annie would have a 4.0 GPA. In fact, Annie has considered becoming a college instructor because she likes to talk and conduct class discussions.

Kenny and Terry

Kenny Kinaesthetic and Terry Tactile are best friends. They have been together since their sandbox days. In the sandbox they built roads, houses, and elaborate castles. As babies they always had to have something in their hands. They clung to their bottles and pacifiers long after other kids had given them up; but, as his mom liked to point out, Kenny was walking by eight months. The boys both learned the alphabet by playing with blocks.

In grammar school they loved working with play dough and messy art projects. Learning to read was a little more difficult for Kenny and Terry. They fidgeted if too much time was spent doing seatwork. If they really needed to concentrate it helped to be able to color, cut and paste, or at least drum a pencil on the desk. The teachers thought they were hyperactive and always told them to sit still. They spent a lot of time in the hall.

When Victor suggested making models of the planets, Kenny and Terry were the first to volunteer to do the job. They got into those science experiments in junior high and for the first time felt good about learning.

In high school they were chemistry lab partners who always got an A on their experiments (except when they blew up the lab because they just had to see what happened when they mixed the pink stuff with the green stuff). Shop classes were their specialty. Their mothers had more knick-knacks, spice racks, and towel holders than any other moms in the PTA. Kenny and Terry had a flair for fixing things, and never had to read the directions to assemble anything. They learned to drive one day by taking Terry's father's car to an empty parking lot while he was taking his Sunday afternoon nap. They both had to take the written test over, though, before they actually got their licenses. It's a good thing PE counts as a high school requirement. They really needed those credits to graduate.

At college both Kenny and Terry do well in lab classes, technical courses, and art courses where there is not too much written work. In English they never read a book if there is a movie version available. They signed up for the fitness center immediately and will probably try out for sports. These two guys are pretty much alike. Terry is better at hand/eye coordination and working with his hands, while Kenny is better in athletics and physical activities.

The Three Basic Learning Styles

From our stories about Victor, Annie, Kenny and Terry we have illustrated some of the strengths of three distinct learning styles: visual, auditory and kinaesthetic/tactile. Visual learners use their eyesight, or vision, as their preferred method of taking in information and learn best by reading or watching a demonstration. Auditory learners use their ears or sense of hearing the most. They prefer to learn by listening to a lecture, discussion, or audio tape. Kinaesthetic/tactile learners are much better at getting information by using their sense of touch. They prefer to learn by doing or becoming physically involved with what they are studying. If they do have to read or listen, it helps if they can move around or do something with their hands.

These learning styles reflect preferences in the way we learn. Knowing that you are a visual learner doesn't mean that you don't understand what you hear. It means that given a choice, you would usually prefer to read or watch. Visual learners usually fare quite well in grade school, where teachers cater to this style. Go into any preschool through fifth grade classroom, and you will be bombarded with visual stimulation. Elementary school teachers all learn how to create effective bulletin board displays. They want to make sure that any kid who is not paying attention is still learning something while he/she stares at the walls, ceiling, windows, or even out the door into the hall. Since reading plays such an important role in education, visual learners who like to read seem to do well, even in high school. They will do well in college if they can take good notes. They should try to get everything important written into their notes to read and look at when studying for a test.

Auditory learners, on the other hand, may find college classes more to their liking because many instructors use the lecture/discussion method of teaching. In the lower grades auditory learners can get bored with too much seatwork and reading. On the whole, though, they probably did fine in school since most teachers at that level explain everything in detail. As they get older, their auditory strengths are used even more as verbal reasoning skills are emphasized.

Tactile and kinaesthetic styles vary slightly. Tactile learners like to use their hands, while kinaesthetic learners use their whole body whenever possible. These two styles are so similar, though, that throughout this chapter we will use the terms synonymously. These learners are probably the least understood in schools. Although some teachers really try to bring in hands-on approaches to learning, others find it difficult to adapt their more audio/visual styles to a kinaesthetic child. Because that child usually needs to be moving around while taking in the information, the typical classroom arrangement makes school more difficult. Not surprisingly, most of the developmental students in my college classes discover that they are kinaesthetic/tactile learners. They never quite "got it" in grade school and high school because they were never given the opportunity to learn most subjects in their preferred style.

So that brings us to the here and now. Perhaps you could see yourself in the stories of Victor, Annie, Kenny, or Terry. You're saying "That's me! That's the way I learn best." Activity 2 is an inventory that will help you determine your learning style. It's great to know your strengths so you can use them to your best advantage. But since life is not always fair, and your instructors will not always teach in your preferred style, you need to learn some strategies to compensate for the other styles that are less developed in you.

Visual learners learn best by:

Reading   Watching demonstrations   Seeing pictures

Strategies for visual learners include:

Printed materials	Movies	Blackboard demonstrations
Diagrams	Charts	Photos
Graphs	Handouts	Illustrations
Reading textbook before lecture	Taking notes to read after lecture	Overheads/transparencies

Auditory learners learn best by:

Listening   Conversation

Asking questions   Discussing

Strategies for auditory learners include:

Study groups	Study buddy	Audio tapes
Movies	Recitation	
Reading textbook following lecture		

Tactile/Kinaesthetic learners learn best by:

Doing   Touching

Moving   Feeling

Strategies for tactile/kinesthetic learners include:

Hands-on learning	Experiments	Interactive learning
Teamwork	Role playing	Workshops
Performance models	Note taking (writing out what you see or hear)	Collecting samples
Becoming physically involved		

Concentrating on how the reading and the listening will benefit you in experimentation.

Find Your Learning Style

Complete Exercise 1: Learning Styles Inventory to find the way you prefer to learn.

Results

Now that you have these results, you can begin to see the way you prefer to learn. The results of the surveys are informal, and if you think you could benefit from a more in-depth diagnosis, you should contact your campus counseling or testing center. They will have other tests which will give you more information.

How Can You Use Your Learning Style?[2]

Going back to the Learning Styles Inventory, look at your preferences regarding auditory, visual, and kinaesthetic. If you have a strong preference for one over the others, you probably have some idea that you learn better if you receive information in a particular way. You would prefer to work with or react to information in that same mode.

If you don't find that you have a strong preference for one learning style over the others, you may have found that you prefer to receive information one way, but you would rather react to it or work with it in another way. Or you may have found that you are well integrated in these areas, and show no strong preferences in receiving or reacting to information.

The following suggestions are categorized according to learning style. It's a good idea to read over all of the suggestions, keeping in mind your strengths and weaknesses. The type of material you are responsible for getting in different classes should also be considered when choosing a strategy to use. Generally, the more senses you can use, the better you learn and remember the information. Sometimes it will be helpful to concentrate on your strong areas especially with difficult material.

Suggestions for Auditory Strengths

General Hints

You will benefit from hearing information—audio tapes, your own voice, or lectures.
You may want to make tapes of reading assignments or class notes.
Pretend that you are teaching someone else the information and explain it out loud.
Reading aloud notes or text material will help you.

Lecture Hints

Use a cassette tape player for pre-testing by asking yourself questions, leaving a 2–3 second blank space, and then giving the answer.
Use a cassette player to record difficult material from your notes and then listen to the information as needed.
Orally test yourself by asking questions from your notes.
Read aloud any difficult material in your notes.
If you can't read aloud, try vocalizing the words quietly.

---

[2] From *Practical Approaches for Building Study Skills and Vocabulary, Second Edition* by Funk et al. © 1996 by Kendall/Hunt Publishing Company. Used by permission.

Textbook Hints

Read aloud summary statements, headings, and subheadings before you begin reading a chapter.

Restate key ideas to yourself as you read material. Keep a "conversation" going with your text as you read (agree or disagree with the author, or question key ideas).

For difficult material, restate in your own words what you have just read.

Read aloud, vocalize, or whisper passages that are difficult.

Read vocabulary words and their definitions before you begin reading.

After reading, quiz yourself (aloud) over the vocabulary.

Orally quiz yourself over selected main ideas.

Tape yourself reading difficult text sections, and then go back and listen to them.

Suggestions for Visual Strengths

General Hints

You will benefit from seeing information—either in print or from videos, charts, or overheads.

It will be easier for you to remember what you read than what you hear.

When given information orally, you should write it down or take some notes.

Lecture Hints

Read the text before attending lectures.

Take notes over lecture material.

For difficult or confusing material, use a mapping technique along with notes (mapping is drawing a diagram of the material read, using only the main ideas, then showing the relationship among the ideas with lines connecting the them).

Use white space on your page as a guide when taking notes (skip lines between main ideas).

To learn material, stare off into space and remember what the written information looked like on your page.

Textbook Hints

Preview chapters by reading the headings, subheadings, and outlines before reading the chapter.

Watch for topic sentences. Reread them to help you stay with the material being read. Underline topic sentences.

Draw a diagram, jot down a list, use mapping, or make a chart to help you retain difficult material.

Underline key words and concepts as you read. Marking your text will be very helpful.

Suggestions for Kinaesthetic Strengths

General Hints

You learn best by doing. The more involved you are with material, the easier it is for you to learn.

You should try to find practical applications for information. When you can, do projects and experiments using what you learn.

Write information down.

Moving your fingers along the lines as you read may help.

Lecture Hints

Take notes and go back over them, making special marks for important material or material you need to go over more.

For difficult or confusing material, answer practice questions in writing.

Write difficult information in the air with your finger.

Use your hand as a marker as you go through your notes.

Textbook Hints

Use your hand or finger as a guide as you read.

For difficult material, draw a chart or diagram to help you understand what you read.

Underline important words and concepts as you study.

Making and using study cards will help you learn difficult material.

Use 3 x 5 cards with a question on one side and the answer on the other. You can also put charts, lists, and diagrams on small cards to use for studying.

Use your finger to point out summary information, main points, and headings and subheadings as you read.

Student Environment

The environment around you is another factor that influences your learning. The time of day when people participate in an activity often will determine how well or how poorly they perform. Students who take courses or study at the times when they are most alert tend to do better. (Don't you wonder how many research studies it took to verify that amazing fact?!) Still, many people do not even consider this when they schedule their classes or plan their study time. Are you a morning person or a night person? Do you peak mid-morning or fizzle in the middle of the afternoon? If you can't keep your eyes open after 9:00 p.m., don't plan to study for your chemistry test after the rest of the family has gone to bed. Complete Exercise 3: Environment Inventory to uncover the best study conditions for you.

Now that you have selected the study conditions that appear to best suit you, be sure that they are indeed the best ones for you. Try experimenting with different classes and study conditions. Students always tell me they can't study without loud music. But actually, they have never tried a quiet approach. If you usually listen to loud music or have the television on while studying, be sure that a quiet room will not be better before you discard the idea. If you prefer to study alone, try working with a friend or group. You may find that you are more effective when learning with others.

The surrounding environment will also have an effect on how you perform. Do you prefer a room that is loud vs. one that is quiet? Must you work on a neat desk, or does it matter whether or not it is cluttered? What about the lighting? Or the room temperature? What is it that makes you comfortable? It is very difficult to concentrate when you are uncomfortable. If the room is too cold, your mind may concentrate more on keeping warm than on your algebra problems.

Activity 1 will help you determine what kind of study environments provide the best "fit" for your needs. Find out for yourself and use the information to your best advantage.

Instructional Styles[3]

Three types of instructional styles most often used by teachers are **independent, student centered,** and **cooperative learning**.

Independent

An independent instructional style is very formal and businesslike. The instructor delivers his/her class material primarily by lecturing, and the student has no input into the class lecture. The student is almost totally responsible for learning independently. He or she is expected to take notes, follow the syllabus, read the textbook, complete the assignments, and prepare for assorted quizzes and exams. This type of learning places the importance on the individual student's efforts and usually takes place in classes with large enrollments.

Student Centered

The student centered type of instructional style is less formal. Discussion is introduced into the classroom along with the lecture. The instructor attempts to involve the group into the learning process by asking probing questions that encourage students to think, answer questions and make comments. The lecture delivery is in a traditional format, but the instructor requires class participation by calling on students, if necessary.

Cooperative

The cooperative type of instructional style makes a concerted effort to involve the students in group dynamics. Not only are lectures peppered with question and answer sessions, but students may be involved in lab work, demonstrations, presentations, and/or group problem-solving exercises. In some cases the teacher does not lecture at all, and the students are totally responsible for discovering the information on their own. The instructor serves as a facilitator and resource person. In cooperative learning the students work as teams and may even do their exams together.

What Teaching Style Suits You?

What teaching style suits you? Answer the questions in Exercise 4: Teaching Style Compatibility Inventory to find out.

You should try to find out about the teacher's instructional style before you sign up for a class. Your best bet is to talk to other students. Find out as much as you can about the person with whom you will be spending the next term. The instructor's personality will also influence his/her teaching methods. Try to select someone whose teaching style is compatible with your learning style. In order to do this, however, you must be prepared to register early so that you can get into the classes you want. Course sections taught by popular teachers fill up very quickly.

---

[3] From *The Community College: A New Beginning, Second Edition* by Aguilar et al. © 1998 by Kendall/Hunt Publishing Company. Used by permission.

When it is impossible for you to find an instructor with a compatible teaching style, make an honest effort to learn. Sit in the front of the classroom to be certain that you do not miss anything. Not only should you listen to what your instructor is saying, but you need to watch for facial expressions and body language. Note where emphasis is placed during a discussion or lecture, pay close attention to board work and/or overhead transparencies used in class, and be aware of the material that will be covered in class. You can always do this by reading your textbook before each class.

Study for the class in your best learning style mode. Rewrite or tape your notes. Read your notes or textbook out loud. Do whatever it takes to learn. Talk with the instructor if you have problems; ask questions when you do not understand. Seek out available tutorial services to provide that extra edge.

Complete the scenarios in Exercise 5 to further consider ways to make the best of a course when the teaching style and your learning style don't match.

Summary

It is important to recognize that all people do not learn in the same way and that there is no single right way to learn. These styles are merely a reflection of your personality and your particular preferences. Just as you prefer to use your right hand or left hand to do certain tasks, your mind prefers to use certain methods for taking in and processing information, coming to conclusions, and functioning on a daily basis. All of us use more than one style. However, you can become more proficient in the other, less preferred learning styles by practicing and using them more often. Try to adapt your style to the conditions under which you must learn.

Once you have determined whether your primary learning style is visual, auditory, or kinaesthetic/tactile, use it to your best advantage. Find the strategies that work for you. Get to know yourself and your preferred study modes. Become aware of your best time of day for learning, and try to study under optimal conditions with regard to room temperature, lighting, noise level, furniture, etc. Finally, make every attempt to take classes with teachers whose instructional styles will motivate you and make it easier to comprehend the material.

Reflect and Apply

1. Which of the learning styles described in this chapter seems to fit you best?
2. Why do you think so?
3. Analyze a course in which you are currently enrolled—or one in which you are doing well and enjoy. Why do you like this class? Why do you think you are doing well?

Name: _____ Date: _____

■ Exercise 1: Learning Styles Inventory

Please choose one response for each of the items on the inventory. Even if more than one statement is true for you, choose only the one that is most true, or that is true more often for you than the others.

1. If I have to learn something new, I would prefer:
    a. to read about it
    b. to have someone explain it to me
    c. to try it

2. The strategy that helps me learn a new spelling or vocabulary word is:
    a. put it on a flash card and look at it often
    b. spell or say it out loud several times
    c. write it over and over until I remember it

3. If I need directions to a new place, I would prefer:
    a. to follow a good map, preferably with landmarks drawn on it
    b. to have someone tell me exactly how to get there
    c. to have someone take me there

4. I do well in classes where:
    a. the teacher uses visual aids and writes important things on the board or overhead
    b. the teacher lectures on the important things to know
    c. there is some kind of hands-on activity like an experiment or lab where I can learn by doing

5. If I had to put something together, I would:
    a. read the manual or watch the instructional video first
    b. ask someone to tell me how to do it
    c. take out all the pieces and start trying to put it together. I read the instructions/ask for help only as a last resort if I can't figure it out.

6. I remember best the things I:
    a. see
    b. hear
    c. do

7. I would rather:
    a. read a story myself
    b. listen to someone else read a story
    c. act out the story in a play

8. In a casual setting when I'm listening to an interesting speaker:
    a. I visualize the people, places and events being described
    b. I listen to the speaker's tone of voice to derive meaning
    c. I need to have some kind of physical movement such as rocking, tapping, etc. to help me concentrate

9. If I need to remember a phone number:
    a. I look it up, then picture the number in my mind
    b. I repeat it to myself several times
    c. I write it down, or remember it by where the numbers are on the phone key pad

57

10. When teaching other people things:
    a. I would rather use a picture, diagram, chart, etc. to show them what to do
    b. I would rather tell them how to do it
    c. I would rather demonstrate how to do something than tell how to do it

11. At a party:
    a. I like to watch people
    b. I like to listen to others talk
    c. I initiate conversations

12. When I shop for groceries:
    a. I take a list
    b. I talk to myself to remember what I need to buy
    c. I walk through the store and remember what I need as I go

13. In order to relax in my leisure time:
    a. I watch TV or read
    b. I listen to music
    c. I am involved in crafts or do-it-yourself projects

14. In math class, I would prefer to:
    a. read and follow the example from the book
    b. have the teacher explain how to do the problem
    c. have the teacher show me how to do the problem, then have me work one on my own

15. When I watch TV:
    a. I look at the screen and pay attention
    b. I can be doing something else in the room as long as I can listen
    c. I have to be eating or using my hands for crafts, or other hobbies

16. When I need to spell a difficult word:
    a. I picture the word in my mind and mentally spell it
    b. I spell it aloud
    c. I must write it out

17. I like to learn something new by:
    a. watching a person demonstrate how to do it
    b. listening to lecturers, speakers, or tapes
    c. getting involved by doing it myself

18. In a group project I would rather:
    a. research other written material to gain knowledge about the project
    b. talk to others about how to do the project
    c. collect the information for the project

19. I learn best when I:
    a. read the textbook
    b. listen to the lecture
    c. design a project

20. When studying for tests, I do best when I:
    a. read my textbook and notes
    b. listen to the tapes from class
    c. explain the information to someone else

21. To make best use of my class notes I:
    a. read them over
    b. read them out loud or on to a tape so I can listen to them
    c. organize the information using charts, diagrams, mind maps, etc.

Now, add up your scores to see which is your preferred learning style.

Total A's _____6_____ Visual

Total B's _____7_____ Auditory

Total C's _____7_____ Tactile/Kinesthetic

Name: _____ Date: _____

■ Exercise 2: Learning Styles Exercise

Your friend Joe Student is taking Spanish. Not only is he becoming overwhelmed by how much he has to learn and remember, he is getting bored with reading lists of words over and over in an unsuccessful effort to memorize vocabulary. Give Joe some help with his studying. Suggest study tools that will help him study and remember more effectively and efficiently. Stretch the study tools across all three learning styles to help Joe enliven his study time.

Joe's vocabulary words for this week:

English translation	**Spanish**
drive	manejar
teacher (male)	maestro
to eat	comer
chair	silla
to learn	aprender
cup	la taza
car	coche
spoon	cuchara
to cook	cocinar
bicycle	bicicleta
to read	leer
pencil	lápiz
stove	estufa

Directions: For each learning style, provide two specific study tools or methods Joe could use to remember his Spanish vocabulary.

Visual

_____

_____

Kinaesthetic

_____

_____

Auditory

_____

_____

Name: _____ Date: _____

Exercise 3: Environment Inventory

Circle the letter that best describes you.

1. I prefer to take classes in the:
   a. morning
   b. afternoon
   c. evening

2. I prefer to study in the:
   a. morning
   b. afternoon
   c. evening

3. I learn best when I study with:
   a. soft background music
   b. loud music
   c. peace and quiet

4. I like to study:
   a. at a desk
   b. on the sofa or bed
   c. in an easy chair

5. I study best:
   a. in my room
   b. at the library
   c. at the kitchen or dining room table
   d. in the living room
   e. in the cafeteria

6. I study best:
   a. alone
   b. with a friend
   c. with a study group

7. If other people are around when I study they:
   a. annoy me
   b. make it impossible to get anything done
   c. do not bother me
   d. help me

8. I like to study in a room that is:
   a. hot
   b. warm
   c. cool
   d. cold

9. I get my best work done:
   a. when I rush to meet a deadline
   b. when I have plenty of time to organize my work
   c. in due time

10. When I study I like to:
    a. eat my meal
    b. drink coffee, tea, juice, or soda
    c. snack on "junk" food
    d. chew gum
    e. avoid food and drink

11. I like to study best:
    a. in a bright room with natural sun light
    b. with a fluorescent lamp
    c. with a desk light rather than an overhead light
    d. with medium to bright overhead lighting

12. I like to study with:
    a. the television set on
    b. the radio on
    c. no distracting noise

13. When studying with a friend I prefer to:
    a. do so with the person present
    b. use the telephone
    c. it doesn't matter

14. I prefer to study:
    a. indoors
    b. outdoors when the weather permits
    c. either indoors or outdoors

15. I enjoy studying:
    a. early in the morning
    b. during the day
    c. in the evening
    d. late at night

Name: _____ Date: _____

Exercise 4: Teaching Style Compatibility Inventory

List three or four of your favorite courses.

_____

_____

_____

What do these courses have in common?

_____

_____

_____

How was the class in each of these courses conducted?

_____

_____

_____

What kind of exams were given in these courses?

_____

_____

_____

Why did you like these courses?

_____

_____

_____

List three or four of your least favorite courses.

_____

_____

_____

Why did you not like these courses?

___
___
___

How was the class in each of these courses conducted?

___
___
___

What kind of exams were given in these courses?

___
___
___

Do you see a pattern?

___
___
___

What is it?

___
___
___

Name: _____ Date: _____

■ Exercise 5: Scenarios

Each scenario below describes a class situation where your learning style and the instructor's teaching strategies do not match. Assume that it is a course you are required to take, so dropping it is not an acceptable solution.

Develop two or three strategies for each class that will enable you to experience greater success in the course. Your instructor may ask you to discuss your answers with the rest of the class.

1. Extroverted teacher with introverted student.
   Instructor emphasizes group work. Introvert could be overlooked or not encouraged to participate fully.

   _____
   _____
   _____
   _____
   _____

2. Strongest Learning Mode: Auditory
   Instructor uses textbook extensively and requires many outside readings.

   _____
   _____
   _____
   _____
   _____

3. Strongest Learning Mode: Visual
   Class is primarily lecture. Grade is determined by two scores: the midterm and final exams, which are based on class notes.

   _____
   _____
   _____
   _____
   _____

4. Weakest Learning Mode: Tactile
   Course has a laboratory component. A large percentage of your grade is based on demonstrations, presentations, and projects.

5. Instructor provides multiple choice questions only.
   You have difficulty answering multiple choice questions.

6. Instructor uses essay questions only on his exams.
   You need concrete objects with which to work (i.e. graphs, charts, diagrams).

7. Weakest Learning Mode: Auditory
   Course is an audio-tutorial or telecourse. Your grade is based on laboratory experiments and oral exams.

8. Weakest Learning Mode: Visual
   Massive textbook and outside readings are required. In class the instructor makes extensive use of overhead transparencies.

   - tape the lecture
   - take heavier notes while in class
   - read aloud, move fingers along the lines

9. Weakest Learning Mode: Visual
   Class is a series of films, diagrams and pictures.
   Assignments—to critique works of art.

   - heavy notes
   - study in groups
   - make study cards

10. Strongest Learning Mode: Tactile/Kinaesthetic
    Lecture class only with extensive outside readings.

    - follow w/ fingers
    - make diagrams
    - study cards
    - practice ?s

Some Examples of Strategies that you might use for this exercise:

A student who prefers to read the textbook will enjoy a lecture more by taking extensive notes and relating them to the text.

A student who prefers to learn by listening is better to read the textbook after the lecture.

A kinaesthetic learner prefers to experiment on his own and can best learn by manipulating or handling the materials involved in the course.

CHAPTER 4
Remembering to Concentrate

Concentration and memory are both important factors in your learning process. The ability to concentrate affects how much you can accomplish while you are studying. The ability to remember information is going to determine how well you will be able to apply this information in your life and how well you will score on tests.

Concentration is a by-product. It only happens when we don't think about it. If you are engrossed in your history book and suddenly realize that you were concentrating, then at that moment you would have broken your concentration on the reading material.

Concentration is the process that permits you to focus your attention on a particular task. This process requires continual monitoring of distractors. You will have a better chance of improving your concentration if you know what causes you to lose it.

Complete the Concentration Checklist to find out "How is your concentration?"

Why Is Concentration Difficult?

Concentrating on a subject is not something that just "happens." Albert Einstein was the typical "absent-minded professor." His enormous intellectual powers were so concentrated on the problem at hand that he lost all connection with routine activities. A good example today would be the teenager engrossed in playing a video game. He loses all touch with routine activities. "I can't concentrate" is a common student complaint. The habit of concentration can be developed by self-discipline and practice in "becoming involved."

From *Practical Approaches for Building Study Skills and Vocabulary*, Second Edition by Funk et al. © 1996 by Kendall/Hunt Publishing Company.

Name: _____ Date: _____

■ Concentration Checklist

DIRECTIONS: Check all statements which you feel apply to you:

- [ ] 1. I "drift off" when listening to a lecture in a class I don't like.
- [ ] 2. I am easily distracted when trying to study—noise, uncomfortable temperatures, or interruptions really bother me.
- [ ] 3. Once I'm interrupted, I find it difficult to get back on task.
- [ ] 4. I find it difficult to work on large/long assignments.
- [ ] 5. If I don't like the instructor, I find it difficult to pay attention in class.
- [ ] 6. I'm usually too tired to concentrate when I begin to read my textbook assignments.
- [ ] 7. If something is on my mind, I usually can't concentrate until the problem is solved.
- [ ] 8. I read the material, but I just don't seem to remember what I've read.
- [ ] 9. It's hard for me to listen to the instructor and take notes at the same time.
- [ ] 10. Some of my classes just don't seem to be important, and I can't pay attention in them.

How's your concentration? If you had five or more checks, you need to pay particular attention to the concentration strategies discussed in this chapter.

What Are Some Problems in Concentrating and Their Solutions?

1. *Problem:* Mental and/or Physical Fatigue—It is difficult to concentrate when you are tired. Studying late at night can be a problem because of this. Mental fatigue can be caused by too many things to do, depression, fear of failure, lack of interest, and many more factors. When you are physically tired, it is hard to care about anything, not to mention trying to concentrate on it. Sometimes boredom can be the cause of the fatigue feeling.

   Solution: Determine the time of day you are most alert. Use this time of day for your most difficult assignments. A proper diet, rest, and exercise will also help you be more alert. If boredom is the culprit, find something in the class that will help you build an interest. Look until you find it! Be alert to ways in which your class relates to your life. Read actively and converse mentally with the author. It also helps to study in a well-ventilated room. Take short breaks and do something active.

2. *Problem:* Too Much to Do—Procrastination is usually the cause here. Often we are more overwhelmed by the idea of all that we need to do than the actual work that needs to be accomplished. When we try to think of several things at once, it is impossible to concentrate.

   Solution: Keep a calendar of test and assignment deadlines. The deadline for one class will probably coincide with the deadline of another class. Make a schedule with definite times for studying and completing specific assignments. Stick to this schedule! One way to do this is to set goals for each study session. Plan ahead exactly what you expect to accomplish in that session. It is important to set realistic goals. Divide long assignments into short sessions. Reward yourself after your objective is completed. Your objective should not be to just cover the pages, but to understand the assignment.

3. *Problem:* A Poor Attitude—If you do not care about what you are studying, you obviously will not be able to concentrate!

   Solution: Accept the fact you need to learn the material. Many people have spent long hours in deciding what courses were necessary to fit a particular program. Decisions are not always based on simply turning out good teachers or lawyers. These people were also concerned with producing good, well-rounded individuals.

   Before you allow your attitude to ruin any hope of good concentration and retention, give the subject a chance. Be an active reader. Dig in and question, agree, or disagree with the author. Talk to students who are majoring in this field and see what interests them. Could it be possible that your lack of background is causing the dislike? Explore this field in an encyclopedia. Look in bookstores for review and workbooks. If you can build a background, maybe you can help your attitude!

4. *Problem:* No Concentration Habit—If you have been out of school for a period of time, did not apply yourself previously, or have not been involved in an activity that required concentration, maybe you have "lost" the habit of concentration.

   Solution: You had it at one time. You have concentrated when you were learning to ride a bicycle, when you learned to read and write, drive a car, and many other basic skills you possess. You can re-develop this skill by being aware of how important it is. This could take some practice!

5. *Problem:* Noisy Study Environment—Are you trying to study with your favorite television program? How about your favorite music? Do you take your textbook to a ball game?

    Solution: Two or three hours of study in quiet surroundings does more good than ten hours of study in a noisy place. It is important to have a designated study place that is used only for studying. Concentrating will be aided by associating studying with a particular locale.

6. *Problem:* Poor Reading and Study Skills—It is difficult to concentrate if you are having problems understanding what you are trying to learn.

    Solution: If your vocabulary is limited, you need to work on this! Practice vocabulary exercises, word games, and read as much varied material as you can. You improve reading by reading. Learn basic effective approaches to textbook study.

7. *Problem:* Deciding Who Is in Control—It is difficult to concentrate if you're not aware of who controls your concentration efforts.

    Solution: You should be cognizant of what contributes to your concentration. If you are in control, then you are the one who can make the decisions necessary to increase your concentration. If the control is something else, is there anything you can do?

What Are External and Internal Distractors?

A learner must be able to cope with internal and external distractors before starting to concentrate and learn.

Internal Distractors

Any form of negative self-talk is an internal distractor. In order to concentrate, your mind must be quiet and controlled. Sometimes a small voice inside that should be full of confidence blurts out, "You are probably going to say something stupid," and, sure enough, this proves to be true. But luckily, there is also another voice hiding in there. You feel confident and knowledgeable about what you are about to say, and it comes out right! These inside voices determine to a great extent the "tone" of your world—whether it is good, bad, or indifferent. We can change how we feel by what we say to ourselves.

Negative self-talk can be produced by insecurity, fear, anxiety, frustration, defeatist attitudes, indecision, anger, daydreams, and personal problems. This self-talk is obviously influenced by your feelings. If your self-talk seems to lean more on the negative side, you are not alone! Richard Fenker says 80–90 percent of students with learning problems have self-talk that is predominantly negative. Fenker believes you can control these negative voices using your right brain and substituting more positive self-talk. If you are afraid of speaking in public, imagine yourself giving a report in front of a class. If you have test anxiety, imagine or picture yourself being relaxed and calm in that testing situation. Spend a few days listening to yourself. When a negative opinion surfaces, try to replace it with a neutral or a positive thought!

What Internal Distractors Affect You?

Take a look at the following list of internal distractors. Do any of these distractors seem to be a problem for you? If so, note the possible answer for this distractor.

Hunger	Eat before you study.
Fatigue	Plan study time when you are most alert and get at least 7 to 8 hours of sleep. Don't forget some exercise!
Illness	Postpone until you feel better.
Worrying about grades or work	Try to focus on the task and better grades will be the result. Focus on work while you are at work.
Stress	Attempt to focus on what you are trying to accomplish.
Physical discomfort	Study in a comfortable place.
Not understanding assignment	Always clarify assignments before you start.
Personal problems	Make a note of the problem and tell yourself you will cope after you study.
Lack of interest	Try studying with someone else, find something that you can relate to, or look at related material.
Negative attitude	Remember negative thoughts take away from getting a job done! Convince yourself there is something positive in the class.

Please note that some of these distractors can be eliminated if you anticipate your needs!

External Distractors

External distractors originate outside of you. They are those things that draw your attention away from a learning task.

Take a look at the following list of external distractors. Do some of them seem familiar? Many of these problems can also be eliminated if you anticipate your needs.

Lack of proper materials	Before you start your study session, have paper, pencil, etc. in place.
Music, television, noise, lighting too bright or too dim, temperature too high or too low, people talking, telephone	Choose your study location carefully. These should be eliminated by just choosing a proper spot.
Party or activity that you want to attend, family or friends wanting you to do something	If possible, plan your study session ahead of activity and use it as a reward.

Do the Concentration Worksheet to determine your specific problems.

Why Is a "Place of Study" So Important?

By looking at internal and external distractors, you can see how many can be controlled by the place you choose to study. It is important to have a definite and permanent place to study. Psychologists believe a conditioning effect is created between your desk and you. Do not do any other activities at your study desk. You should associate your study place with studying alone. Don't write letters, daydream, plan activities, or visit with friends in your study place. You need a study place where you feel comfortable and where you are likely to have few distractions.

A Program to Increase Concentration while Studying

Purpose

This program is designed to help you learn deep and effective concentration while studying.

How Does It Work?

Primarily by capitalizing on the concentration powers you already possess. This is done by developing an extremely strong association between one particular physical location (such as the desk in your room) and deep concentration on your studies.

What Must You Do?

To set up a strong association such as this, you must: Remove old associations that your "study spot" might have for you. This means removing pictures, telephones, souvenirs, etc. from your study area. When seated in your "study chair" only materials being studied at that moment should be seen. This sounds simple and in fact it is not extremely difficult, but it does require some self-discipline—especially at the beginning. You learn this new association by merely making sure that the only time you are in your study spot is when you are concentrating on your studies. Get up and move to another chair, or at least turn around in your chair so that you are looking at an entirely different set of visual stimuli every time your mind wanders, a friend comes in to talk, your roommate asks you a question, etc. Don't be discouraged if you have to change locations or turn around every few minutes for the first several days. It takes this long to develop this new association for most people. It's vital that you do absolutely nothing except concentrate while in your study spot. If you feel like letting your mind wander, go ahead . . . but make sure you move out of your study spot or turn around in your chair. Also, don't force concentration, or you'll end up associating your study spot with discomfort rather than concentration. Concentration is also helped if you switch study subjects every half hour or forty-five minutes, rather than working so long on one particular subject that you tire of studying for that course.

What Can You Expect?

Between 75 and 90 percent of the students who try this program find they can dramatically increase their periods of deep concentration within a period of a week or so, if they have been faithful to the system. Going from periods of concentration as short as two minutes to more than 45 minutes within several weeks is not at all unusual. But remember, the first three or four days will be the hardest, because it is during that time you will not notice much change. After the third or fourth day (assuming you have studied several hours each day), you will begin to notice a difference. Some students find the number of times they have to turn around in their chairs the first few days to be discouraging, and feel that the system results in their wasting time. However what is probably the case is that they have finally become painfully aware of just how much time they have actually been wasting in the past!

How Do You Improve Concentration while Reading?

Dr. Walter Pauk, noted study skills expert, believes the best way to gain and maintain concentration while you read is by having a lively conversation with the author. (No one will have to know!) Agree or disagree with the author. Interject your thoughts and ideas. This will also lead to more comprehension.

One reason your mind may wander during reading is because material is unfamiliar or too difficult. You cannot concentrate on what you can't comprehend. Formulate a purpose for reading! It also never hurts to look up words when you do not know the meanings!

What Are Some Strategies to Strengthen Concentration?

1. Learn to beat boredom—If boredom is causing a problem with concentration, study in small groups occasionally, buy review manuals and workbooks and look at the material from a different angle. Perhaps a tutor could provide new insights.

2. Become more active in studying—Highlight, underline, make questions out of the material, paraphrase, construct mnemonics, and/or form imagery associations. Think about your learning style and put it to work.

3. Ignore external distractions—A vibrating tuning fork held close to a spider's web sets up vibrations in the web. After the spider makes a few investigations and doesn't find dinner, it learns to ignore the vibrations. If a spider can control external distractors, a student should be able to eventually ignore external distractions.

Memory

Your brain is constantly being attacked with all kinds of information. You need to learn to process all of this by selective attention. Unimportant information signals are discarded immediately, such as a dog barking, a bird chirping, or the wind blowing. Other signals are only recalled for a moment. These signals will either be stored or dropped. As you are reading, you may recall the sentence you just finished. But, it may be difficult to recall that sentence when you finish a paragraph. The exact wording of that sentence has probably been dropped. If you can remember the concept of the sentence, you have probably stored that information in your memory.

It is important to note that without memory, there would be no learning.

Before you start reading this portion of the chapter, complete the Memory Worksheets.

What Are the Three Stages in the Memory Process?

1. Respond—If you don't understand material you are trying to remember, you don't have a chance to respond. One method we have of understanding new information is to relate it to what we already know. It will be helpful when starting a new chapter in a text to stop and think about what you already know about the material. What does this information mean to you before you learn anything new about it? To help you respond to information it is advantageous to use all of your senses: Listen to the lecture, take notes on it, and read about it.

2. Reserve—The key to reserving or retaining information is to make a conscious effort to remember. You need to find a reason to remember! One of the best ways to reserve information is to use or practice this information.

3. Remember—Our mind enables us to remember or recall information we have retained. Organization is an important factor in recall. Using your preferred learning style is also an asset. Review is vital for recalling information.

The immediate memory is called your short-term memory. This information is either discarded and forgotten or it is transferred into your permanent memory. This permanent memory is your long-term memory. Not all information stored in your long-term memory is in a form that can be retrieved. Short-term memory plays an important role in our everyday life. It is also vital in reading and study situations. The transfer of memory from short-term to long-term is enhanced by organization, repetition, and association with what we already know.

A study conducted at Southwest Missouri State University by Dr. Charles Tegeler revealed information on the value of review to help you remember. Students were given information and they studied it until they had 100 percent mastery. The group was divided into two groups. One group did not review the material and at the end of 63 days when they were retested, they averaged 17 percent comprehension. The other group reviewed once a week. At the end of the 63 day period, they averaged 92 percent comprehension! (See Figure 1.)

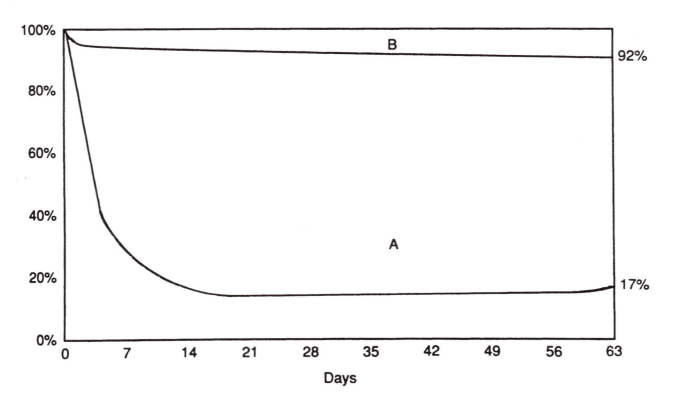

A - no review
B - review once a week

Figure 1

Why Do You Forget?

Forgetting can be defined as a failure or loss of memory. Your mind remembers only what you need and discards the rest. Do you remember grades you made in your classes in the eighth grade? Do you even remember what classes you had? You probably don't remember. Information that is not used is forgotten.

Research has proven over and over that the greatest amount of forgetting occurs during the first day. Remembering what you have heard is even more difficult to remember than what you have read. When you read, you have control over the material. You can slow down, regress, or speed-up your reading.

People often say they forgot something when they actually never knew it. If you just met someone and didn't really catch their name, you didn't forget it—you probably never knew it.

There are a variety of theories about forgetting. Think about these as you read them and see if you can understand how the theory relates to your own "forgetful" experiences.

1. It's There Somewhere!—Some psychologists believe once we have thoroughly learned something, it remains in our memory our entire life. This theory suggests that the concept is there, but we are just having trouble finding it in order to be able to retrieve it.

2. Interference Theory—Old facts and ideas cause us to forget new facts and ideas. The reverse is also true. New ideas and facts can cause confusion with old ones. We are continually adding ideas to our memory bank. If you learn three similar facts at three separate times, the middle one will have the most difficult time surviving. This is also true of lists you need to remember. The first and last items are easier to remember than the middle ones.

3. Use It or Lose It—If you don't use a fact you have learned, it gets more difficult to remember it. This is why review is so important!

4. Motivation and Attitude Theory—Here are our two favorite words again! Sometimes we choose to forget. Things we associate with unpleasant memories or mistakes we have made we would like to forget. A poor attitude in class can definitely affect memory ability. You have the power to influence both remembering and forgetting.

How Can You Enhance Your Memory?

Our most powerful attack against forgetting is cognitive processing. This simply means deep thinking. It is deep thinking that makes a long-lasting memory trace. According to Walter Pauk, there are three steps in cognitive processing or deep thinking:

1. Understand the fact thoroughly; be able to explain it in your own words.

2. Analyze the fact by viewing it from all sides.

3. Relate the fact to information you already have.

Using memory effectively is being able to recall information at the right time. Our memory system needs to be flexible.

The following ideas should help improve your memory:

1. *Organization*—The first step in organizing is to get a broad overview. Learn general concepts before you learn specifics. If you have a "feel" for the general idea, the details will have a place to fit.

   Research has shown that our short-term memory has a limited capacity. Seven unrelated items are about maximum for most people to remember. In various college classes, you will need to remember more than seven unrelated items. The way to handle this is through meaningful organization.

   Chunking or Clustering—This is a method whereby you categorize similar items you need to know. For example:

   As you walked to the grocery store, you realized you didn't have your list with you. You did remember there were twelve items. The items you had on your list were:

   onions, lettuce, ice cream, bananas, green beans, eggs, cheese, peas, apples, grapefruit, milk, and oranges.

   Look at these items for 15 seconds. Close the book and see how many you can recall. You are doing well if you remember 6 or 7.

   By clustering or chunking these items, we can make them manageable. We can have 3 major items instead of twelve.

Vegetables	Dairy	Fruits
onions	ice cream	bananas
lettuce	milk	apples
green beans	eggs	grapefruit
peas	cheese	oranges

   When we think of the major headings, the individual details fall in place. The thought of dairy products automatically reduces our thoughts to dairy products. This procedure will work well in your textbooks. Learn to associate details with the major headings.

   John Morris suggests a similar organizational technique. A good way to consolidate and summarize information you need to remember is to use the "poker-chip" strategy. In the game of poker, the blue chips are worth the most, followed by red chips and then the white chips. By analogy, the most important ideas in any message are the blue chips. Next to the blue chip ideas are the red chip, and subordinate to the red chip are the white chip ideas, which may be considered details.

   Around a poker table, you'll usually find a player has many more white chips than red or blue. Usually he will also have a few more red chips than blue. A writer has few blue chip ideas, a few more red chip, and many more white chip ideas. When you are summarizing, mark white chip ideas with a W, the red chip ideas with an R, and the blue chip ideas with a B. This technique makes main ideas easy to remember. The main ideas act as magnets holding together the subordinate ideas and the supporting details.

2. *Visualize Relationships and Associations*—Knowing individual facts does not help you understand a topic. Relating details provides a basis for the main idea. Also, it is important to relate new ideas to what you already know. Visualizing uses a different part of your brain than when you just read. This will also aid in reten-

tion. Often students will remember a picture, table, or graph that explains a theory easier than they will remember the words that described it. The better our background, the easier this will be.

3. *Make It Meaningful*—We remember things better when we can apply them to ourselves. If we can match the information we need to remember to a goal we have set, it will be easier to recall.

4. *Intend to Remember*—Your mental attitude plays an important role in your memory. Intending to learn can create a positive attitude that will include other important characteristics, such as active learning, paying attention, and writing to understand.

5. *Motivated Interest*—Research has shown that interest is important to learning, but remembering is almost impossible without interest. If you are not interested in a class you are taking, find some way to create an interest. We tend to forget information that contradicts our opinions. If you feel bored, consider the possibility that you are creating your boredom. Take responsibility for your attitudes.

6. *Recitation*—This technique is probably the most powerful one that will allow transfer from short-term to long-term memory. When you want to remember something, repeat it aloud. Recitation works best when you put concepts you want to remember into your own words.

    Arthur Gates did a series of recitation experiments in 1917. His experiments suggest that when you are reading a general text (psychology, sociology, history), 80 percent of your time should be spent in reciting and 20 percent in reading. It is also more effective to start recitation early in the reading process. Do not wait until you have read everything before you start to recite.

7. *Spaced Study*—Marathon study sessions are not effective. It is much better to have intermittent spaced review sessions. A practical application of this would be using the small blocks of time you are now wasting during the day. It is also important to take breaks while you are studying. After 45–50 minutes, reward yourself with a short break. When you come back, you will be more alert and more efficient. If significant learning is taking place and you are really engrossed, go for it! You don't have to stop, but memory is more productive when you space your studying instead of trying to accomplish everything in one long session.

8. *Brainstorming*—If you are having a problem recalling an answer on a test, try brainstorming. Think of everything you can that is related to what you are trying to remember. For example, if you are trying to remember your fifth grade teacher's name, think of other elementary teachers you had. By association the name you are trying to remember should pop up during this brainstorming.

9. *Reflecting*—It is important to give information time to go from short-term memory to long-term memory. This is considered consolidation time. Researchers vary on their opinions, but a safe rule is to leave information in your short-term memory 4–15 seconds. This gives information time to consolidate and transfer to your long-term memory. This is important to remember when you are reading quickly and not stopping to think about what you have read. The information will be discarded quickly if you do not allow time for transfer. Stop and think about what you have just read, recite it, paraphrase it, and relate it to what you already know.

10. *Use All Your Senses*—The more senses you involve in studying, the better your memory process will work. Read and visualize, recite key concepts, devise questions, and write answers.

11. *Combine Memory Techniques*—You can combine organizing, reciting, and reflecting in one task. Different techniques can reinforce each other.

12. *Repetition*—Simply repeating things will aid memory. Advertisements hook us in this way. We learn a jingle by hearing it repeated again and again. For example:

    "You Deserve a Break Today" . . . McDonalds

    "It's the Real Thing" . . . Coke

    "Ring around the Collar" . . . Wisk Detergent

    "You've Got the Right One, Baby" . . . Diet Pepsi

13. *Mnemonics*—Mnemonics are easily remembered words, rhymes, phrases, sentences, or games that help you remember difficult lists, principles, or facts.

    An example of a rhyming association could be:

    "In fourteen hundred and ninety-two Columbus sailed the ocean blue."

If you have a group to remember or a list of items, you can make-a-word mnemonic. An easy way to remember the Great Lakes is by the word HOMES—Huron, Ontario, Michigan, Erie, and Superior.

Similar to this is an acronym. An acronym is formed by the first letters of the words you want to remember. A good example of this would be the note taking system introduced in this text.

> ***TRQ: T** ake notes*
> ***R** evise notes*
> ***Q** uestion main points*

Another mnemonic device is to make a sentence you can remember. You make the sentence using words you devised from the first letter of the words you need to remember. For example:

You need to remember the factors that are involved in the quality of your sleep. These factors are the habit of your sleep, the environment where you sleep, the duration, your general health, and the use of drugs.

Your mnemonic sentence could be: "Hey everyone, don't have drugs."

You made these words using key words in the list you needed to remember:

> *Hey—habit*
>
> *everyone—environment*
>
> *don't—duration*
>
> *have—health*
>
> *drugs—drugs*

It is important to note that mnemonics do not help you understand the material. They assist in rote memorization.

General Study Skills

The next section is to make you think of different areas in general study skills. Answer the questions honestly and, after each major section, write a brief paragraph describing your habits in these areas and whether they are potential problems. Awareness of the problems in these different areas is the beginning of more efficient study.

Summary

The best way to improve your concentration is by identifying and eliminating internal and external distractors. You are in control of internal distractors. External distractors may be beyond your control, but you can learn to control your reactions to them. A proper place to study and how you study also affect concentration. Take frequent breaks and reward yourself!

Recall ability is controlled by your memory processes. Forgetting occurs very rapidly unless you take certain steps to prevent this. Realizing the importance of organization, visualization, intention to remember, interest, recitation, combining memory techniques, spaced study, brainstorming, reflecting, using your senses, and mnemonics will help you in strengthening your recall ability.

Reflect and Apply

Complete the following worksheets to apply what you learned in this chapter to your study sessions.

Name: _____ Date: _____

■ Concentration Worksheet

During your next study session, keep a record of internal and external distractors. On the chart below, write what the distractor was. After your study session, determine whether the distractor was internal or external. Write a brief solution.

Distraction	External/Internal	Solution
1.		
2.		
3.		
4.		
5.		
6.		
7.		
8.		
9.		
10.		

Name: _____ Date: _____

Your Memory Habits

Answer yes or no to the following questions:

	YES	NO
1. Do you intend to remember your course work?	____	____
2. Do you try to get interested in your classes?	____	____
3. Do you honestly focus your full attention while studying?	____	____
4. Do you review lecture and textbook notes once a week or more?	____	____
5. Do you use organization in your study sessions?	____	____
6. Do you study in short spaced (45–50 minutes) sessions with breaks?	____	____
7. Do you keep an open mind when being introduced to new material?	____	____
8. Do you recite material you are trying to remember?	____	____
9. Do you make an effort to understand the material, not just read it?	____	____
10. Do you use several methods to reinforce memory, i.e., reciting, discussing with friends, and effective note taking?	____	____

If you answer yes to 7 or more of these, you are on the right track! If you have 3 or more no answers, you need to evaluate your study habits.

Write a brief paragraph explaining what you intend to start doing to develop your memory.

_____

_____

_____

_____

_____

_____

_____

CHAPTER 5
Active Listening and Note Taking Skills

Introduction[1]

Listening and Note Taking Skills

Good note taking skills are critical to your college success. They begin with the process of active listening, are developed through practice and skills analysis, and end with learning to use your notes as a part of your total study system.

This chapter will help you to identify your note taking strengths and weaknesses and will introduce you to several "user friendly" note taking systems. You'll also learn to assess your instructor's lecture style and develop strategies which will allow you to take good notes even when the lecturer isn't super organized.

Active Listening and the Importance of Note Taking

Why take notes? As a student, you are asked to "listen"—to receive and absorb information—on an ongoing basis. You will need to process this information and later will be asked to show how well you understand the material by testing or some other formal evaluation process. Use the following exercise to identify your current note taking strengths and weaknesses.

---

[1]From *The Community College: A New Beginning, Second Edition* by Aguilar et al. © 1998 by Kendall/Hunt Publishing Company. Used by permission.

Note Taking Skills Inventory

Note Taking Skill	Yes	No
PREPARING FOR CLASS		
1. I check my course syllabus on a daily basis to make sure I'm aware of upcoming assignments.	✓	
2. I read the textbook assignment before class so that the lecture material will seem familiar to me.	✓	
3. I have a three-ring binder and looseleaf paper for classroom note taking.	✓	
4. I have reviewed the table of contents of my textbook to have a general idea of how the information for this course is going to be organized.		✓
5. I have "tuned in" to my instructor's style and have a general idea of how s/he will deliver the material.	✓	
PAYING ATTENTION IN CLASS		
1. I am able to keep my attention on the subject matter even if the instructor wanders from the point or makes comments with which I don't agree.	✓	
2. I am alert and actively listening during both lecture and discussion periods.	✓	
3. I feel comfortable in asking questions if I don't understand the material presented in the lecture.	✓	
4. I can identify introductory and concluding statements and can recognize transition words and phrases when the teacher is lecturing.	✓	
5. As I listen, I can usually pick out the main ideas and supporting details without difficulty.	✓	
NOTE TAKING TECHNIQUE		
1. My notes are complete enough for me to understand them even when I look back over them many weeks later.	✓	
2. I use my own words rather than trying to write down exactly what the teacher says.	✓	
3. I make sure to copy down information put on the board and to include in my notes any examples the teacher used.		✓
4. I leave space to allow me to clarify my notes to add to them at a later point.		✓
5. I use a "personal shorthand" system of abbreviations and symbols which allows me to write down information more quickly.		✓
REVIEW AND USE OF NOTES		
1. I review and edit my notes as soon as possible after class.		✓
2. I use my notes to think of possible test questions to prepare for quizzes/tests.		✓
3. I summarize the important ideas from each lecture on a daily basis.		✓
4. I compare my notes with the text material I've read to make sure I fully understand the material.		✓
5. In reviewing my notes, I can understand the connections between main ideas and supporting details and examples.	✓	

Look over your responses to the inventory questions. In which sections did you have the most "Yes" responses? Which area needs the most improvement? Use the following sections on listening skills, preparing for note taking, recording information, note taking systems, and using your notes for test review to help you develop your notetaking abilities.

Listening Skills[2]

Hearing is a physiological, involuntary, natural reaction that does not require interpretation. We know the "Muzak" was on in the elevator, but we can't name the song we just heard. In contrast, listening is a psychological, voluntary action that requires interpretation or the assignment of meaning. You must be able to respond to information heard in classes. These are critical skills for a student to develop. Ability in this area will affect your ability to take effective notes that will enhance your success in many classes. Effective listening involves paying attention and concentrating on what the speaker is saying. In order to listen effectively, you must be physically present and mentally alert in class.

PHYSICALLY PRESENT. Being physically present means attending class regularly. If you are not attending regularly, you need to honestly evaluate your situation. Circumstances often necessitate a change in plans. If attending class is not a priority, maybe you need to sit down with an advisor and discuss your academic goals.

Physical presence also means sitting in class where you can hear and see the speaker, focusing on the speaker, and maintaining eye contact. Finding a place to sit where you can see and hear enhances your ability to concentrate. As a general rule, the closer to the front you sit, the more focused and attentive to the lecturer you will remain. In fact, research on college students and academic success has proven that students who sit closer to the instructor achieve higher grades. Those students appear to be more focused on the instructor. From the instructor's perspective he/she may feel that a rapport has been established with those students.

MENTALLY ALERT. Being mentally alert means avoiding distractions, thoughts, and behaviors that inhibit or block your ability to listen effectively. Bringing your body to class and allowing your mind to be someplace else sabotages your goals for effective listening. If you are preoccupied, worried, daydreaming, or thinking about something else while trying to listen, you will most likely miss a lot of the information being given. Financial concerns, academic difficulties, family problems, roommates, weekend plans, etc., etc., are all examples of things that compete for a student's attention. For some students, class time is the only quiet time they have. It is during this quiet time that personal problems and concerns begin to enter into consciousness and compete for attention. What can you do when you are sitting in class and your mind begins to wander, or you begin to think about things unrelated to the class?

- Jot down these thoughts on a piece of paper. Tell yourself that you will get back to them later.
- Give yourself permission to attend to these problems at a later time.
- Set aside time during the day to work on problems.

Aside from personal distractions, many students have difficulty listening to lectures because they lack the basic course knowledge. They are unfamiliar with the material be-

---

[2]From *Your Utah State Experience: Strategies for Success, Fourth Edition* by Utah State University Academic Support Services. © 1998 by Utah State University Academic Support Services. Used by permission of Kendall/Hunt Publishing.

ing presented and become overwhelmed. This is often the result of failing to do assigned readings or poor class attendance. By attending class regularly, doing supplemental readings to build background, and coming prepared, you are able to keep on top of assignments and avoid being overwhelmed.

WAYS TO IMPROVE LISTENING. There are ways to improve your listening skills. The following is a list of some basic techniques for effective listening in class.

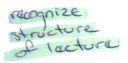
recognize structure of lecture

- *Recognize how ideas are organized.* Lectures usually begin with some type of introduction followed by a thesis statement. This statement is what they hope to cover in the day's lecture. The thesis is supported by additional information. Most professors bring closure to their lectures by summarizing what they have covered. Learn to identify the lecture style that is used by your professor.
- *Become involved in what is being said.* If there are prepared notes for the course, read these before coming to class. Think about the purpose of the lecture, identify key points, make connections between ideas, and write down specific examples. Mark possible test questions.
- *Screen out distractions such as:*
  - background noise;
  - unusual accents, dialects, and language mistakes;
  - speaker disorganization, emotion, or habits;
  - superfluous material; and
  - your own inner voice.
- *Organize statements into main points and supporting reasons.* Use an outline form if it is helpful. Add information to prepared notes or outlines.
- *Discriminate between relevancies and irrelevancies.* Remember that not all information is important.
- *Maintain an active body state.* Sit with your back fairly straight and your pen poised to take notes. Sit in front and have eye-contact with the speaker.
- *Develop a positive attitude about the class.* You may have to use "self-talk" statements such as, "I'm going to listen carefully for the key points so I will be ready for the discussion in my study group."

In order to improve your listening skills, you will need to practice using the suggested techniques for effective listening until they become automatic. There are many situations in which you will have this opportunity in class, at work, and with friends, family, and strangers.

Note Taking Strategies

Over 50% of what we hear is lost within the first hour. This makes it pretty clear that we can't depend on our memories for the material but need to have a written record for reference. Since college instruction is primarily lecture-oriented, good note taking skills are especially important.

It is difficult to separate listening and note taking. Note taking actually aids in effective listening. By taking notes, you are forced to listen carefully and critically to what is being said. You can build your interest in a subject through concentrated listening. Note taking provides a written aid for the retention of information. When you take notes in class, you are actively processing information.

Taking notes in class involves more than showing up to class with a pen and a piece of paper. It is an active process that involves three stages: before the lecture, during the lecture, and after the lecture.

BEFORE THE LECTURE. Being prepared to take effective notes involves thinking about the process before the actual class period.

- For each class use a different standard sized notebook (8½" by 11") or use colored dividers to create sections in one notebook. The larger size allows you to take notes and jot down questions and comments.
- Read the syllabus and discover the topic for that day. Write the date and the topic at the top of the paper.
- Create a note taking format for that particular class. Formats vary and there is no right way, only the way that works best for you and matches the information in the class. Figure 7 is an example of a popular format called the Cornell method. Divide your paper into separate sections. Choose a main section to take notes and smaller sections for pertinent information such as key terms, vocabulary, important people, and dates. Include a section for questions and an area to write a short summary in your own words. Additional sections may be added for supplementary information, for example, a comparison with the textbook information or possibly a section on problem solving.

pre-read
review

- Be prepared for the class by reading the textbook assignment and taking notes or reviewing information from the previous class.
- If the instructor has provided prepared notes for the class, read these before coming to class. (See Figure 8) This will provide you with background knowledge which will increase your understanding of the lecture.
- Review your notes from the previous class and your reading notes just before class.

DURING THE LECTURE. Now that you have prepared yourself for the process, you are ready for the actual recording of the notes. Complete Exercise 1: Evaluating Lecture Styles, to better correlate your note-taking with each lecture type.

repeated
emphasis

- Only record the essential points. Instructors usually indicate important material in a variety of ways, such as:
  - Writing important information on the board.
  - Putting important information onto overheads.
  - Emphasizing important information through tone or voice level.
  - Reviewing or summarizing possible exam material.
  - Restating the same material in several ways.
- Listen for "signal words" from the instructor. These words indicate what direction the instructor is headed. Your notes should reflect the signals they gave you such as "There are *four* important parts of this concept." Then your notes should be labeled accordingly.
- Write on every other line allowing room for additional material.
- Skip lines to show the end of one idea and the start of another. Indicate sub-ideas and supporting details with numbers or letters under the major idea.
- Use abbreviations and symbols when possible. You will want to develop your own personalized vocabulary of symbols that you can use without extra thought. Be careful that you don't use so many types that you can't decipher your notes later. Common symbols are "?" placed by confusing information or "*" by important information to remember. Use abbreviated words as "i.e." for "in other words" or "ex" for example.
- Write legibly. Do your notes right the first time. This will save you time as well as giving you practice in listening and taking effective notes.
- Purchased notes should also include active processing during the lecture:
  - Add additional examples given by the instructor or classmates.
  - Star important points stressed by the instructor. (Colored pens are a helpful tool.)
  - Mark confusing points with a question mark. Ask instructor or take questions to a SI section or study group.

- Draw lines to connecting information.
- Add additional information to charts, graphs, or diagrams.

AFTER THE LECTURE. Even though class time is over, the note taking process continues until you have processed your notes for future study.

- ZAP 1: Review your notes as soon as possible. Read through them, making corrections and filling in information you remember. Add questions to your Cornell notes.
- ZAP 2: Within 2 or 3 days after class, compare your lecture notes to the assigned reading. Make study tools with essential information.
- ZAP 3: Within one week, make consolidation notes from your lecture and reading. Put the information into your own words.

Selecting What to Record[3]

Knowing *what to write down* is a key to good note taking. How do you decide what's important? Your first step takes place when you complete the reading assignment before class. You enter the classroom with a general idea of what's likely to be covered. During class, you need to **pay close attention to the clues your instructor will use** to signal important ideas and concepts. Remember that your instructor wants you to understand and process the information being presented. S/he will use both verbal and nonverbal signals to help you pick out the main ideas and supporting details.

Verbal Signals:

1. DEFINITIONS—Definitions will generally show up as multiple choice or matching questions on quizzes or tests.

2. ENUMERATIONS—are signaled in ways such as "The four steps in the process are . . .," "Five characteristics of . . .," "The two effects of . . .," etc. Be sure to include a clear heading that identifies the topic.

3. TRANSITIONAL WORDS—While major points may not always be enumerated, instructors often use transitional words or phrases such as "Another reason is . . .," "then," "consequently," "furthermore," etc. These words are definite signals to help you with your note taking.

4. DIRECT ANNOUNCEMENT—Instructors sometimes say "This is an important point . . .," "The basic idea here is to . . .," or "Pay special attention to," etc. They're telling you up front that this information is important.

5. REPETITIONS—If a point is repeated, you can usually assume that the information is important. Try writing an "R" in the margin of your notes to show that this point was repeated.

6. EXAMPLES—Examples help you to understand important points. If you don't write examples down, you probably won't be able to remember them later and may not understand the idea or concept being explained. Try to come up with your own examples when you review your notes, as your own examples will be easier for you to remember.

---

[3] From *The Community College: A New Beginning, Second Edition* by Aguilar et al. © 1998 by Kendall/Hunt Publishing Company. Used by permission.

Nonverbal Signals:

1. VISUALLY PRESENTED INFORMATION—When an instructor puts information on the board or overhead or provides handouts, s/he is giving you a signal that this information is important. Be sure to copy down information placed on the board!

2. INSTRUCTOR MANNERISMS—Frequently when instructors are about to introduce a new topic, they will pause for a minute or glance down at their notes to gather their thoughts. This is a clear signal that you should space down and get ready for a new topic.

Recording Information

Now that you're prepared for class and are tuned in to watching for instructor signals, you need to develop a personal note taking system. This system will include a general note taking style and the use of certain personalized note taking strategies which will make your notes uniquely yours.

In reviewing note taking styles, we'll look at three "user friendly" systems—the informal outline with a "key word" or "recall" column, the Cornell system, and the visually oriented "mind-mapping" or "cluster system." Experts use different terms to describe these note taking systems, but the ideas behind each system are similar regardless of the names used to identify them.

Note Taking Styles

Taking notes in a formal outline format by grouping information into main ideas or topics, secondary topics, and supporting details or examples is one of the oldest note taking systems around. This system can be very effective when the lecturer is well organized and the information is delivered in a logical, step-by-step way. This technique is also useful when taking notes on assigned reading, as textbook chapters tend to be fairly well organized.

Many instructors are very knowledgeable but often don't seem to present the lecture material in a way that is easy for students to follow. They may also stray off the subject on a regular basis or have other mannerisms that make it difficult for you to come up with nicely outlined notes. I bet you can easily think of several teachers who fit this description!

Two of the note taking systems we'll review are variations on the formal outline, and their linear format on a divided notebook page makes them very easy to follow.

The Informal Outline

The informal outline (sometimes known as the indented topic system) lets you get down the major topics and shows secondary points and supporting details by indenting them under the major headings. Figure 1 presents a set of student notes on "The Great Depression" using the informal outline system. This system leaves a 2 ½" margin on the **right** side of the paper. After class, you can jot down key words which serve as "memory prompts." This "recall" column provides you with a built-in review technique when you begin test preparation review.

1/16/96
Hist 104

MAJOR CAUSES OF THE GREAT DEPRESSION

A. Federal Reserve Board Influence
   - No bank rep. or depositor's insurance
   - Didn't bail out first banks which closed
   - Raised interest rates
   - Too many loans to brokers & mkt. speculators

B. Market Speculation
   - Investors borrowed to buy stocks – used stocks as collateral to buy more "Margin"
   - Business spec. instead of reinvesting
   - "Anything goes" attitude

C. Unequal Distribution of Income
   - Companies kept prod. goods, but didn't raise wages
   - Consumers forced to "credit" buying
   - Credit dried up
   - Hawley-Smoot Tariff – kept imports out but Europe couldn't buy our goods

---

Impact of FRB policies

"Margin" Buying

"Get rich quick" attitude

Production ⇑ Wages & Credit ⇓

Hawley-Smoot Tariff

Figure 1 ■ Informal Outline

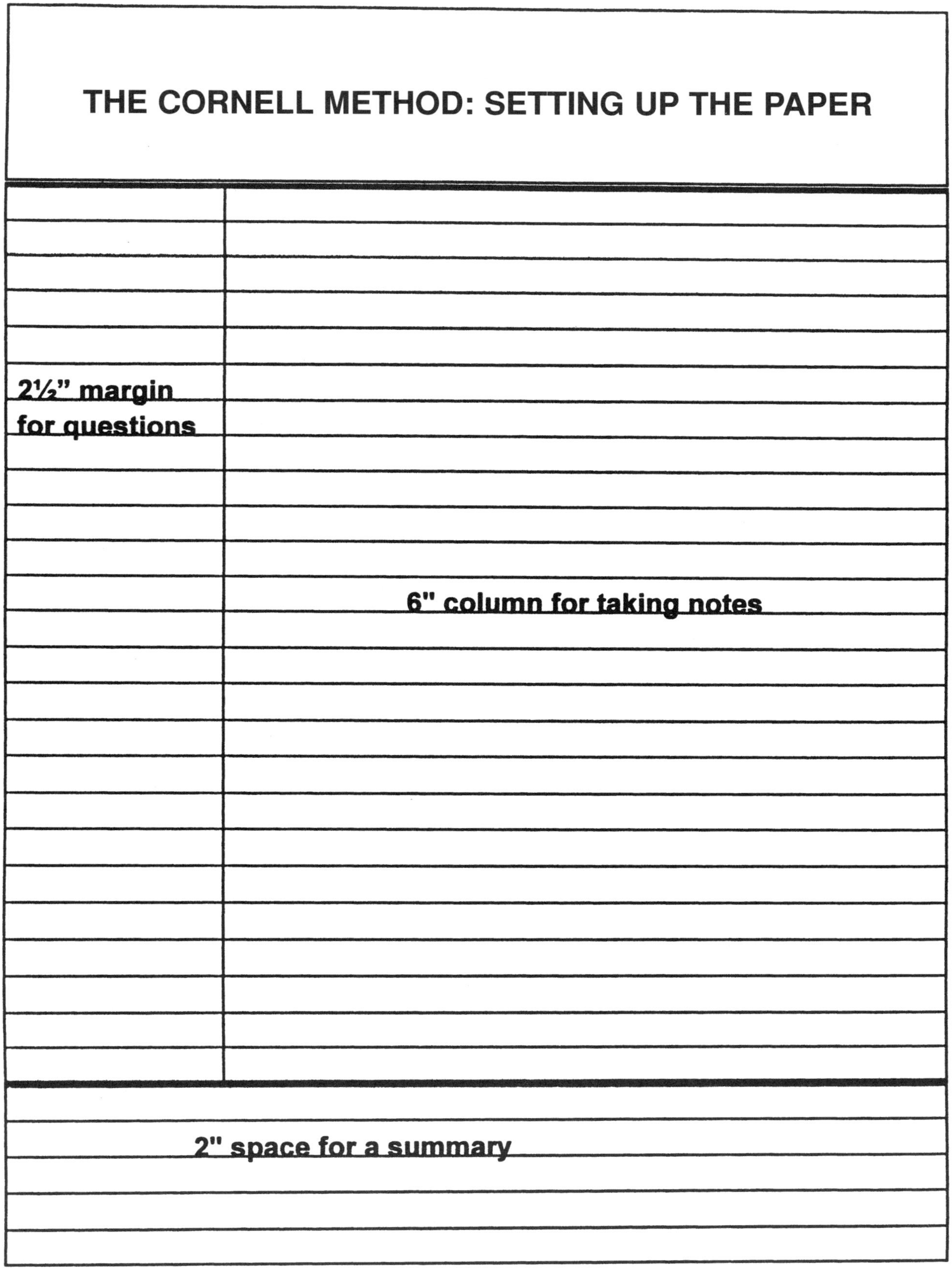

THE CORNELL METHOD: SETTING UP THE PAPER

2½" margin for questions

6" column for taking notes

2" space for a summary

Figure 2 ■ The Cornell Method: Setting Up the Paper

THE CORNELL METHOD

1/16/96
Hist. 104

	CAUSES OF THE GREAT DEPRESSION
	LOSS OF CONTROL BY FED. RESERVE BD.
WHAT IMPACT DID FRB POLICIES HAVE ON THE ECONOMY?	1. No bail out for first banks to close
	2. Raised interest rates
	3. No bank regulation
	4. No bank insurance for depositors
	5. Banks made too many loans to brokers and speculators
	MARKET SPECULATION
HOW DID THE LACK OF MKT. CONTROLS CONT. TO THE "CRASH"	1. No controls – "anything goes" attitude
	2. Investors borrowed to buy stocks and used them as collateral to buy more
DESCRIBE "MARGIN" BUYING	3. Business sector speculated instead of re-investing in their own companies.
WHAT WAS IMPACT OF THE HAWLEY-SMOOT TARIFF?	HAWLEY-SMOOT TARIFF – Kept imports out but then Europe couldn't buy goods from us.

SUMMARY: NO ONE CAUSE OF THE CRASH. "MARGIN" BUYING, POOR ECONOMY AFTER POST-WAR BOOM, POOR FRB POLICIES WERE MAJOR INFLUENCES.

Figure 3 ■ The Cornell Method

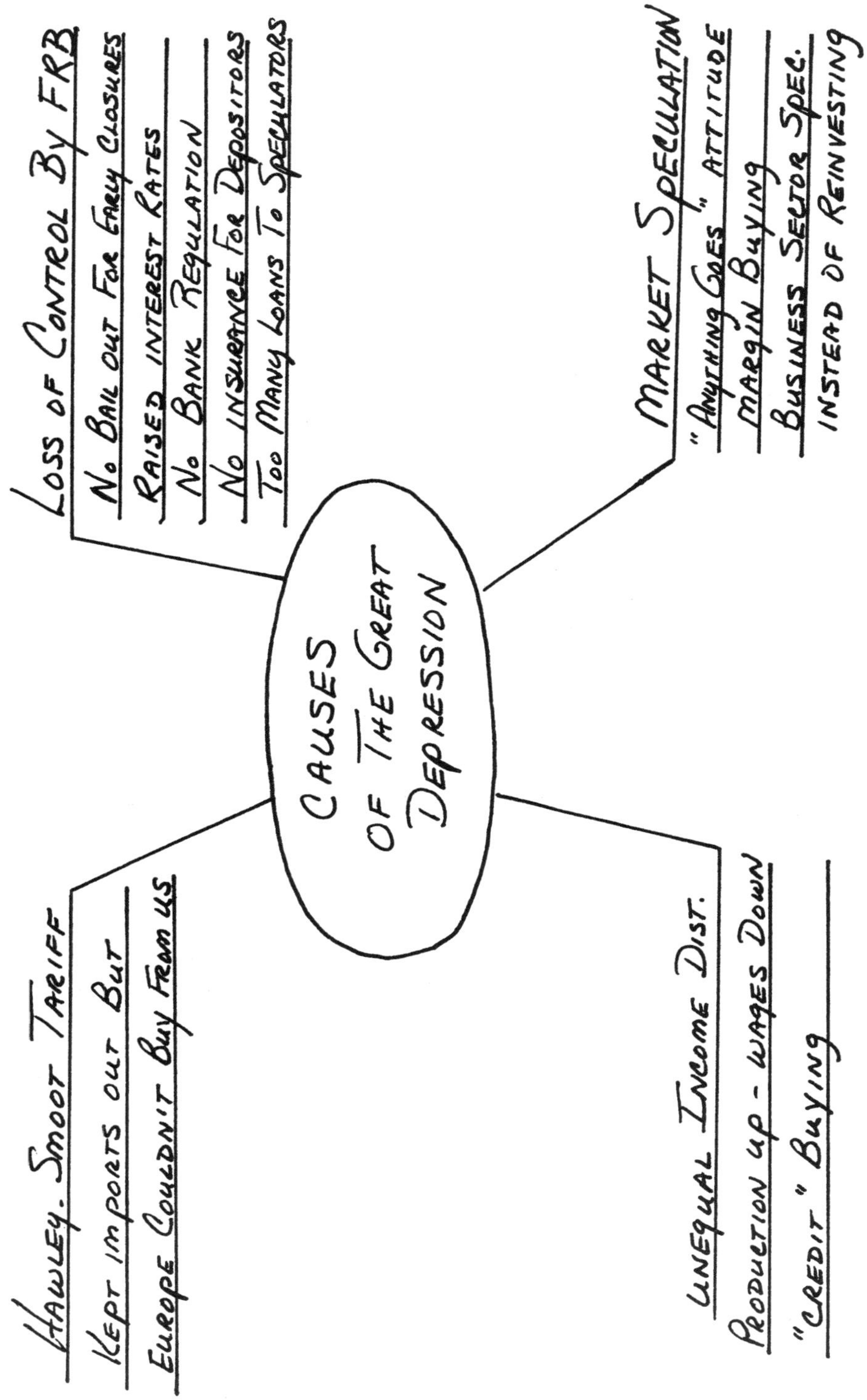

5: ACTIVE LISTENING AND NOTE TAKING SKILLS

Causes of The Great Depression

- **Hawley-Smoot Tariff**
  - Kept imports out but Europe couldn't buy from US

- **Loss of Control By FRB**
  - No Bail out for Early Closures
  - Raised Interest Rates
  - No Bank Regulation
  - No Insurance For Depositors
  - Too Many Loans To Speculators

- **Market Speculation**
  - "Anything Goes" Attitude
  - Margin Buying
  - Business Sector Spec. Instead of Reinvesting

- **Unequal Income Dist.**
  - Production up - Wages Down
  - "Credit" Buying

Figure 4 ■ Mind-Mapping

The Cornell System

The Cornell system, developed by Dr. Walter Pauk of Cornell University, is a second and widely used note taking system. Figure 2 divides the notebook paper into the three sections of the Cornell system, and Figure 3 shows lecture notes on the Depression taken in the Cornell style. Unlike the informal outline system, the Cornell system places the narrow column on the left and uses this column to develop questions about the lecture material. This system also uses a horizontal column across the bottom of the page to summarize key points.

Mind-Mapping

The "mind-mapping" or cluster system of note taking is a totally different approach. This system starts with the main idea or topic in the middle cluster and branches out with supporting details. It is very effective for visual learners. Figure 4 shows the same lecture material on the Great Depression presented in the mind-mapping style. If you like to visualize or "picture" information in your mind, this style could be your best bet. When reviewing, the individual mind maps are arranged to present a visual picture of all the information covered.

As you develop your note taking skills, you may find that you use the same style for all of your classes or you may change styles depending upon the course content. Any system, however, is only as good as you make it. Paying attention in class to get down the important information and then editing and reviewing your notes will definitely pay off when you are tested on the material.

Personalized Note Taking Strategies

Most instructors speak at the rate of 125–150 words per minute. You can't expect to record everything your instructor says, nor do you want to do so. Your job is to listen for main ideas and supporting details and to put the information down in *your own words*. You'll need to be listening for connections and relationships between main topics and trying to get down as much information as you can. Developing a system of "personal shorthand" which includes the use of abbreviations and symbols will help you to get the job done.

Figure 5 provides you with a list of commonly used abbreviations and symbols. You'll want to add to this list with abbreviations and symbols common to the vocabulary for your major or for technical terms which you'll probably use frequently. As you develop your own shortcuts, make sure that you'll be able to remember them!

Other personalized strategies include using a "lost" signal—a circled question mark (?) —to show places in your notes where you think you missed something. After class, you can ask classmates or the instructor to fill in any gaps. You may also want to clearly indicate examples used by putting a large "X" by them. Board work can be shown by using a large "B," and direct announcements of important facts can be shown with a "DA," etc. You get the idea.

Review and Use Your Notes

Now that you've *Read* the text prior to class and *Recorded* your notes during class, it's time for the final "R" of good note taking—the *Review*. Your first review of classroom

COMMON WORDS AND TERMS	ABBREVIATION OR SYMBOL	COMMON WORDS AND TERMS	ABBREVIATION OR SYMBOL
AMOUNT	Amt.	LESS THAN	<
AND	&	MONTH(S)	Mo(s).
CHAPTER	Ch.	NEGATIVE	–
COMPANY	Co.	NOT EQUAL	≠
CONTINUED	Cont'd.	NUMBER	#
DECREASE	Dec.	ORGANIZATION	Org.
DEFINITION	Def.	PAGE	Pg.
ECONOMIC	Econ.	PARALLEL	∥
EQUALS	=	POSITIVE	+
EXAMPLE	Ex. or X	PRINCIPAL	Princ.
GENERAL	Gen.	SIGNIFICANT	Sig.
GOVERNMENT	Gov.	SOCIAL	Soc.
GREATER THAN	>	SUMMARY/ SUMMARIZE	Sum.
HOUR/HOURLY	Hr./Hrly.	THEREFORE	∴
ILLUSTRATE	Illus.	VERSUS	Vs.
IMPORTANT	Imp.	VOLUME	Vol.
INCREASE	Inc.	WITH	w/
INFORMATION	Info.	WITHOUT	w/o
INTRODUCTION	Intro.	YEAR	Yr.
LEADS TO	→		

Figure 5 ■ Abbreviations and Symbols

notes should take place as soon as possible after class while the information is still fresh in your mind. This first review is used to clean up or "edit" your notes. Some editing steps to include are:

- Rewriting illegible words
- Completing incomplete thoughts or ideas
- Filling in ?
- Clarifying any abbreviations you used which you aren't sure you'll remember later.

As you complete this editing process, you are also reviewing your notes for organization and content. This step allows you to silently repeat the material and serves as a rehearsal step to help move the information into long-term memory.

At the end of each week, you should complete a second review of your notes. This time you can concentrate on relationships, time sequences, and other organizational patterns as well as on general content. You may want to highlight key concepts at this point and think about how the lecture material and the text overlap or support one another. This second review serves as a repetition to build your memory of the material.

If you are a kinaesthetic or tactile learner who benefits from rewriting notes, especially if you have access to a word processing system, you may want to rewrite or computerize your notes at this point. Word processing functions allow the use of boldface type, italics, and other features to highlight specific content.

The next review of your notes should take place as a part of test preparation. If you know that the test will include essay as well as multiple choice questions, review your notes and try to predict several questions from the way in which you've organized your notes. Look for connections, relationships and the organizational patterns we've already mentioned.

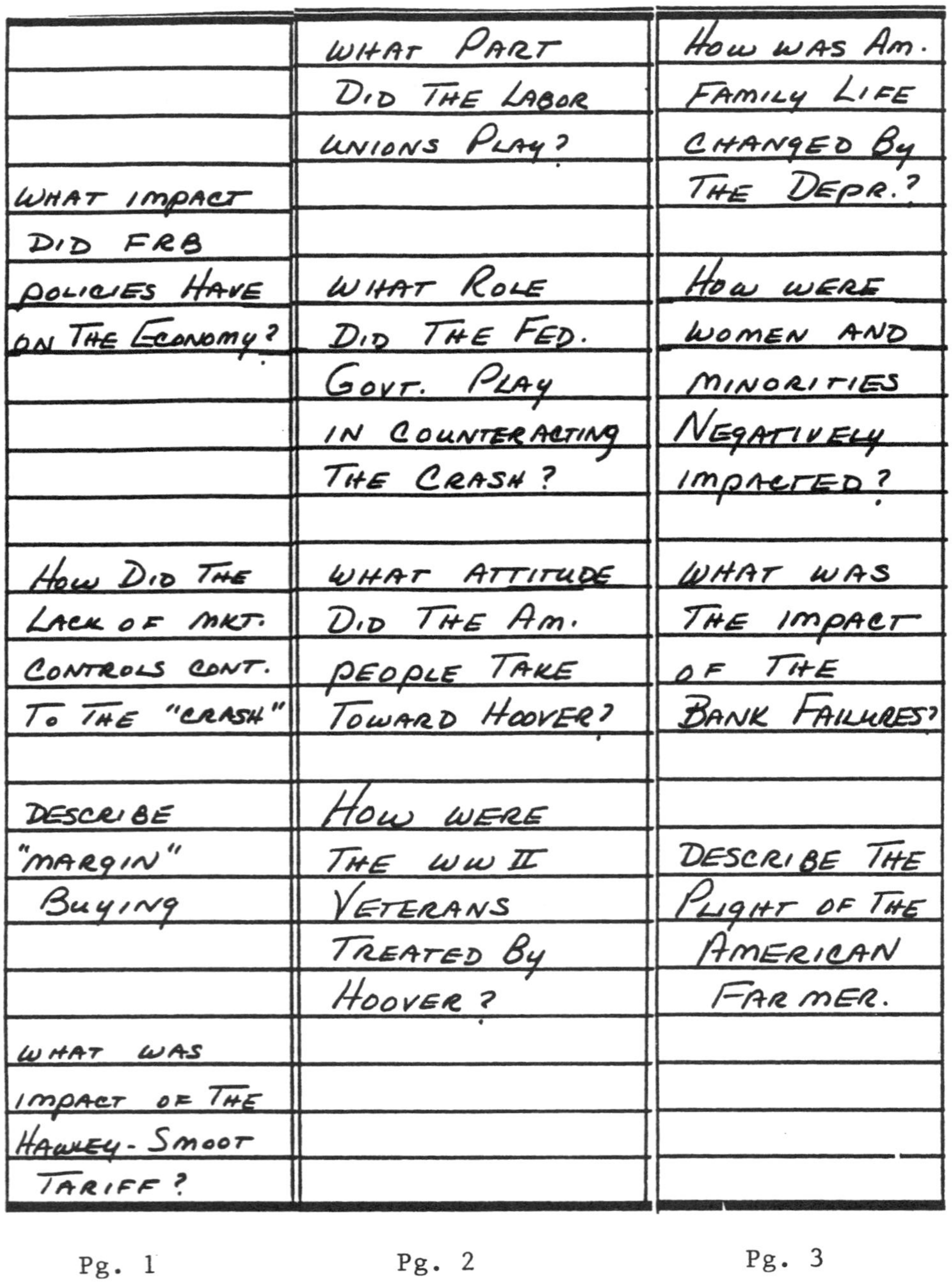

Pg. 1	Pg. 2	Pg. 3
	What part did the labor unions play?	How was Am. family life changed by the Depr.?
What impact did FRB policies have on the economy?	What role did the Fed. Govt. play in counteracting the crash?	How were women and minorities negatively impacted?
How did the lack of mkt. controls cont. to the "crash"	What attitude did the Am. people take toward Hoover?	What was the impact of the bank failures?
Describe "margin" buying	How were the WW II veterans treated by Hoover?	Describe the plight of the American farmer.
What was impact of the Hawley-Smoot Tariff?		

Figure 6 ■ Overlapping Study Notes for Test Review

Multiple choice and true/false questions might ask you to recognize differences among details or to recall specific facts or data. Use your notes as a guide to think up possible test questions. Remember to look for your symbol showing the information was shown on the board or that a direct announcement was made that the material was important.

If you are using the Cornell system or any modification which divides the paper by showing questions or key words in one column and your notes in another, you have a built-in review system. Take your one-sided notes from your binder and overlap them so you can see only the question/key word column. Use a blank sheet of paper to cover your notes for the top sheet (See Figure 6).

Looking only at the questions/key words, begin to review aloud what you know about each topic. If you need a "prompt," you can lift the paper above to see your notes on the subject. Once you feel you have mastered the material, put a check mark beside that question or key word. Once your understanding of each topic has been shown with mastery checks, return the page to your binder. Continue to review any topics/material on which you still need to refer to your notes for "prompts."

Remember that if you had used a spiral binder for note taking rather than looseleaf pages, this super effective test review system wouldn't work. This approach allows you to complete an honest, productive review. You can easily tell which material you have down cold. Material you haven't yet mastered is also clearly identifiable. Reciting the information aloud in your own words also helps you to process the information for long-term memory storage so that you'll be able to retrieve it for the test.

The final review of your notes should come *after you've reviewed your test results.* Were you prepared? Were your notes adequate? If not, what kind of information were you missing—main ideas, supporting details, examples? If you completely missed some questions, what information was missing from your notes? What percentage of the test questions seemed to come from the lecture material compared to the text? Were the questions objective (multiple-choice, true/false, etc.) or essay? If essay, did your notes show the connections you needed to answer the questions? What do you need to improve before the next test? This type of review, rather than just looking at your test score, will help you to make effective use of your notes.

Right Brain/Left Brain Dominance

Now that we've reviewed three common and "user friendly" note taking systems, how do you know which system will work the best for you? First, look over some of your previous note taking efforts. How are your notes arranged? Which of the three systems described are closest to your efforts. Secondly, think about how you've used your notes in the past. If you spent plenty of time reviewing for the test, did your notes provide you with the information you need? Are you comfortable with the system you've been using, or is it the only method you've ever tried?

When thinking about the three systems described, you'll probably have an instinctive positive response to one of these methods. Check out your instinctive response by reading the following information on right-brain versus left-brain information processing.

Psychologists and neurologists who study how the brain organizes information suggest that we are primarily right-brain thinkers or left-brain thinkers. An understanding of how we personally organize and process information will help us pick the note taking style with which we feel most comfortable.

Right-brain thinkers use a spontaneous, intuitive approach to information processing and problem solving. They like to see the whole picture (holistic) and respond strongly to visual stimuli. Left-brain thinkers use a language processing approach. They like things to be logical and use rational, step-by-step problem solving techniques. Where do you think you fit? Look over the characteristics identified with right and left brained thinkers and check those which seem to be true for you personally.

Where do most of your checks fall—under the right-brain or left-brain thinkers group? If you are a LB dominant, you will probably be more comfortable with a linear note taking approach which allows you to organize information as you listen. You'll want to clearly separate major points and supporting details. Either the outline format or the Cornell method will probably work best for you.

Right-Brained Thinkers

- ☐ Usually have a messy desk or work area
- ☑ Study whenever time allows; sometimes have energy bursts and work non-stop
- ☐ Like to study/review with others
- ☐ Sometimes work on several projects at once
- ☐ Use visual notes—charts, diagrams, color coding, etc.
- ☑ Often procrastinate, but work well under pressure and get the job done
- ☐ Class notes may use arrows or lines to show connections and relationships
- ☑ Not worried about time—deals with the present
- ☐ Use intuitive feelings and "hunches" to problem solve
- ☑ Use visuals & colors when getting down ideas

Left-Brained Thinkers

- ☑ Prefer to work at a neat, orderly desk
- ☐ Use a planned, organized study/work schedule
- ☑ Prefer to study alone
- ☑ Complete one assignment/project before beginning another
- ☑ Notes are usually in linear, outline format
- ☐ Use a planned approach to completing assignments on schedule—comfortable with deadlines
- ☑ Main ideas and details are easily identifiable—frequently in outline or indented topic format
- ☐ Keep track of time
- ☑ Use facts and reasoning to come up with answers or solutions
- ☐ Make lists

If you are a right-brain dominant, you will probably be more comfortable with a more creative note taking method. Using the mind-mapping (also known as the cluster system) method will allow you to visually focus on the centrally placed main ideas while adding connectors and supporting details as necessary. This note taking style allows you to see the whole picture at one glance. Symbols and diagrams may easily be added, and color coding can be used to show relationships between ideas.

What if you seemed to be evenly balanced between both areas? This does happen, and it means you have strengths in both areas. You can use the best of both "brains" to accomplish what needs to be done. For example, your left-brain side generally has you planning your work and following an organized schedule for getting things done. One night, however, your right-brain side might have a real energy burst, and you keep working as long as the adrenaline rush lasts.

Once you've identified a preferred note taking style, you need to personalize your note taking to help you get down the information you need as quickly and accurately as possible.

Summary

This chapter introduced you to the concept of active listening and how our listening skills influence our note taking ability. Good note taking requires advance preparation—having the right supplies, reviewing the course syllabus, reading the text, and recognizing your instructor's lecture style.

Knowing what to record is the hardest part of the note taking experience for many students. This chapter introduced you to verbal and nonverbal signals which the instructor uses to let you know what is important.

The next step is developing your own note taking style. Three note taking systems—informal outline, Cornell system, and mind-mapping were demonstrated. Each system is usable, and you should try them out until you find a comfortable "fit." You were also encouraged to develop a system of "personal shorthand," and were provided with a list of standard abbreviations and symbols to help you along.

Finally, you were shown how to edit and review your notes for test preparation. Your notes are only as good as the information you record and the way in which you use them. Students who do well on tests have generally used their notes for serious test review. Try the techniques demonstrated in this chapter and see if your performance doesn't improve too.

■ Reflect and Apply

After reading the chapter and completing Exercise 2, describe at least three specific changes you can make in your note taking. Focus on both the way you actually take notes and the way in which you use your notes.

Name: _____ Date: _____

■ Exercise 1: Evaluating Lecture Styles

DIRECTIONS: Use the statements listed below to evaluate the lecture style of one of your instructors for this semester.

Course Name   Yes   No

1. My instructor begins by giving a quick "recap" of the last class session. _____ _____

2. My instructor clearly introduces each new topic. _____ _____

3. Lecture pace is comfortable—neither too slow nor too fast. _____ _____

4. Instructor's voice level and pronunciation are satisfactory—I can clearly understand what is being said. _____ _____

5. My instructor keeps "on target" and generally doesn't wander too far off the topic. _____ _____

6. Lecture material includes illustrations and examples which help me to understand the material. _____ _____

7. Vocabulary level used is in my comfort zone. I don't feel overwhelmed with terms I don't understand. _____ _____

8. My instructor encourages classroom discussion and is open to questions. _____ _____

9. My instructor frequently uses the board or overhead projector to provide me with visual input. _____ _____

10. The last few minutes of class are used to summarize main ideas covered and/or to clarify new assignments. _____ _____

Discussion: If your checklist reveals several checks in the "No" column, it is critical that you use the note taking strategies discussed in this chapter to get the most you can from the lecture and classroom discussion.

Name: _____ Date: _____

Exercise 2: Editing Your Notes

Select and photocopy a set of lecture notes from one of your classes for this semester (at least two pages). Using a different colored pen or marker, edit these notes using the techniques described in the chapter. Rewrite any illegible words, complete incomplete thoughts or ideas, fill in any blanks, clarify abbreviations used, check your text or a friend's notes to fill in any information you might have missed.

Next, review your notes and jot down either "key words" or questions in the margin to identify the main ideas and topics covered.

CHAPTER 6
Reading and Note Taking

Introduction[1]

In this chapter you will learn about several strategies to make your reading and note-taking more efficient and productive. First, we'll look at ways to use your textbooks more efficiently, how to read for better understanding and use a formal study system called SQ3R. Then, we will focus on more specific reading skills: finding the main topic and summarizing paragraphs. To make efficient use of your reading time, we will look at ways to make text-notes to improve your comprehension and create study tools. Before you begin, complete the following "Reading and note-taking habits" survey.

Reading and Note-Taking Habits

1. Do you like to read fiction? ✗
2. Do you read books not related to classwork? ✓
3. Do you formulate questions while reading? ✓
4. Do you read newspapers and magazines? ✓
5. Do you feel you read too slowly? ✓
6. Dos your mind wander when you read? ✓
7. Do you daydream in class? ✗
8. Do you often not finish the amount of reading you intend? ✓
9. Is your best reading done at a certain time of day? ✗
10. Do you read word-for-word? ✓
11. Do you preview the material before reading? ✗
12. Does the mood you are in play an important role in your reading? ✓
13. Does your weak vocabulary cause you to read slowly? ✗
14. Do you read for leisure? ✓

---

[1] From *Your Utah State Experience: Strategies for Success, Fourth Edition* by Utah State University Academic Support Services. ©1998 by Utah State University Academic Support Services. Used by permission of Kendall/Hunt Publishing Company.

15. Do you organize and plan your reading sessions for school? ✗
16. Do you take notes while you read? ✓
17. Are your notes hard to follow when you use them to review? ✓
18. Do you get caught in the details of a reading, sometimes missing the author's main point? ✗
19. Do you highlight or underline key points when you read? ✓
20. Do you often summarize sections of your reading in your own words? ✗

■ College Reading Strategies

You may have arrived on campus feeling confident in your academic reading skills. Having a reading section in this book may appear unnecessary to you. Reading in your high school courses may have varied from being able to pass the class without looking at the text, to required reading of several texts, novels, or supplemental readings. You may have heard rumors that college reading is "different," however, the only problem you currently anticipate is the expense of the text.

Often, by mid-semester, students realize why college reading may require more skills than they previously had to demonstrate. This section, "College Reading," explains active study/reading approaches to textbooks that will involve you in using your textbooks to gain information. College classes usually require a text, often expensive, and reading assignments that must be completed to pass the class. You may find the text difficult to comprehend. The reading assignments contain more facts and ideas per page and are written at a higher reading level than high school texts. In fifteen weeks, you may have to be responsible for the amount of information you covered in an entire year in high school. The chart in Figure 1 lists common reading problems and suggested study strategies to help you with this area.

Active study reading is not "speedreading." Research has shown that speedreading is only effective when you are reading information that you already know and understand. What students do need are active reading/study strategies and a flexible reading rate. In some instances you will be able to speed up your reading, but often new information requires more than one reading and an interactive approach. Active reading strategies involve you in the reading process so that you are able to effectively read and comprehend the material in the textbook. With the use of time management skills, concentration techniques, and study strategies, you can feel in charge of all the reading required in college.

What Affects Reading Comprehension?

Before you begin an exercise program, you check your physical readiness. Similarly, you want to check your reading readiness by identifying your **Purpose, Background, Interest,** and **Difficulty.** These four factors affect your comprehension of textbook material. Assessing yourself in each area and knowing what to do with problems in each area will help you plan how to read effectively.

6: Reading and Note Taking

Causes of Reading Problem	Active Reading Strategies
1. Lack of motivation.	■ Evaluate your reading purpose, your background knowledge, your interest in the material, and the difficulty of the reading. ■ Do the most difficult reading first. ■ Arrange your schedule so that you read at your most productive study time. ■ Find a way to personalize the information. ■ Join a study group, divide the reading responsibility so that each person creates a summary and study guide for the group.
2. Lack of background knowledge and understanding of the subject.	■ Skim the chapter headings, pictures, charts, graphs, and diagrams. ■ Read the summary or conclusion first. ■ Get a tutor to explain difficult concepts. ■ Form a study group to discuss topics. ■ Allow additional time to reread the text 2–3 times.
3. Inability to concentrate.	■ Formulate a purpose for reading. ■ Practice a study strategy such as SQ3R. ■ Annotate the text. ■ Look for signal words to follow the organization of the text. ■ Break the reading time into manageable blocks.
4. Frustration with inability to recall the information.	■ Make connections between old and new information. ■ Review the main concepts daily. ■ Create study guides that reflect the type of test for that class.
5. Course and textbook contain difficult vocabulary and terminology.	■ Make a course vocabulary notebook or 3 x 5 card system, listing new words and definitions. ■ Review the vocabulary daily. ■ Learn common prefixes, suffixes, and root words to hope you build your vocabulary. ■ Use color to highlight similarities and differences in word parts.

Figure 1 ■ Reading Comprehension Problems and Strategies

Purpose. Students often sit down to read with only the thought that they have to "study" this chapter and hopefully retain "something." Take a minute to identify the purpose of the reading, that is, what is your reason for reading the textbook? Textbooks are read for different reasons:

- To build background knowledge so you can understand the lecture.
- To add supplemental information to your class notes.
- To learn details, such as the classification of types of rock or the time sequence of events that led up to the Civil War.
- To be prepared for a class discussion: the causes of the Civil War and the effect it had on the future politics of the South.
- To understand principles, processes, and concepts such as Mendel's Law of Genetics, Newton's Three Laws of Motion, or the properties of real numbers.

How do you know the purpose of the text for each class?

1. Read the syllabus, and pay careful attention to the relationship between the reading assignments and the class topics.
2. Talk to the instructor.
3. Talk to other students who have had the class or are in class with you. Find out how they used the text for the class.
4. If Supplemental Instruction sessions are available for the class, attend, and the SI leader will model how to use the textbook.

Background. Your reading comprehension is strongly affected by your background knowledge or what you already know about the subject. This is why:

- If you have high knowledge of the subject, then it may be easier for you to read the material. You will be able to meet your purpose quicker than if the information is totally new to you.
- If your knowledge of the subject is low, then you will have to build up your knowledge base. Some lectures are intended to build background before attempting textbook reading. Often, you will be expected to do this on your own. Time management becomes a factor, as you may have to reread your text three times to build up enough knowledge to comprehend the information.

How do you check your background for reading?

1. Before reading the chapter, skim the chapter headings, pictures, charts, graphs, and diagrams.
2. Read the summary and think about what you know about the subject.
3. Read the syllabus, and mark the topics that you know something about.
4. Review your notes, and look for connections between the lecture and the reading.
5. Discuss new information with other students in a study group or at an SI session. This will enhance your knowledge base and help you comprehend the information.

Interest. Students often complain that they don't like to read the text because it is not interesting. In many cases this is a true statement, but it doesn't remove the fact that in many classes if you do not read the text, you will not pass the class. If you avoid the text because of lack of interest, then you need to take some action to make the reading bearable for that semester.

How do you create interest in what you need to read?

1. Break your reading session into small time units. Twenty minutes of concentrated reading, then a small break, then twenty minutes more of focused reading.
2. Create questions before you read. Pretend they are real test questions, and you must know the answers to pass the class.
3. Use a specific reading strategy such as SQ3R to keep focused.
4. Do something with the information as you read the text. Write lists or notes in the margins. Create a picture of the information in your mind. Write an outline, or draw pictures of the process.
5. Share the reading with study partners. Divide up the chapter into sections, and make each student responsible for reading and teaching the concepts from their section to the other members of the group. Be aware that the section you learn best will be the one that you teach.
6. Talk to the instructor and ask questions about the subject matter. Ask him/her how they would advise you to read and comprehend the text. The instructor may say something to spark your interest.
7. Reward yourself for reading and studying material that is not interesting to you.

Difficulty. The difficulty of the reading material can encourage or discourage a student from reading and studying the text. Sometimes the format of the text is more difficult than the actual course material. You have little control over the choice of the text, but you do have options if the reading is difficult.

How do you cope with difficult reading material?

1. Think again about your purpose for reading, your prior knowledge of the subject, and your interest in the course and material. Are any of these factors making the reading difficult? Reread the suggestions in this section and the reading solutions chart.
2. Get a tutor for the class or attend Supplemental Instruction sessions. Difficult information is explained and discussed. This may make the reading less complex and more interesting.
3. Read another text that is on the same subject, but is written in a different style or reading level. You can check out textbooks at the library or other resource centers.

The SQ3R Reading Strategy

After you have evaluated your purpose, background, interest, and difficulty, then you are ready to begin your study session. Just as when you begin a journey to a new destination, you follow a map or plan, so should your reading session have a plan. SQ3R is a basic reading system that is often used by college students to improve their reading and studying.

How Do I Use SQ3R?

S = SURVEY. (Gather the information necessary to focus and formulate reading goals.)

- Read the title, headings, and subheadings of the chapter or the article. This helps your mind prepare to receive the information.

- Read the introduction and summary to get an overview of the main ideas. This will familiarize you with the concepts and how the chapter fits the author's purposes.
- Notice the graphics—charts, maps, diagrams, etc. are there to make a point—don't miss them.
- Pay attention to reading aids—italics, bold face print, chapter objectives, end-of-chapter questions are all included to help you sort, comprehend, and remember information.

[Margin note: GET AN INITIAL IDEA OF WHAT READING IS]

Q = QUESTION. (Question as you survey. This helps your mind engage and concentrate as you actively search for answers to questions.)

- Ask yourself what YOU already know about the subject
- As you read each of the above parts, ask yourself what is meant by the title, headings, subheadings, and captions. One section at a time, turn the boldface heading into as many questions as you think will be answered in that section. Write these down on 3 x 5 cards or create a study guide.
- Add further questions as you proceed through the section.
- Ask yourself, "What did the instructor say about the assignment in class? What handouts support the reading? What is the purpose of the reading assignment?"

[Margin note: ? YOU WANT ANSWERED]

R = READ. (Read and think actively. Fill in the information around the questions and structure you have been building.)

- Look for main ideas and supporting details. Use outlining, underlining, and text marking skills.
- Read to answer the questions that were raised in the question step.
- Read carefully all of the underlined, italicized, boldface words or phrases.

R = RECITE. (Recite right after reading an assignment. This trains your mind to concentrate and learn as it reads.)

- Use good judgment about places to stop and recite.
- Use outlining and underlining skills. (Do not underline long passages. Use a pencil to first underline important information. Only mark after you have read a passage AND understood it.)
- Write a summary statement of each section.
- Quiz yourself on the main points. See if you can answer from memory. If not, look back again, don't go on to the next section until you can recite.
- Connect new material with what you already know about the subject.
- Write questions on any material you do not understand, and ask your instructor to explain it.
- Write the answers to the questions you created.

R = REVIEW. (Review after you recite; daily, weekly, and before a test. This refines your mental organization and puts information into long-term memory.)

- Look over your outlines, underlining, and any notations you made in your textbook.
- Recite briefly the main ideas to keep the information fresh in your mind.
- Make practice test questions from review notes.
- Relate the textbook information to the Levels of Knowledge in Bloom's Taxonomy. Can you use the information beyond the basic knowledge level?

Course	Concepts	Study System May Include:
Social Sciences	Major theorists in the field. Theories and principles of behavior.	Underlining and marking as you read. Making charts to compare theories. Attending SI sessions.
Foreign Languages	Vocabulary words, meanings, pronunciations, and tenses.	Practicing translation and pronunciation at the language lab. Adding flash cards and conjugation charts to your review step.
Literature	Elements of writing: plot, characters, point of view, theme, style, and tone.	Interpreting, evaluating, and writing about the selection.
Math	Formulas to learn, Sample problems and exercises.	Include a practice step for solving problems; a math tutor.

Figure 2 ■ Adapt the SQ3R Study System

Apply the SQ3R System

Now that you know the framework and purpose of SQ3R, try applying the system. Complete Exercise 1: Practice using SQ3R.

HOW TO ADAPT THE SQ3R STUDY SYSTEM. There is not one study system that works for everyone all the time. Finding a study system the helps you read, understand, and remember the information depends on many factors that have been discussed in this book. For each class, you will have concepts to learn that are presented in distinct formats. Your commitment to identify the concepts, then create and practice a study system you choose, is more important than the type of system used.

When creating a study system, SQ3R can be a starting point. You can then adapt the steps to fit the concepts in the class and your preferred way to learn. Your system may include outside resources as a tutor or a study group. Figure 2 summarizes suggested ways to adapt your study system.

USING SIGNAL WORDS AND PHRASES. Signal words can help you understand relationships between ideas. They can guide you through a textbook passage, showing where you need to concentrate more, or where you may speed up on your reading. The words will help you anticipate where the author will lead the discussion. By observing the words carefully, they can be a useful tool in marking a text for main ideas. Figure 3 lists some commonly used signal words and their meanings in a textbook pattern.

Read the following paragraph. As you read, identify each signal word and think about its meaning in the sentence. How does the word guide you in following the author's thoughts? What do you think will be the main subject of the next paragraph?

> *"Geography is what geographers do."* This statement by A.E. Parkins is an effort to define the discipline of geography. The word geography comes from Greek "geo" meaning "earth" and "graphicus" meaning "to write a description." Geography, therefore, deals with descriptions of the earth, especially how space is occupied on our earth. It is concerned with the investigation of spatial variations of people, places, things, or any other observable phenomena on earth. As a discipline, geography is divided into two main areas

of focus, i.e., human and physical. Human geography is concerned with global cultures, histories, economics, and politics, to name a few areas of study. Physical geography, on the other hand, deals with the interrelations of the atmosphere, hydrosphere, biospheres, and lithosphere. Due to the vastness of each of these natural spheres, it is helpful for the physical geographer to have a working knowledge of scientific notation.

Using Your Textbooks[2]

Reading for Understanding: What's in a Paragraph?

The basic building block of all reading material is the simple paragraph. Most paragraphs contain three major parts. The **topic sentence** states the main idea or point the author is trying to get across. The **body** of the paragraph contains one or more supporting sentences which develop or prove the point being made. The **conclusion** will either re-state the main idea or topic, or will provide a transition to the next paragraph. Let's look at the three main parts of this sample paragraph:

It is time that America elected a woman President.

TOPIC SENTENCE: States the main idea, the author's point of view.

Many women have a great deal of experience in the political arena; from being Senators or Representatives, to state Governors, to powerful executives in large companies. Some women have learned about the role of the President from close observation, such as being members of the Cabinet, or even relatives of the President himself. Many times it has been obvious that inherent feminine personality traits could be very useful in the role of Chief Executive. For example, women may use compassion for the feelings of others to come to fair judgements on sensitive issues. Furthermore, there are many issues of great importance to women that male-dominated government has not yet addressed; such as affordable child care.

SUPPORTING SENTENCES: Gives facts or opinions to support the main point.

These are some of the many excellent reasons why the idea of a female President should be taken seriously by Americans today.

CONCLUSION: Re-states the main point, sometimes summarizes the supporting statements.

Train your mind to identify topic sentences. Topic sentences contain the broader topic or category under which the supporting sentences fit. For example, in the following group of words: *stove, blender, refrigerator, kitchen;* "kitchen" is the topic. It could be made into the topic sentence of a paragraph with the other three words developed into supporting sentences.

Understanding a paragraph doesn't always happen in sequential order. Sometimes, you pick out the main topic, but change or alter that choice after reading the supporting sentences. With careful consideration of the supporting points "stove," "blender," and "refrigerator," it is evident that the topic "kitchen" should be narrowed further to "kitchen

---

[2] From *The Community College: A New Beginning, Second Edition* by Aguilar et al. © 1998 by Kendall/Hunt Publishing Company. Used by permission.

appliances." Because any topic sentence should reveal the scope of the paragraph, the topic must point you, the reader, in the right direction. If you choose a topic from a paragraph, that is too broad, such as "kitchen," then you might expect the paragraph to contain information about all parts of a kitchen from dishes to food. Therefore, when looking for the main topic of a paragraph, ask yourself whether the topic you locate is too broad, too narrow, not right or just right as you read the supporting sentences.

Locate the topic among the supporting details in the following list. Also, locate the one supporting detail that is off topic, or shouldn't be in the group below.

a. Compare your reading notes and lecture notes and research any gaps or questions that arise.
b. Review daily and weekly not just the night before a test.
c. Create study guides by adding questions to the left margin of your Cornell notes.
d. Begin your essay answers by restating the question
e. Make practice questions

For further practice in locating topic sentences, complete Exercise 2.

Variations of the Standard Paragraph

Sometimes a paragraph will contain no topic sentence, but a series of supporting sentences (facts or opinions) leading to a conclusion. The preceding example, minus its topic sentence, would work this way. Another stylistic variation might be a paragraph which has no formal conclusion, but invites the reader to come to his or her own conclusion from the evidence provided. Here's an example of this variation:

> *What will you find at Founders' University? At Founders' you'll find a beautiful, wooded campus with a lovely blend of old and new architectural styles. At Founders' you'll find the latest scientific and technical equipment, always available for your use. At Founders' you'll find an enthusiastic and friendly student body. And at Founders' you'll find the finest instructors ready and willing to give you plenty of time and individual attention.*

The paragraph might have concluded with a sentence like, "Everything you're looking for, you'll find at Founders'." Instead, the author chose to leave the paragraph open-ended, inviting the reader to draw the obvious conclusion about the merits of Founders' University.

Summarize

Now that you understand the basic structure of a paragraph, your goal is to summarize the main points in your own words. This is often a difficult task, because it is easy to get caught up in details. To find the main points, you need to consider whether each phrase is key to understanding the main topic. To do this, you need to be an active reader. Engage your mind in questioning, "What is the author most wanting me to learn or understand from this paragraph?"

A good way to avoid getting caught up in the details, is to read the paragraph, then look away and think about, "What was the main topic." By not looking at the paragraph, you will also get a better start at summarizing in your own words.

With practice you can train your mind to not get distracted or diverted by details. Complete Exercise 3: Summarize. Then compare your results with a classmate's summary.

In summary, to understand a paragraph, find the topic sentence and grasp what the author is trying to tell you. Read the support sentences and learn what they are explaining about the topic. Remember that reading is a dialogue with the text, not a one-way communication from the paragraph to your mind. Ask questions and make connections while you read to help yourself stay alert and better understand the material. Form opinions about the support sentences, for example, "Are the support sentences facts or opinions?"

READING AND MARKING TEXTBOOKS. When you read a chapter in a textbook, the quickest way to focus on the information that you need to learn is to mark the information. Information that is marked in an organized format will be learned in an organized manner.

Why Mark the Textbook?[3]

"Why would I want to mark up my textbook?" you ask, "I can sell it to the bookstore at the end of the term and get some of my money back!" Think of the cost of your textbooks as an investment in your education. If you want to save money, buy used textbooks to begin with!

There are three good reasons to mark your textbooks for your own study. First, the marking process itself forces you to concentrate as you read—you can't be physically marking the book while falling asleep at the same time! Marking also helps you understand the material as you go along—it helps you organize the reading in your mind. Finally, because you summarize the main point when marking, you'll have ready-made focal points for later review and for making study guides. Do your marking in two steps: first highlight or underline, second annotate.

Highlighting and Underlining

First you'll want to mark certain items with highlighting or underlining:

1. The topic sentence (main idea) of the paragraph
2. Main (key) words of the supporting sentences
3. Names and dates if studying history, psychology, etc.
4. Definitions

Here is an example of a highlighted paragraph:

Language is a system we infer from the sounds that come out of the mouths of speakers and the marks that come from the hands of writers. Variation within a language is of two main kinds. From one kind, we identify those who use the language: we infer where they come from, what groups they belong to, when they learned the language, and what they are like as individuals—their age, sex, education, and personality. Such variation is called dialect. From the other kind, we identify the uses to which language is put: the subjects it treats, the circumstances in which it is used, the medium of its expression (for example, speech versus writing), the social relationships among its users, and the purpose of its use. Such variation is called register.

---

[3]From *The Community College: A New Beginning, Second Edition* by Aguilar et al. © 1998 by Kendall/Hunt Publishing Company. Used by permission.

6: READING AND NOTE TAKING

1. **Example Words: To indicate that another point or an example follows:**

to illustrate	for example	for instance	another
also	furthermore	moreover	for example
such as	specifically		

2. **Emphasis Words: To indicate that the next information is important:**

most important	remember that	pay attention to
above all	a key idea	the main point
most significant	of primary concern	

3. **Cause and Effect Words: Check to be sure you know the cause for each effect word:**

because	since	due to	consequently
as a result	effect	cause	for
accordingly	if . . . then	therefore	thus, so

4. **Summary Words: To indicate that a conclusion follows:**

therefore	finally	consequently	in conclusion
so	to conclude	in a nutshell	to sum up

5. **Time Words: To indicate that a time relationship is being established:**

numbers	steps	stages	next
finally	first, second, etc.	the four steps . . .	

6. **Compare/contrast Words: To indicate concepts are to be looked at from more than one angle:**

similar	like	disadvantages	different	pros and cons
in contrast	equally	contrary to	on the other hand	conversely

7. **Swivel Words: To indicate an exception to a stated fact:**

however	although	but	nevertheless
though	except	yet	still

Figure 3 ■ Signal Words for Note Taking and Reading

Annotating

Next, use the margins of the page to make annotations. To annotate means to summarize. In this case you will annotate by adding marks. By using a system of symbols and notation, you mark the text after the first reading so that a complete rereading will not be necessary. The annotating should include important points that you will need to review for an exam.

When should you annotate your text? Annotating should be done after a unit of thought has been presented and the information can be viewed as a whole. This may mean marking after only one paragraph or after three pages, as what you mark will depend a great deal on your PBID. If you mark as you read, too much is marked and you are unable to see the "big picture" or main concepts. It takes time for the brain to organize information; so if you read, think, and then mark, the main points will develop and you can decide what you need to mark to remember later.

Return to the sample highlighted paragraph and add annotations. Compare your annotations with a classmate. Then, turn to Exercise 4: Marking for Further Practice in Highlighting and Annotating.

Summary

Take control of your learning and implement the reading comprehension skills covered in this chapter. Begin by organizing your reading session with a method such as SQ3R. Assess the difficulty level of the reading and decide how much time it will take to complete. Give your concentration a break and tackle one small section of the reading at a time. Mark your text when you locate the topic sentence and main points. Then, after each small section, summarize and reflect on what you read. Remember that the texts you are reading in college are difficult, because they are frequently packed with information that will be new to you. The more you read, the more you will learn, and the easier reading will become.

Reflect and Apply

1. Without referring back to the chapter, make a quick summary of what you learned on the lines below. After you are finished, check your comprehension by comparing your summary to the chapter. What did you miss? If you missed something, why do you think you didn't remember it?

_____
_____
_____
_____
_____
_____
_____
_____
_____
_____
_____
_____

The above exercise was a way to engage you in the reading. Reading doesn't have to be a chronological progression through the text. Check your comprehension and stay focused using summarizing and review.

Name: _____ Date: _____

Exercise 1: Practice Using SQ3R

Directions: The following exercise is designed to give you practice in the steps of SQ3R.

Section I. Survey

1. Name of textbook:

2. List at least two questions or thoughts which the title suggests to you:
   _____
   _____

3. List at least two major points the author makes in the Preface:
   _____
   _____

4. List at least two major points the author makes in the Introduction:
   _____
   _____

5. Take at least three chapter titles listed in the Table of Contents and turn them into questions:
   _____
   _____

6. If there is an Appendix, what does it contain?
   _____

7. Does the book contain a Glossary? Yes _____ No _____ An Index? Yes _____ No _____ If the answers are yes, look over the Glossary and/or thumb through the Index looking for familiar names, places, or terms. How much do you think you are going to know about the contents?

8. Look through the first two chapters of the book and check any of the following aids used in them.

   ___ headings   ___ footnotes   ___ pictures
   ___ subheadings   ___ bibliography   ___ graphs
   ___ italics   ___ study questions   ___ bold vocabulary words
   ___ summary   ___ assignments   ___ other

121

Section II. Question

Use the textbook you surveyed. Pick one chapter or an assigned reading.

Title of Chapter: _____

1. What do you think is the main idea of the chapter?

   _____
   _____

2. Turn three headings into questions.

   _____
   _____
   _____

3. Write the answer to one of the questions in your own words. Use a format that will help you remember the information: an outline, list, drawing, diagram, etc.

   _____
   _____
   _____

Section III. Read, Recite, Review

Now, think about how you will actively **Read** the text, **Recite** the information, and **Review** the material.

1. Describe your active reading techniques. (Did you annotate, answer questions, etc.?)

   _____
   _____

2. Describe what will you do when you review the material? (Will you create an outline, study sheets, study cards, etc.?)

   _____
   _____

3. Attach a photocopy of a page from your textbook and show how you annotated the important information.

CHAPTER 7
Critical Thinking and Analysis

Finally, you say to yourself, it's Friday night! After a long, hard week you're ready to "cut loose," relax, and unwind. What better way to start the weekend than by going to the movies? Okay, you're psyched! This will be fun. What should you see? You turn to the entertainment section of the local newspaper and look at the ads for the movies currently playing. You're not quite sure what's good, so you read the various endorsements. "Two thumbs up!" reads one ad. Another states, "One of the year's ten best!" Still another comments, "Hugely entertaining." The accolades continue for movies in other ads: "Breathtaking!" "An extraordinary film!" "Spectacular movie making at its best . . ."

Wait a minute, you think to yourself, something is wrong here. The films now showing in the theaters can't all be great. Suddenly and without warning, one of the few Latin phrases you learned years ago springs to mind, *"Caveat emptor!"*—let the buyer beware! Of course, the goal of advertising is not to present "the truth," but rather to persuade you to make a decision that might not be in your best interest (although it certainly is in the best interest of the filmmakers to get you to forfeit some of your hard-earned cash to see their show). You realize that a dose of healthy skepticism is warranted to bridle the enthusiasm of the ads and to curtail the degree to which they influence your decision-making.

Eyeing the ads in this new light, on further inspection, you examine the various authors to whom the above quotes are attributed. Familiarity with the critics might affect your evaluation of the ad's validity. For example, while you often agree with the movie critic's "two thumbs up," you are a bit incredulous of a glowing recommendation when the critic's name doesn't ring any bells. Similarly, while you may have some confidence in the credibility of a source quoted in *Rolling Stone* or seen on NBC-TV, you are less eager to spend your money on a film when you don't recognize the point of origin of some phenomenal sound-bite (would you be persuaded to see Kevin Costner's *The Postman* when its most exuberant endorsement was by a commentator from UPN News 13?). Whether you know it or not, you have just engaged in critical thinking and analysis to help you decide which movie to see.

From *Making Connections, Achieving Success, Understanding Others, 2nd edition* by Bocchi et al. Copyright © 1999 by Bocchi et al. Used with permission of Kendall/Hunt Publishing Company.

What Is Critical Thinking?

What exactly is "critical thinking?" Philosophers, psychologists, educators, communication experts, scientists, mathematicians, and the man (or woman) on the street all have an interest in critical thinking. While a single definition that satisfies all constituents has yet to be devised, most would agree that critical thinking entails "skills in applying, analyzing, and evaluating information" (Ruminski and Hanks, 1995, p. 5). Many experts in the field (e.g., Kurfiss, 1988; Levy, 1997; Zechmeister and Johnson, 1992) have characterized critical thinking with reference to the following concepts: objectivity, open-mindedness, systematic investigation, problem-solving, distinguishing fact from opinion, questioning assumptions, discerning implicit values, avoiding logical flaws and personal biases, tolerating uncertainty and ambiguity, searching for alternative explanations, respecting the viewpoints of others, and maintaining a willingness to change one's beliefs if the evidence warrants it.

While there are many definitions of critical thinking in the literature, the one we like best is as follows: critical thinking entails a set of intellectual skills and habits of mind to help people make decisions in the face of uncertainty. The fact that much of life is uncertain and unknown dictates the need to become effective critical thinkers. When answers are known, critical thinking is unnecessary.

Examples of Critical Thinking

For example, the solution to arithmetic problems, such as $3 + 5 = X$ or $8 - 2 = Y$, can be answered from memory alone if the person knows the basic facts of addition and subtraction. In contrast, an algebraic problem, such as "solve the equation for a: $(a \times 5) + (a \times 3) = 56$," requires not only knowledge of certain algebraic principles, but also familiarity with thinking strategies in order to work through a solution not immediately apparent, nor intuitively obvious. (Hint: "a" is equal to a lucky number.)

Similarly, when facing many everyday problems, differences occur in the ways in which people cope with difficulties—sometimes they rely on memory alone. Other times they require thinking strategies to help find a solution. For example, once you've chosen a major, there will be certain required courses you must take, no matter what. No need for critical thinking here. However, there also may be components of the major's curriculum where you have a choice—select one course from among the following three alternatives. Which should you take? What factors might you consider in making your selection? Should you base your decision on the relevance of the courses for helping you to fulfill your long-term career goals? Might you consider the reputation of the professors teaching the alternative courses, with one having a better reputation as a teacher or another known to wreak havoc on a student's GPA? Should you consider in your decision the problem of finding time for both your classes and your job, selecting a less desirable course that nonetheless fits into your schedule?

In answering the question, "Which course should I take?" you may find that you reach a different conclusion when the issue is examined in light of the different considerations above. As if life weren't complicated enough, you now must decide how to prioritize these concerns and determine which factor to give the most weight in making an informed, well-reasoned decision. Should you assign priority to your professional objectives? Of course, but what if you eventually change your career path? How about choosing the course based on the professor, only to find when you take the course that he or she doesn't live up to expectations? Or you could decide to take the course that is most convenient given your current commitments and obligations, but then get a promotion at work requiring you to change your entire schedule!

How can you decide which course to take when the future is so unpredictable? It is said that nothing in life is certain except death and taxes. While alive, leave your tax bill to your accountant. Be certain to leave your body after death to an undertaker. For everything in between, use your critical thinking to make decisions in the face of uncertainty!

Skills and Attitudes That Facilitate Critical Thinking

It is not possible to review here all the wisdom currently available concerning how to think critically. One could take an entire course on the subject or read several books and just begin to scratch the surface. Therefore, we will instead do the following: first, we will discuss a few examples of critical-thinking skills and attitudes; second, we will focus on one particular aspect of critical thinking that often causes people some consternation—arguing and argument; then we will examine how critical thinking can be of use not only when dealing with words, conversations, and logic, but also when analyzing statistics, reviewing quantitative information, and examining graphs in which the data are represented pictorially. Finally, we will discuss the importance of critical thinking for aiding learning and enhancing your education.

Fallacies in Reasoning[A]

As critical thinkers, it is important to be able to recognize fallacies in reasoning.[1] Fallacies are patterns of incorrect reasoning. Recognizing these fallacies can help you to avoid them in your thinking and writing. You can also be aware when others are using these fallacies to persuade you. They may use these fallacies for their own purpose, such as power or financial gain.

Appeal to Authority. It is best to make decisions based on reviewing the information and arguments and reaching our own conclusions. Sometimes we are encouraged to rely on experts for a recommendation because they have specialized information. Obviously, we need to have trust in the experts to accept their conclusions. However, when we cite some person as an authority in a certain area when they are not, we make an appeal to a questionable authority. For example, when a company uses famous sports figures to endorse a product (a particular brand of athletic shoes or breakfast cereal, for example), they are appealing to a questionable authority. Just because the athletes are famous, they are not experts in the product they are endorsing. They are endorsing the product to make sales and earn money. Notice the commercials you see on TV. Many of them are appeals to a questionable authority.

Jumping to Conclusions. When we jump to conclusions, we make hasty generalizations. For example, if a college student borrows money from a bank and does not pay it back, the manager of the bank may conclude that all college students are poor risks and refuse loans to other college students.

Making Generalizations. We make generalizations when we say that all members of a group are the same:

- All lawyers are greedy.
- All blondes are airheads.

---

[1] Information on fallacies in reasoning was adapted from the Institute for Teaching and Learning and their interactive Web site called Mission Critical: http://www.sjsu.edu/depts/itl/index.html

[A] From *College and Career Success* by Marsha Finley Fralick. Copyright © 2000 by Kendall/Hunt Publishing Company. Used by permission.

Your occupation does not determine whether or not you are greedy, and the color of your hair does not determine your intelligence. Such thinking leads to harmful stereotypes and reasoning fallacies. Instead of generalizing, think of people as unique individuals.

Attacking the Person Rather than Discussing Issues. To distract attention from the issues, we often attack the person. For example, during the Clinton administration, much time was spent attacking the person rather than discussing the issues. Rather than focusing attention on health care and education, attention was focused on real estate deals and extramarital affairs. Political candidates today are routinely asked about personal issues such as extramarital affairs and drug use rather than focusing on political issues. Of course personal integrity in politicians is important, but attacking the person can serve as a smokescreen to direct attention away from important political issues. Critical thinkers need to avoid reacting emotionally to personalities and need to use logical thinking to analyze the issues.

Appeal to Common Belief. Just because it is a common belief does not mean that it is true. At one time people believed that the world was flat and that when you got to the edge of the earth, you would fall off. If you were to survey the people who lived in that period in history, the majority would have agreed that the earth was flat. A survey just tells us what people believe. The survey does not tell us what is true and accurate.

Common Practice. Appealing to common practice is the "everyone else is doing it" argument. Just because everyone else does it, doesn't mean that it is right. Here are some common examples of this fallacy:

- It is okay to cheat in school. Everyone else does it.
- It is okay to speed on the freeway. Everyone else does it.
- It is okay to cheat on your taxes. Everyone else does it.

Appeal to Tradition. Appeal to tradition is a variation of "everyone else is doing it." The appeal to tradition is "we've always done it that way." Just because that is the way it has always been done, doesn't mean it is the best way to do it. With this attitude, it is very difficult to make changes and improve our ways of doing things. While tradition is very important, it is open to question. For example, construction and automotive technology have traditionally been career choices for men, but not for women. When women tried to enter or work in these careers, there was resistance by those who did not want to change traditions. This resistance limited options for women.

Two Wrongs. In this fallacy, it is assumed that it is acceptable to do something because other people are doing something just as bad. For example, if someone cuts you off on the freeway, you may assume that it is acceptable to zoom ahead and cut in front of their car. The "two wrongs" fallacy has an element of retribution and getting back at the other person. The old saying "two wrongs do not make a right" applies in this situation.

The Slippery Slope or Domino Theory. The slippery slope or domino theory is best explained with an example. If I fail the test, I will fail class. If I fail this class, I will drop out of college. My parents will disown me and I will lose the respect of my friends. I will not be able to get a good job. I will start drinking and end up homeless. In this fallacy, the consequences of our actions are remotely possible and negative and are assumed to be certain. These dire consequences are given to influence the decisions and change behavior. In this situation, it is important to evaluate these consequences. One does not necessarily lead to the other. If you fail the test, you could study and pass the next test. As a child you were probably cautioned about many slippery slopes in life:

- Brush your teeth or your teeth will fall out.
- Do your homework or you will never get into college and get a good job.

Wishful Thinking. In wishful thinking an extremely positive outcome, however remote, is proposed as a distraction from logical thinking. For example, a new sports stadium may be proposed. Extremely positive outcomes may be given, such as progress, downtown redevelopment, recreation, professional sports teams, increased revenue and creation of jobs. On the other hand "slippery slope" advocates may see increased taxes, lack of parking and neglect of other important social priorities such as education and shelter for the homeless. Neither position is correct if we assume that the outcomes are certain and automatic. Outcomes need to be evaluated realistically.

Appeal to Fear or Scare Tactics. Sometimes people use an emotion such as fear to interfere with rational thinking. I once saw a political commercial that showed wolves chasing a person through the forest. It was clearly designed to evoke fear in those who watched it. The message was to vote against a proposition to limit lawyers' fees. The idea was that if lawyers' fees were limited, the poor client would be a victim of limited legal services. Lawyers wanted to have the freedom to charge whatever they chose. The proposition was defeated and lawyers retained the right to charge exorbitant fees, resulting in higher insurance costs for everyone. The commercial used scare tactics to interfere with rational thinking.

Appeal to Pity. In an appeal to pity, emotion is used to replace logic. It is what is known as a "sob story." Some appeals to pity are legitimate and are used to request charity and empathy. However, the sob story uses emotion in place of reason to persuade and is often exaggerated. College faculties often hear sob stories from students having academic difficulties. Here are some examples:

- Please don't disqualify me from college. I failed all my classes because I was emotionally upset when my grandmother died.
- Please don't fail me in this class. If you fail me, my parents will kick me out of the house and I will not be able to get health insurance.
- Please don't give me a speeding ticket. I have to get home right away. My cat is sick.

Appeal to Loyalty. Human beings are social creatures who enjoy being attached to a group. This fallacy involves acting according to the group's best interests without considering whether the actions are good or bad, right or wrong. An example is the saying, "My country, right or wrong." Critical thinkers consider whether the actions are right or wrong and do not support ideas just to support a group with which they identify. We can feel this loyalty to our friends, family, school, communities, teams and favorite musicians.

Peer pressure is related to the loyalty fallacy. With peer pressure, members of the group act in a certain way because they think members of the group act that way. Another variation to the loyalty fallacy is called "bandwagon." It involves supporting the group ideas just to be part of the group. This emotion is powerful when the group is perceived to be powerful or "cool." In elections, people often vote for the candidate that is perceived to be the most popular. If everyone else is voting for the candidate, the candidate must be the best. This is not necessarily true.

Appeal to Prejudice. A prejudice is judging groups of people or things positively or negatively, even if the facts do not agree with the judgment. A prejudice is based on a stereotype in which all members of a group are judged to be the same. By appealing to a prejudice, speakers seek to gain support for their causes. Listen for the appeal to prejudice in "hate" speeches or literature directed against different ethnicities, genders or sexual orientations.

Appeal to Vanity. An appeal to vanity is also known as "apple polishing." Using this strategy, the goal is to get agreement by paying compliments. Students who pay compliments to teachers and then ask for special treatment are engaging in "apple polishing."

Post Hoc Reasoning or False Causes. Post hoc reasoning has to do with cause and effect. It explains many superstitions. If I play a good game of golf whenever I wear a certain hat, I may conclude that the hat causes me to play a good golf game. If I lose my lucky hat, I may not be able to play golf as well. The hat is a false cause (or post hoc) for playing a good game of golf. I may feel more comfortable wearing my lucky hat, but it is a secondary reason for playing a good game. I play a good game of golf because I practice good golf skills and develop my self-confidence. In scientific research, care is taken to test for false causes. Just because an event regularly precedes another event, it may not be the cause of it. For example, when the barometer falls, it rains. The falling barometer does not cause the rain. A drop in atmospheric pressure causes the rain. If falling barometers caused the rain, we could all be rainmakers by adjusting our barometers.

Straw Man (or Woman). Watch for this fallacy during election time. With this strategy the politician creates an image of someone else's statements, ideas or beliefs, much as we create a scarecrow to scare away the birds from the garden. For example, politicians accuse their opponents of being liberals and raising taxes. Maybe that is only part of the story. Maybe their opponents also voted for many tax-saving measures. When politicians or anyone else uses the straw man (or woman) fallacy, they are falsifying or oversimplifying. Use your critical thinking to identify the straw men or women (political opponent) during the next election. Of course you don't have to be a politician to use this strategy. People often use this strategy when they spread gossip or rumors about someone they want to discredit.

Burden of Proof. Burden of proof simply refers to the person who should provide the evidence for the truth of a statement. Generally the person making the statement is the one who should provide the evidence of the truth of the statement. However, the speaker may attempt to shift the burden of proof to another person to distract attention. Here is an example of shifting the burden of proof from the popular TV show, *The X-Files*:

> *Scully:* Your sister was abducted by aliens? Mulder, that's ridiculous!
> *Mulder:* Well, until you can prove it **didn't** happen, you'll just have to accept it as true.

Mulder shifts the burden of proof to Scully. If she can't prove it didn't happen, it must be true. It is actually Mulder who needs to prove that what he says is true. It is not up to Scully to provide the evidence for or against the possibility of alien abduction. Mulder is making the claim, and he needs to provide the evidence of the truth of his statement.

False Dilemma. This fallacy is called the "either-or fallacy" or the "black-and-white fallacy" because you think that you have to choose one option or the other. For example, think about this statement:

> *My country, love it or leave it.*

In this statement you are presented with two opposite choices: love it or leave it. Are these the only options? Maybe if I disagree with my country's policies, I could work to change them or exercise my right to vote for a different political leader. Maybe I could leave my country and still love it. Most social issues today are so complex that we need to examine many options to find the best answers. When students say that they need an

"A" grade or will drop the class, they are using the false dilemma fallacy. It is possible to earn other grades and make progress toward graduation. Critical thinkers are not limited by either-or choices, but look to find creative solutions.

Viruses of the Mind. No, it's not a real virus; it just acts like one. Viruses of the mind refer to beliefs for which hard evidence is lacking.[2] These beliefs survive like viruses in that they need a host to ensure their survival. Some person or group believes the idea and promotes it. The ideas jump from person to person, much like a virus. An example is the Heavensgate cult:

> *It all seems perfectly ludicrous: 39 people don their new sneakers, pack their flight bags and poison themselves in the solemn belief that a passing UFO will whisk them off to Wonderland.*[3]

Cults and new millennium doomsday forecasters spread unorthodox and sometimes harmful beliefs with great fervor. These thoughts are perpetuated through mind control techniques. With mind control, members of a group are taught to suppress emotion and accept the ideas of the group in exchange for a sense of belonging. These groups survive because they do not allow members to think critically or question the belief system. Mind control is the opposite of critical thinking. It is important to use critical thinking about beliefs for which there is no hard evidence.

How to Become a Critical Thinker

Use a Critical Thinking Process

When thinking about a complex problem, it is helpful to use a critical thinking process:

1. **State the problem in a clear and simple way.** Sometimes the message is unclear or obscured by appeals to the emotions. Stating the problem clearly brings it into focus so that you can identify the issues and begin to work on it.

2. **Identify the alternative views.** In looking at the different views, you open your mind to a wider range of options. The diagram entitled "Alternative Views" below gives a perspective on point of view. For every issue, there are many points of view. The larger circle represents these many points of view. The individual point of view is represented by a star on the larger circle. Experience, values, beliefs, culture and knowledge influence the individual point of view.

3. **Watch for fallacies** in reasoning when looking at the alternative views.

4. **Find at least three different answers.** In finding these different answers, you force yourself to look at all the possibilities before you decide on the best answer.

5. **Construct your own reasonable view.** After looking at the alternatives and considering different answers to the problem, construct your own reasonable view. Practice this critical thinking process using the critical thinking exercises at the end of this chapter.

---

[2] Geoffrey Cowley, "Viruses of the Mind: How Odd Ideas Survive," *Newsweek*, April 14, 1997, p. 14.
[3] Ibid.

Alternative Views[4]

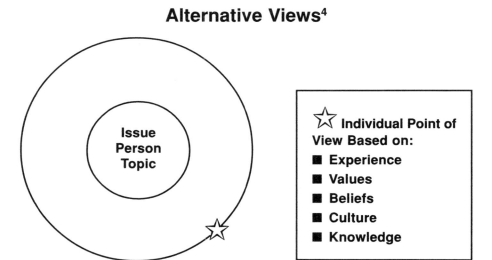

Tips for Critical Thinking

1. Beware of your mind-set. A mind-set is a pattern of thought that you use like a habit. You develop these patterns of thinking based on your personal experiences, culture and environment. When the situation changes, your old mind-set may need to be changed.

2. Be willing to say, "I don't know." With this attitude you are open to explore new ideas. In today's rapidly changing world, it is not possible to know everything. Rather than trying to know everything, it is more important to be able to find the information you need.

3. Practice tolerance for other people's ideas. We all have a different view of the world based on our own experiences and can benefit from an open exchange of information.

   If there is any secret of success, it lies in the ability to get the other person's point of view and see things from his angle as well as from your own.

   —Henry Ford

4. Try to look for several answers and understand many points of view. Remember the false dilemma fallacy of reasoning? The world is not either-or, or black-and-white. Looking at all the possibilities is the first step in a creative solution.

5. Understand before criticizing. Life is not about justifying your point of view. It is important to understand and then offer your suggestions.

6. Realize that your emotions get in the way of clear thinking. We all have beliefs that are important to us. It is difficult to listen to a different point of view when someone questions your personal beliefs that you consider important. Open your mind to see all the alternatives. Then construct your reasonable view.

7. Examine the source and outlook of the message. If the material downplays the hazards of smoking to your health but is written by the tobacco industry, you will gain some insight about the message and motivation of the authors. Political announcements require that information about the person or organizations paying for the ad be provided. Knowing who paid for the advertisement helps you to understand the point of view that is being promoted.

---

[4] Idea contributed by Vangie Meneses, Dean of Counseling, Cuyamaca College, El Cajon, CA.

8. Ask the question, "What makes the author think so?" In this way you can discover what premises the author uses to justify his or her position.

9. Ask the question, "So what?" Ask this question to determine what is important and how the author reached the conclusion.

Critical Thinking over the Internet

The Internet is revolutionizing the way we access and retrieve information today. Through the use of search engines, Web sites, electronic periodicals and online reference, it is possible to find just about any information you need. The Internet is also full of scams, rumors, gossip, hoaxes, exaggerations, and illegal activity. Anyone can put anything on the Internet. You will need to apply critical thinking to the information that you find on the Internet.

Author Reid Goldsborough offers suggestions for thinking critically over the Internet:[5]

- Don't be fooled by appearance. It is easy to create a flashy and professional-looking web site. Everyone is jumping on the e-commerce bandwagon. Some products or services are legitimate, but some are scams.
- Find out about the person or organization providing the information. There should be links to a home page that lists the author's background and credentials. You need to be skeptical if the author is not identified. If you cannot identify the person who authored the web site, find out what organization sponsored the site. Most of the Internet resources in this text are from educational or government sources. It is the goal of these organizations to provide the public with information.
- Look for the reason the information was posted. What is the agenda? Keep this in mind when evaluating the information. It is the agenda of many web sites to sell a product or influence public opinion.
- Look for the date that the information was created or revised. A good web site posts the date of creation or revision because links become outdated quickly.
- Try to verify the information elsewhere, especially if the information does not match common sense or is at odds with what you believe. Verify the information through other web sites or your local library.

Critical Thinking as Argument[B]

"Don't be so argumentative!" "I don't want to argue . . ." Ever hear comments like this from people you know? Most of us have. Often people equate arguing with fighting, seeing both as negative. They're wrong! Actually, communication researchers have found that arguing is an important critical-thinking skill. They've found that adults who are good at arguing are more creative, have higher self esteem, and are better at learning, problem-solving, and seeing things from other people's perspectives (Rancer, Whitecap, Kosberg, and Avtgis, 1997). Adults who can argue skillfully, that is, who are good at defending their positions about controversial topics, seem to be less likely to attack the person whom they are arguing with—either verbally (by attacking their character or their self-concept) or physically (Rancer et al., 1997). So, actually, being argumentative is a good thing.

---

[5] Reid Goldsborough, "Teaching Healthy Skepticism about Information on the Internet," *Technology and Learning*, January, 1998.

[B] From *Making Connections, Achieving Success, Understanding Others, 2nd Edition* by Bocchi et al. Copyright © 1999 by Bocchi et al. Used by permission of Kendall/Hunt Publishing Company.

In fact, any time you are trying to convince someone of anything, you are making an argument. Whenever you write a paper for a class (at least a good one) or a proposal for something at your job, you also are making an argument. So the question isn't really whether you argue or not, the only question is, are you good at it? Can you convince people of your position, not because they feel intimidated or hurt or are bored with the discussion, but because they come to see that your point of view makes good sense? This is the difference between what communication researchers call arguing and what they call verbal aggression: can the people you are talking with walk away from the discussion feeling good about themselves and having changed their minds? If they can, then you've succeeded in attacking their position on the issue without attacking them. That's the essence of a good argument. And again, developing solid arguments is an essential component of critical thinking.

To be really good at arguing, you have to understand what an argument is. Basically, any argument has three components: a main point that you are trying to convince someone of, some evidence to back up your point, and then some things that you take for granted (assumptions) that connect the evidence to the conclusion. We make arguments all the time, but often we don't think about it as arguing. For example:

Please let me borrow the car tonight, Dad. I have a drama club rehearsal at school from 7 to 10, and that way you or Mom won't have to spend all night driving back and forth to school.

This is a nice simple argument like the ones we make every day. If her dad agreed right away to lend her the car, the girl in this example probably would not even think of what she said as an argument. But it is; she has a main point: that she should be allowed to borrow the family car for the evening. She offers some evidence to convince her parents: a) she wants to get to school for a rehearsal and b) driving there herself would spare them the inconvenience of dropping her off and picking her up. She's also assuming some things as she speaks—that her parents support her drama club participation, that there isn't some other obvious way for her to get to school besides either borrowing the car or having her parents drive, and that there aren't other factors that are more important to her parents than convenience.

If, for example, her parents have told her she can't be in the drama club until her grades improve, they aren't likely to be persuaded to lend her the car so that she can go to rehearsal (but they might be eager to lend her the car if she were going to a tutoring session). Similarly, if the school's next door, the rehearsal there isn't much of a reason to give her the car keys. And finally, if she's wrecked three cars in the last month, her parents probably would rather drive around town all night than let her anywhere near the driver's seat of whatever car they have left!

One of the important things about this example is that the strength or weakness of the student's argument has as much to do with the things she's assuming as it does with what she actually says. This is true of most arguments. One difference between people who are good at arguing and those that aren't is the ability to focus on this hidden part of arguments—both their own and those of the people with whom they disagree.

Before we get too far into tracking down assumptions, though, let's make sure you understand the other pieces: the **evidence** and the **main point** or the **conclusion.** Sometimes the actual words someone uses will tip you off as to which part of what he or she is saying is the evidence and which is the conclusion. For example, anything that starts with "therefore" or "thus" or "as a result" is pretty definitely the main point. And anything that starts with a "because" or a "for example" or "for instance" is usually evidence. But often people aren't so generous, and you have to figure it out using common sense. Evidence should answer the question "why?" or "why should I believe that?" In our example above, our student said, "You should lend me the car." If her Dad had then asked "Why," the rest of her argument would be a good answer to that question.

Analyzing an Argument

DIRECTIONS: Try the following examples; circle the conclusion and underline the evidence. The answers are at the end of the section. (If you get stuck, try adding "because" to the beginning of different pieces of the argument. If it still makes sense when you do that, the piece you added "because" to is evidence.)

1. No, I can't come out with you guys tonight. I always spend too much money when we go out, and I need to save money for Christmas presents.

2. I think dark colors make me depressed. The only dark clothing I own is my raincoat, and every day I wear it, I feel totally gloomy.

3. Your cat is very overweight. Regular cat food is designed for active cats of normal weight. You should feed her special diet cat food.

4. Susan is really interesting—she's an avid hiker and works at the Yerkes Primate Center doing language research with the apes there. Every time I see her, I realize how many things you two have in common. You really should let me set you up! Oh, and she's really cute, looks a little like your old girlfriend Jane.

5. SOUP will be signed to a record contract soon. They have talented musicians and a range of lively musical styles.

6.

Name: _____ Date: _____

Creating an Argument

DIRECTIONS: Now let's take this beyond our own canned examples and into your life: think of a recent situation in your own life when you were trying to convince someone of something. What was the point you were trying to convince the person of?

_____
_____
_____
_____

This is the "conclusion" of your argument, even if you say it first. Sometimes in other contexts it gets called the "thesis." But whatever you call it, it is the main idea that you want to get across to the other person or people involved, whether it is your son, your wife, your boss, or your professor. If they agree to this idea, you feel you've accomplished your goal.

Now, list the facts you used in trying to convince the person:

1. _____
   _____

2. _____
   _____

3. _____
   _____

4. _____
   _____

In general, the more separate facts (or "evidence") you can offer to back up your point, the stronger your argument will be—assuming your facts are accurate. Most of the time, when people argue, they try to use accurate evidence. They know their argument will fall apart immediately if their evidence isn't solid.

Sometimes you think you've got great evidence, but you don't, because there's information you're unaware of that's relevant. For example, maybe the girl in our example on the previous page doesn't know that her father has a meeting at the high school tonight from 7 to 10 for some civic organization he belongs to. It wouldn't be at all inconvenient for him to drive her to her rehearsal, since he's going to her school at the same time anyway. So much for her argument to use the car, right? It always pays to check the evidence, in case it's not true, but it's equally important to realize, as we've already shown you, that even if the evidence is accurate, the argument may not be bulletproof. There are always assumptions out there to deal with, and like evidence you offer directly, the assumptions may be very good ones or may actually be completely wrong.

Take, for example, the following argument. *You should go vote before the polls close. It's important for informed citizens to participate in the election process.*

There is one major assumption that is necessary to get from the evidence (which in this case is really an opinion rather than a hard fact) about the importance of informed citizens participating in elections in order for the listener to conclude that she should vote. Pause for a moment and see whether you can identify it:

_____

_____

_____

Consider a graduate student named Johan. He grew up in California, in a little town outside Fresno. He went to college in California and then grad school in New York. If you met him and talked to him for a while, you would probably have assumed, as do most people, that he was your average American grad student. But Johan, California accent, black hair, dark eyes and all, is a Swedish citizen. His dad was Swedish and his mom's Japanese (hence the very un-Swedish coloring!). No matter how informed Johan was about American politics, he wouldn't have voted in a presidential election—he's not a U.S. citizen.

Our argument above wouldn't work to convince him to vote, since it incorrectly assumes that he's an informed citizen. The same argument would be equally ineffective directed at people who are citizens, but who don't know anything about the issues. They could agree with my comments about the importance of informed citizens voting, but for people who aren't informed or aren't citizens, this won't be persuasive evidence that they, personally, should vote.

Sometimes finding the assumptions is incredibly easy. This is usually when they are really bad assumptions. For example, respond to the following argument: "Fritz is a cat. Therefore, Fritz must be a reptile." You probably immediately thought, "Wait a minute. That doesn't make sense—cats aren't reptiles!" The assumption that cats are reptiles jumps out at you pretty easily. But sometimes assumptions aren't so obvious, and we read right past them. At other times, the exact assumption being made is a little trickier to pin down. Take a look at an example you saw earlier:

SOUP will be signed to a record contract soon. They have talented musicians and a range of lively musical styles.

Try to identify the assumption that links the evidence to the conclusion.

_____

_____

_____

Often, when we've used this example in class, people have gone overboard in stating the assumption on this one. They say something like, "The only way to get a record contract is to have talented musicians and a lively range of musical styles." But actually, to get from the information about SOUP's talents and musical style to the conclusion that they'll be signed, you don't need to assume that this is the *only* way to get a contract, just that these characteristics are *enough.* So the correct assumption is something more along the lines of: "Talented musicians and a lively range of musical styles are enough to get a band a recording contract" or "One sure way to get a recording contract is to have talented musicians and a lively range of musical styles." See the difference? It might still be possible for someone else to get a record contract with lousy musical ability and one dull style, as long as he or she was willing to marry the son of the record company owner.

Name: _____ Date: _____

Assumptions in an Argument

DIRECTIONS: Try to find the assumptions in the rest of the arguments in the practice exercises:

1. No, I can't come out with you guys tonight. I always spend too much money when we go out, and I need to save money for Christmas presents.

   _____

   _____

2. I think dark colors make me depressed. The only dark clothing I own is my raincoat, and every day I wear it, I feel totally gloomy.

   _____

   _____

3. Your cat is very overweight. Regular cat food is designed for active cats of normal weight. You should feed her special diet cat food.

   _____

   _____

4. Susan is really interesting—she's an avid hiker and works at the Yerkes Primate Center doing language research with the apes there. Every time I see her, I realize how many things you two have in common. You really should let me set you up! Oh, and she's really cute, too—looks a little like your old girlfriend Jane.

   _____

   _____

5. [Triangle sign: SLOW CHILDREN AT PLAY]

   _____

   _____

Now go back to the argument from your own life. Can you find assumptions that you are making?

_____

_____

_____

_____

Challenge Assumptions

So why all this obsessive attention to assumptions? Because these are usually the points at which arguments (our own and other people's) are vulnerable to attack. If you want to strengthen an argument, one good way to do it is to provide facts that support your assumptions. If you want to weaken an argument, find the assumptions, and see if you can come up with facts that challenge them. Graduate schools believe that these skills are so important that they test them on major entrance exams that many of you will be taking.

The Law School Aptitude Test and Graduate Record Exam test these skills through multiple-choice questions, and the GMAT tests them when applicants write the required essays. One of the required essays is an analysis of an argument, and you score big on this essay if you can find the assumptions and show what problems they create. Even the MCAT essay section requires that you construct a nice balanced coherent argument. But even if you aren't planning to go to grad school, these skills are important for success in life.

When you are writing a paper for a class, you or someone else should read the paper, looking for things someone could question or challenge (again, usually the assumptions). Then you should directly address these counter-arguments in your paper. Think of yourself as a lawyer, trying to anticipate opposing counsel's every move. Similarly, when you are trying to convince someone in your life of something important, it pays to take some time to think about both sides of the argument to see if you can do anything to either support your assumptions with fact or draw attention to the weak assumptions made by your opponent.

Let's briefly look at how this might work with a couple of the same examples we've been using. We've already seen that our student driver's argument that her parents should lend her the car is much weaker if her dad has to go to a meeting at (or near) her school at the same time as her rehearsal. This fact would challenge her assumption that having her parents drive her to rehearsal would be inconvenient for them. On the other hand, if her parents are big sports fans, and an important game is on TV that night, this fact might support her argument, since letting her drive would mean that they could watch the game without interruption.

What about the argument that "my dark raincoat makes me depressed?" This argument assumes that the fact that these things occur together regularly (their correlation) indicates that the raincoat causes "me to be depressed." This is a common logical error that people make. Just because two things reliably happen together, doesn't necessarily mean that one causes the other ("correlation does not imply causation"). It's certainly possible that "wearing dark colors makes me sad," or it's possible that "if I'm miserable, I tend to choose clothes to match my mood." But it's also possible that there is some third factor that drives the whole relationship—in this case, it might be that "the rain in the forecast causes me to wear the raincoat," and that "when the rain actually falls, I feel lousy about the bad weather."

What facts might strengthen or weaken this argument? Well, information about rainy days when the speaker isn't wearing the raincoat would help. If the speaker isn't in a bad mood on those days, too, then that would weaken the argument that it's the dark clothes that make him sad, since that would suggest that the rain would be a more likely cause. On the other hand, if he's in a good mood on the rainy, non-raincoat days, then it doesn't seem like the rain is enough to put him in a bad mood by itself.

And if he's still in a bad mood on days when he wears the raincoat, but the weather guys were wrong and it's sunny all day, that would be another point for the raincoat rather than the rain. Again, the point is that these facts address the assumption that there's nothing else special about the days when he's depressed and wearing the rain coat—specifically, the role of the rain which might make a good alternate explanation.

There's another really common assumption that people make when they argue which is worth looking at. That is what I'm going to call the "assumption of representativeness." Take a look at this argument:

Most of the customers at the A&P near Peachtree Battle must be senior citizens. Every time I shop there, all the other customers are retired folks.

Every time—that sounds like pretty good evidence, right? Only if the times that the speaker goes shopping are typical of the average shopping time during a given week—that is, if these times are representative of shopping days at this supermarket. The hitch is that this may be a bad assumption. Suppose that I always go shopping on Tuesday, since it's a day when we don't teach and we figure the stores will be less crowded than on weekends. And suppose that the A&P also has a policy of providing senior citizen discounts on Tuesdays. That would mean that older shoppers in the neighborhood (at least budget-conscious ones) would be more likely to shop on Tuesdays than the average person (and less likely to be there on other days of the week, since they would be waiting to shop when it was less expensive). So Tuesdays would not be representative of the usual shopping day at all, and our conclusion about the overall demographics of shoppers at the local grocery would probably be wrong. When you are reading or talking with someone, keep this logical problem in mind—it's a really common weakness in many arguments. In fact, it's even a weakness in some published research.

Sometimes researchers draw conclusions about behavior in general from a study of a small group. That's fine if the group is representative of people in general. Facts that show that the example group is representative will strengthen an argument of this sort. But samples aren't always representative; for example, lots of early psychology research was done on 20-year-old men at Ivy League colleges—and they didn't always behave in the same ways as older adults or women at Ivy League schools or people without college backgrounds. Recent researchers have revisited a lot of early research questions in the field for exactly this reason—to be sure that conclusions drawn from Harvard undergraduates still hold up when the same issues are explored with a more diverse group. So keep an eye out for the assumption of representativeness in your own arguments and in those of other people.

Name: _____ Date: _____

Reviewing Assumptions

DIRECTIONS: As a final step in thinking about how to strengthen or weaken arguments, go back to the little argument you wrote based on your own life. Look at the assumptions you identified. What facts might support those assumptions? List a couple here:

_____

_____

_____

These will strengthen your argument. What facts might contradict these assumptions?

_____

_____

_____

These facts would help your opponents weaken your argument, unless you can come up with some good points to use to counter them. It's always a good idea to know where your own arguments are vulnerable, so that you can do damage control. Even if all you can do is admit they are there, but point out that the strengths are more numerous, you have helped your cause. Researchers have found that arguments which are "two-sided," that is, which acknowledge the opposing position, are actually more persuasive than one-sided ones. They sound more reasonable and balanced and often anticipate the listener's objections and answer them. This is an excellent tactic to use when writing term papers. Look for your assumptions and the objections that your professor could raise while reading the paper, identify them, and show your reader why they are not big concerns. Your professor will think you're brilliant for anticipating his or her objections and addressing them, and you are likely to end up with a much stronger grade.

Answers to the Activities

Activity 1

In 1–6, the conclusion is in italics, and the evidence is underlined:

1. *No, I can't come out with you guys tonight.* <u>I always spend too much money when we go out, and I need to save money for Christmas presents.</u>

2. *I think dark colors make me depressed.* <u>The only dark clothing I own is my rain coat, and every day I wear it, I feel totally gloomy.</u>

3. <u>Your cat is very overweight. Regular cat food is designed for active cats of normal weight.</u> *You should feed her special diet cat food.*

4. <u>Susan is really interesting—she's an avid hiker and works at the Yerkes Primate Center doing language research with the apes there. Every time I see her, I realize how many things you two have in common.</u> *You really should let me set you up!* <u>Oh, and she's really cute, too—looks a little like your old girlfriend Jane.</u>

5. *SOUP will be signed to a record contract soon.* <u>They have talented musicians and a range of lively musical styles.</u>

6.

Activity 3

1. Tonight will be like the other nights we've gone out (no one else will pay for my expenses tonight).

2. There is nothing else happening consistently on the days when I wear the coat that could be making me depressed instead (like rain, perhaps . . .)

3. The cat is fat due to her diet, rather than to some other medical condition. There are not other important differences between diet and regular cat food which might matter more to you than the degree to which the food contributes to your cat's weight problem.

4. You would want to date someone who looks like your ex, is interesting, and has a lot in common with you. You don't mind being "set up" with people.

5. Driving slowly helps avoid hitting children. You don't want to hit children.

Critical Thinking with Numbers and Graphs

A useful way to present evidence in order to convince others (or yourself) about a point is to use numbers, and many numbers are often more convincing than one number. For example, if you want your manager to increase your salary, a list of the salaries (higher than yours, we hope) of people in similar positions would be useful. Or, if you want money from an investor, good profit and growth numbers are important. A lot of numbers, and therefore a lot of information, can be given in a table, but it is much easier to understand that information if it is given in a graph. Below is a table containing information from the Census Bureau concerning the mean family income of people who have completed different amounts of schooling.

Mean Annual Family Income, by Education, 1995	
Below First Grade	$26,000
High School Dropout	$30,000
High School Graduate	$43,000
Some College	$51,000
Associate's Degree	$54,000
Bachelor's Degree	$73,000
Master's Degree	$88,000
Doctoral Degree	$106,000
Professional Degree	$130,000

Figure 1

The relationship between income and education is clear enough in the table, but it is even clearer in the following graph.

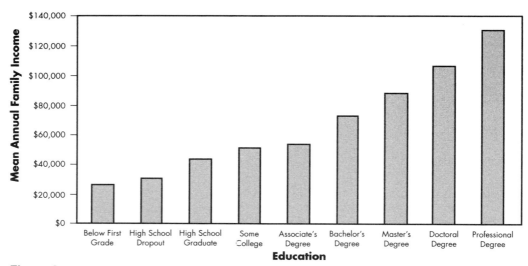

Figure 2

When we see this graph we can immediately grasp the relationships. For example, we do not need to do any arithmetic to know how much more the family of the college graduate makes than the family of the high school drop out.

As good as graphs are, you still need to look at them critically to make certain that they mean what they appear to mean. To be persuasive, the makers of graphs often want to emphasize certain things and hide others. The most common way to make a graph deceptive is to leave out a part of it.

Look at the relationship between the income of the family of someone with a doctoral degree compared with that of someone with a professional degree in Figure 3. It looks like a huge difference. Now look at this same relationship back in Figure 2. There, the difference does not seem as big. By not starting with zero on the y-axis, and by increasing the vertical size, a large difference appears to be a huge difference. This "trick" may have been done intentionally to be deceptive and provides further support for the maxim, "there are lies, damn lies, and statistics!" Therefore, *"caveat emptor!"* Use your critical thinking to analyze quantitative information so that you will not be manipulated by those who count on you to have math anxiety and expect you to simply accept the numbers without thoughtful consideration.

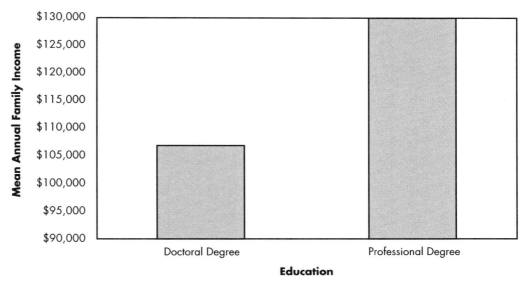

Figure 3

A less common, but just as misleading way to draw a graph is to represent the amount by the height and width, instead of just the height.

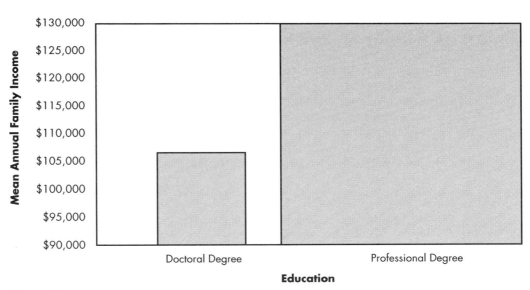

Figure 4

We are predisposed to perceive the amount of something by examining its area, rather than just its height. This, again, may have been done to mislead the audience.

Sometimes, it can be more difficult to misconstrue the meaning of a graph than misinterpret a single number, at least if the number is the wrong type of statistic. Graphs can show us things that are hidden from view when we only are given one or two numbers to examine. For example, the mean price for housing in the Atlanta area might be $120,000 (remember that the mean is obtained by adding all the prices and then dividing by how many prices there were), but we can get a clearer idea about how much we need to pay for a house by looking at the graph in Figure 5.

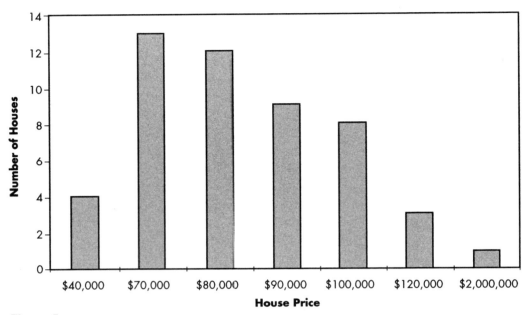

Figure 5

The mean can be misleading when we have a distribution made up of things such as prices or incomes, where a few large examples can bring up the mean tremendously. This is the case for incomes and home prices because there is a definite lower limit to these numbers, but the sky is the limit (think of Ted Turner) for the largest amount. When you have extreme cases (outliers), it is best to avoid using the mean when describing a distribution of numbers, because the mean will be drawn to these outliers—will be deceptively large if the unusual cases are larger than the rest, or deceptively small if the unusual cases are much lower than the rest. A much better way to describe the central tendency for these types of numbers is to use a median—the number halfway between the largest and the smallest value. The median value for an Atlanta home in the example above is $80,000, which is $40,000 less than the mean! Maybe you can afford to buy into the American dream?

A story in the June 24, 1997 issue of the *Atlanta Journal-Constitution* shows how confusing things can be when types of statistics are confused. The story begins with the sentence. "The typical American house sold for $92,500 in 1995, but in Atlanta the price was $126,000, according to a Census Bureau survey and new data compiled for the *Journal-Constitution*." The article later explains that the Census Bureau used medians and the *Journal-Consitution* used means. In reality, the difference between national and Atlanta housing prices is much smaller than the article suggests, evident when the proper comparison is made using median housing prices.

Further examples of how the truth can be distorted with graphs and statistics can be found in *How to Lie with Statistics*, Darrell Huff, W. W. Norton, New York, 1954. Clearly, when it comes to numbers, critical thinking is required!

Critical Thinking, Learning, and Education

It is much easier to remember things that have meaning for you, such as information for a test or the important phone numbers of your relatives. Briefly look at Figure 6. How easy would it be for you to remember it well enough to duplicate? Probably not too difficult because the picture is not terribly complex. But what if the picture was indeed complicated? Would your memory improve if we supplied the picture with meaning by labeling it, "Ants crawling through spilled champagne?" Of course it would!

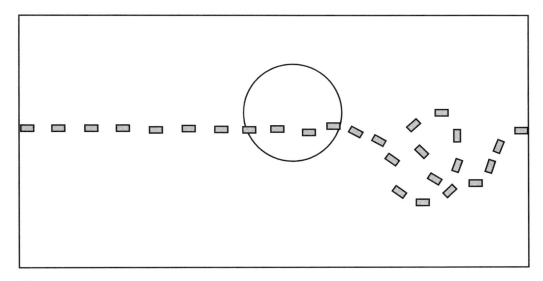

Figure 6

Thinking critically about something gives it meaning and attaches it to the rest of our knowledge. The more we work with a piece of information and the more we compare it with other things that we know, the better we will remember it. Remembering information is vital for a successful career in college and in life.

For example, a basic dimension in the classification of personality is introversion-extroversion. The introvert is quiet, unsociable, and cautious. The extrovert is talkative, sociable, and takes more social risks. Some people are very extroverted, others are somewhere in-between. The distinction between extrovert and introvert isn't too difficult to remember, but if we think about it—if we analyze it—we can remember it even better.

Let's bring time into the personality equation. Do people change in the extroversion dimension over time? Is an introvert always an introvert? Have you ever seen someone who is usually talkative? When did this occur? Could it happen when the person loses his or her inhibitions (among other things) through the use of alcohol? What would an extroverted person do in the same situation? Is it likely that the only difference between the two types of personalities is that the extrovert has a natural supply of something like alcohol in his or her veins? Why or why not? (We assure you that the answer is "not.") After going through this exercise, do you see why it would become more difficult to forget the meanings of extroversion and introversion?

Improving your memory is not the only reason to think critically about what you learn in college classes. Seldom is what you are taught the truth in its entirety. The world is complicated, and college courses present a simplified view of the world to make it palatable. For example, you might have learned, while taking a course in world history, that the assassination of Archduke Francis Ferdinand in Sarajevo was the cause of the first World War. However, unless other things had also occurred—such as Austria's fear of unrest among its ethnic minorities, Germany's reliance on one plan for war, or the weakness of the Russian army—the war might not have started at that time, and might never have started at all. Everything you learn in college (or anywhere else, for that matter) has its limitations and may not be "the truth." It is well worth critically examining even a portion of it if you hope to comprehend and appreciate the complexity of what we know. Remember, in the information age of the 21st century, knowledge is power!

Problem Solving System[c]

The first step in our problem solving system is to REORGANIZE. If you reorganize the problem, and put it into your "own words," then you will be able to understand exactly what is being asked of you. A good way to do this is to underline the verbs in the question, like COMPARE AND CONTRAST, ANALYZE, and DISCUSS.

The next step in the system is to make HYPOTHESES. Hypotheses are "educated guesses" or trial solutions to your problem. This is where you can let your mind roam, or brainstorm, for ideas. At this stage, everything that can possibly answer the question is fair game. No judgments about the hypotheses are made at this time; that comes later.

The next two steps can be combined together because they are RULE OUT THE IRRELEVANT and SET CRITERIA. These two steps are meant to take all of the ideas you came up with during the hypotheses step and start to weed out those that won't work. Setting up criteria means that you determine what your solution must have in it or the criteria it must meet. For example, if you are answering a question that wants you to compare and contrast two things, then any answer you give must compare and contrast. There can be any number of criteria, and they are usually determined by what the question is asking and what you want to say.

The way to determine if something is irrelevant is to look at a hypothesis and ask one question: does this satisfy my criteria and answer my question? If the answer is yes, then keep the hypothesis. If the answer is no, then discard it. Many times hypotheses that seem to work when they are first thought of really don't when they are examined more closely.

The next step in the system is TIME. In order for you to get the best answer possible, you must give yourself enough time to think. If you allow plenty of time, you can explore each hypothesis thoroughly and even go back and do more research if you need to. It is possible to finish assignments or write a paper in one night, but no one does their best work on such short notice.

The next two steps are RECALL and SIMPLE TO COMPLEX. These steps will help you use information you may already have and present your answer in a logical fashion. The recall step is there for you to put to use any prior knowledge you have of the problem. For example, if you read a book about the invention of the steam engine in high school and you are asked in college to write a paper about the Industrial Revolution, you can use the prior information you have from the steam engine book to help you with your present paper. Always use any prior information you have to help you because it can only enrich your answer.

---

[c]From *The Essential Handbook for Academic Success Skills* by California University Regents. Copyright © 1998 by Kendall/Hunt Publishing Company. Used by permission.

The simple to complex step is there to help you stay on track and keep your answers organized. If you start with a simple premise and fill in complex details, your answer will be logical and easily understood by others. If you try to work from the complex backwards towards the simple, your answer will end up being confusing and not make much sense. Another advantage to forcing yourself to go from the simple to the complex, is that you avoid impulsive jumping around in your answer.

The last step in the system is BE PERSISTENT. By never giving up and sticking to your system, you will eventually get the answer to whatever problem you have to solve.

This is the end of the problem solving section of the chapter. The next section of the chapter will focus on ways to get the old creative juices going.

Be Creative

Organizational methods and analysis are things that most people commonly associate with critical thinking. However, these are just the basics to becoming a great critical thinker. You also need to integrate creativity into your thought processes. Think for a moment about all the people you know or know of that you would consider to be great critical thinkers and why you feel that way about them. Through our experiences as workshop presenters, we have found that a great number of people answer something like this: "My friend Mike is one of the best critical thinkers I know of. He always seems to be able to come up with a solution to everything, no matter how hard it is. In fact, even when I do come up with an answer, his always seems to be better." So what can we do about our own critical thinking skills. Well, we've already covered all the technical stuff, the organizational skills, the analysis and the persistence, and how they can help us in our "quest" for answers. But we really haven't touched upon the other half of critical thinking: CREATIVITY!

So what exactly is involved in the creative process? Well for our purposes, let's define it as the expansion of our boundaries, the pushing out of our mental wall, if you will. What do I mean? Well, ever since we were little we've been conditioned by society to think in a certain manner, to have a certain point of view. And through this process of socialization, we have developed a "sense of the conventional." As a result, in our problem solving, we tend to function within the boundaries of this convention. Therefore, our goal should be to break down these "walls," or at least push them out further, and consider things that normally wouldn't lie within our normal thought processes. How do we do this you ask? Well, we just happen to have a few exercises that may move you along in the right direction and get those juices flowing.

Name: _____ Date: _____

■ Be Creative

Think of as many uses for a toothpick as you can.

(For now, just come up with eight.)

1. _____
2. _____
3. _____
4. _____
5. _____
6. _____
7. _____
8. _____

Giving this workshop, we have gotten some incredible ideas for what you can do with toothpicks. For example, one of our favorites is to use them to roast tiny marshmallows over a tiny fire that you made from them. My personal favorite is one that was suggested to me by one of the other workshop presenters. She suggested that I use them to make noiseless wind chimes. Now that you have a few more ideas, go back to the previous exercise and come up with a few more uses before going any further.

1. _____
2. _____
3. _____
4. _____
5. _____
6. _____
7. _____
8. _____

Now that you have completed the exercise the second time, I want you to look back and compare the two sets of answers. Are they different? How? What we have found is that the answers given the first time around are usually the more common and conventional uses such as picking up food and the ever popular cleaning of teeth. But the second time, after we have given some of our favorite examples, the answers get more, shall we say, wild. What happened to make things different? Well, when we shared our ideas, we brought down the walls of conventional thinking. You were no longer confined to just that small realm of ideas and were free to "roam" around a bit and consider uses that you may have eliminated previously because you felt that they were irrelevant. Here are a few more exercises you can use to help bring those walls down.

Job Interview

You have a job interview at 10:00 a.m. the next morning, but your car just broke down that afternoon and won't be fixed for two weeks. The place is 20 miles away, and you need to be dressed well. Also keep in mind that the traffic will be horrible between 8:00 and 10:00 in the morning. List as many possible ways you can get to the job interview.

Term Paper

You've been working on a term paper for weeks and as you arrive at school that morning, you realize that you left it at home sitting on top of the computer. This paper means everything. If you get an A, you get an A in the class; if you fail, you don't graduate. The bell for class starts to ring and you realize that you're stuck since you won't be allowed to leave for any reason. What do you do? (Don't forget to use those creative juices that are flowing now.)

_____

_____

_____

Here are some things to keep in mind as you are working on things in the future:

- **Be original.** Look for new ways to do the same thing. Examine the problem from different points of view and go beyond the conventional. You may find a new solution that works just that much better than the one you just had. It's going to be a bit difficult at first, but it'll get easier and easier the more you practice.
- **Remember not to be judgmental when you're brainstorming.** Jot down your ideas. Many great ideas can be lost at this stage by making quick judgments. Make the judgment calls later on.
- **Be flexible to change.** Change is another one of those double-edged swords, so be careful as to how you wield it. Make sure you know when it is time for change and when you need to stay with convention. Keep in mind that something is only effective as long as it is effective.
- **Keep an eye out for opportunities to use your creativity.** There are opportunities everywhere. This one might be difficult at first, but the more you get in the habit and practice, the easier it is going to get.

Keep in mind these four steps and keep reminding yourself that you can do this, because you can. You do it everyday and probably don't even recognize it.

Connect the Dots

Instructions: Using only four lines and without removing your pencil from the paper, connect the nine dots noted below.

```
    0         0         0

    0         0         0

    0         0         0
```

For the solution, see next page

Answer to Nine Dots Problem

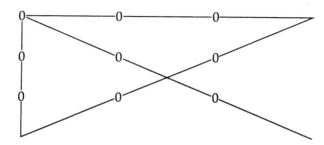

What do you think of the answer? Did you limit yourself just to the dimensions of the imaginary square? You cannot solve the problem if you did. This is a perfect example of how thinking conventionality can hinder you from coming up with the best solutions. Remember, don't be caught up in rules that haven't been set for you

CHAPTER 8
Writing a Research Paper

Writing is hard. Even for many professional writers, the act of sitting down each day and putting thoughts on paper is a difficult, even daunting, task. So why is writing so difficult? Perhaps because, in a way, writing is sales. As writers, you must "sell" your readers on your arguments, your stories or your particular take on a given subject—but you must do so minus all of the communicative apparatus that you normally have at your disposal. You don't have your hand gestures and your eye contact, you don't have your smiling face or nice suit. Yet you must still persuade your readers and you must do so only on the strength of your writing. **Knowing your audience and understanding the parameters and expectations of the particular writing assignment are the first steps** you must understand before beginning the process. What does your instructor want you to learn from this assignment? Is the audience just your instructor? Is there some other real or implied reader? What are the particular instructions for this assignment? What skills do you think the instructor wants you to demonstrate? Refer back to the assignment or criteria sheet for this assignment frequently.

cover the basis your instructor require.

In this course, you will be asked to write a **research paper**. The research paper is the cornerstone of a college or university education because professors and instructors want you to leave their courses knowing what the scholars in that field are saying. Research can be an exhilarating task as you discover the breadth and depth of intellectual activity around topics that interest you. Writing a research paper requires that you have a firm grasp of how to access text and on-line materials suited to your topic and how to incorporate and document these materials in your own essays.

Research papers also (usually) require that you **establish a thesis about your topic**. A thesis is an argument or bias about a given subject which includes some indication of how you will prove this argument **(controlling ideas)**. At this level of education, you are no longer merely entitled to your opinions. You must prove them! Many students find writing a thesis statement a difficult task, but if you think about **the thesis as an organizing structure** which allows your argument to unfold logically and coherently, it becomes a much easier task. Thesis writing employs all of the critical thinking skills you've learned. In the process of researching a given topic, you'll be sifting through the materials and questioning their validity. By forming your own opinion about your topic, you are now closer to having an original idea about it. **Your thesis will help you to establish an outline for your paper and to control the direction of your argument.**

Your writing should never be boring. Even though you don't have your actual voice to work with, your writing should have a **voice**—a tone and rhythm and sound particular to you. Even though you'll be incorporating the thoughts of others, as demonstrated in this chapter in the sections on quoting, paraphrasing and summarizing, you'll be expected to retain your own voice. Always remember that your voice—as well as the quality of your research, your thesis, the organization of your argument, etc.—is a crucial part of selling your ideas to your reader.

Your **conclusion** is there to let you summarize your thesis and main points, but always use different language. Of course your conclusion is not the place to add new information, but that doesn't mean you can't have a clever "illumination" about your topic. If you think about your thesis as a pound of unground coffee beans—something which in and of itself is not all that useful, but provides the promise of something quite useful—then you can think of your conclusion as that same pound of coffee beans ground and ready to be used. It's the same coffee but it's in a different form. And it's very useful now. Strive to keep your reader thinking about what you've written.

Besides finding and incorporating scholarly research into your academic papers, you will be expected to **document your sources** honestly and accurately. There are many different referencing styles, but in this course you will be expected to become proficient in APA (American Psychological Association) style referencing.

Expect to spend some time on a research paper. It is next to impossible to pull off a research paper in a day. Chart your tasks on a time line and leave yourself enough time to let your paper go cold. It's amazing how a day or two can help you to detect errors. Leave yourself enough time to edit, revise and proof your work and enlist the help of a trusted friend or classmate to honestly comment on (peer edit) your paper.

The ability to write a quality research paper is a great skill which will help you throughout your life. Of course you'll be expected to write several research papers while at school, but many of these skills will be useful in your careers and personal lives. Put some time into the process and enjoy the results. There is nothing quite as satisfying as convincing your readers to "buy" your argument. Once you've sold an idea, you're equipped to change the way people think . . . and maybe even change the world.

The Research Writing Process in 20 Steps

The dreaded research paper! It can seem like such a huge project. How can you know where to begin? After you begin, where do you go from there? By breaking the research paper into twenty manageable steps, this overwhelming assignment becomes a series of small tasks. Of course, completing the tasks is up to you. After reading through the following twenty steps to completing a research paper, add any steps you feel might be missing. Then make a research-writing schedule and follow it. The looming dread of procrastinating such a project as this will only lead bring stress. Also, because this paper is valued at a high percentage of your final grade, putting off the assignment puts your grade in danger. Now take a deep breath and get started, because with determination, planning, hard work, and requesting help when you need it, you will excel at research writing.

1. *Select* a topic. (Have a contingency plan ready.)
2. *Brainstorm on that topic* and make a scratch outline. What do you already know about it? What do you want to find out about it?
3. Begin *researching*. Always remember to make note of the source and location of the materials you are collecting. This information will be necessary for your "References" page and for any follow-up research you may need to do.
4. *Narrow* topic
5. Complete a *Contract for a research paper* (Exercise 1) and turn it in to your instructor.

6. *Continue researching.* Get more sources than are required for your research paper. Consider a 3 to 1 ratio. Only one of each three articles you find will be a good resource for your final topic.
7. Create a *thesis statement.*
8. Begin *raw data collection.* Don't forget to note page numbers for any quotes. You will need to include page numbers for quotes in your in-text citations.
9. *Read over your notes* from raw data collection.
10. Refine your *thesis statement.*
11. Write an *outline.*
12. Write the *first draft* (sentences and paragraphs, including quotes and in-text citations)
13. Always make a *back up.* Save your paper to the hard drive and to disk. If you don't have your own computer, *print off a copy* and save your paper to disk.
14. *Edit, revise, rewrite.*
15. *Get help.* Find a friend, fellow student, or family member who can read through your paper. Another person's perspective and input is always helpful.
16. Create a *"References" page.* (Provide complete APA references for all in-text citations.)
17. *Proof.* Check your spelling, grammar, APA style, and essay format.
18. *Peer editing* workshop in class.
19. Write *final copy.* Include the title page, outline, introduction, body with in-text citations, any diagrams, conclusion, and references page.
20. *Photocopy* and *turn in your paper.* Then, relax.

Make a Research-Writing Schedule

Now that you see the steps to writing a research paper, draw up a schedule for yourself. On a calendar, indicate when you will complete each step. First, record due dates. Do you have to bring a draft of your paper to class for peer editing? When is the final draft of your paper due? Now, consider how much time and how many days you will need to spend on each step to research writing. Add these steps to your calendar, giving yourself sufficient time for each. Remember to leave a day or two of lag time between drafts of your paper. When you return to edit and revise, the time away allow you to better expand ideas and identify errors.

Get Started by Committing Yourself to the Project

Essay Structure: The Funnel

Think of your research paper as a funnel. Catch the attention of your reader with a noteworthy opening line. Then, narrow down to the main topic or thesis of your paper. The body paragraphs should propel the reader through your paper. Begin the first body paragraph with an important or strong argument; from that point on, save the best for last. Build the body of your paper so it finishes with the strongest argument; but don't end there. Make a strong conclusion reminding your reader of your argument and pointing to the broader implications of this issue.

Introduction

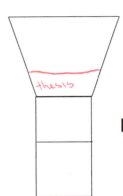

- Hook your reader with an interesting but broad opener.
- Give details and explanation that grab reader's interest and, if needed, provide essential background information.
- Your thesis statement should fit the scope of your paper.
- If appropriate, give a short a road map providing the subtopics.

thesis = argument + (3) controlling ideas

Body

- The body is a paragraph by paragraph development of the arguments in support of your thesis.
- It contains four or five subtopics that argue the thesis. Develop each subtopic in a paragraph or group of paragraphs.
- Start the body with a good opening subtopic, one that is relatively strong.
- Arrange subtopics by emphatic order, with the most important or strongest argument coming last.
- For each subtopic, provide evidence or support in the form of quotes, paraphrases, or summaries. And don't forget your own ideas.

Conclusion

- Restate the thesis. Make it interesting; don't just change a couple of words.
- Avoid introducing new ideas; yet,
- The conclusion is a good place to show broader implications or the wider significance of your topic or argument.
- Aim to keep your reader interested to the last word.

Understanding Essay Structure

Now that you have an overview of essay structure, let's dig further into the parts of an essay. The following explanations and exercises will allow you to deconstruct texts to develop a better understanding of how to:

- Write an introduction and thesis statement
- Learn to state the thesis as an argument
- Develop controlling ideas in a thesis that act as a road map for body paragraphs
- Recognize common thesis pitfalls
- Create a hook that catches readers at the start of an introduction
- Plan the structure of a paper using an outline
- Avoid plagiarism by integrating source material into the structure of a paragraph.

The Introduction

The introductory paragraph of a paper is probably the most frequently rewritten paragraph of a paper. Your introduction requires a **hook** in which you catch the reader's interest and introduce your topic within the first couple of lines. The hook is followed by a short discussion that gradually narrows the discussion and leads the reader to the **thesis statement** at the bottom of the paragraph. Some people refer to the introductory paragraph as a "funnel" (refer back to the diagram for "The Funnel") as it moves from a general introduction of the topic to a very specific argument about that topic.

Writing a thesis strikes a cold fear in many students. For one thing, it seems like everyone has a different idea about what a thesis is and how it is constructed. *What are some of the ideas you've been taught about thesis statements? Use the space below to jot down what you've been told about thesis statements. Share your ideas with classmates.*

The Thesis

At the college level, we share some common ideas about what a thesis statement should be. A thesis statement should:

- appear in your introductory paragraph, usually at or near the end of that paragraph. *Why?*

- be in the form of an argument. *Why?*

- have at least three controlling ideas. *Why?*

- provide the organizing structure for the paper. *How?*

- be between 1–3 sentences long.

Stating the Thesis as an Argument

There are a few common traps that students sometimes fall into when writing a thesis. Sometimes students fail to state their thesis in the form of an argument. An argument implies that someone could argue the opposite of it. *Practice changing the following statements to arguments:*

Example: special needs students

Special needs students should be enrolled in regular school classes.

1. public transportation

2. private schools

3. college fees

Developing Controlling Ideas in a Thesis Statement

Another problem students have is providing support, in the form of **controlling ideas**, as part of the thesis. The controlling ideas are important to your thesis because they immediately show the reader why s/he should believe your argument. But the controlling ideas also provide the structure for your paper. These are the ideas that will advance your argument in the body of your paper. Controlling ideas can come before or after your argument, but they should be part of the 1–3 sentence parameter for the whole thesis statement.

Directions: *In the example below, underline and number the controlling ideas that support the argument.*

Example: Special needs students should be enrolled in regular school classes because such students learn more within this environment, they will avoid the harmful effects of early stigmatization and they will help to create an atmosphere that accepts difference, not sameness, as the norm within our schools.

Take the arguments you have devised in numbers 1, 2 and 3 above and provide at least three controlling ideas for each.

1.

2.

3.

*Practice providing controlling ideas on a few more examples, always being careful that you are proving **your** argument:*

1. Owning an automobile is a necessity

2. Socialized medicine provides a better level of healthcare for the majority of people.

3. Privatizing healthcare is the best option for improving our level of healthcare.

Other Problems with Writing a Thesis Statement

- **The backwards approach.** Be careful not to begin researching with your ideas already too firmly set. This can make it difficult to find materials appropriate to the argument. As outlined later in this chapter in "Steps to Writing a Research Paper," it is important to begin with a topic first; then, by rooting around in the research materials and familiarizing yourself with the various expert opinions on the chosen topic, you can formulate your particular stance vis-à-vis the topic.
- **The too obvious argument.** *(Example: Cramming the night before exams can lead to stress among students.)* Strive to say something original and interesting about your topic. If you can't, perhaps you will need to assess whether you are really interested in this topic. If you're bored, your reader will be too.
- **Controlling ideas do not advance your argument.** *(Example: Owning an automobile is a necessity because everyone has one.)*
- **Controlling ideas are spread out too far away from your actual argument.** Keep your controlling ideas connected to your thesis. They can come before or after your argument, but they must be close by!

The Hook

Think of the advertisements you saw on your way to school. Some of the billboards and posters were easy to ignore, they didn't grab your attention. Other advertisements made you want to stop and read on, to notice the product for sale. Your attention was grabbed by a hook. That hook is something that appeals to you and is presented in just the right way to attract an intended audience.

The hook of an introduction has a similar function, but its goal is to sell readers on your argument. The goal of the hook is to start the readers on that path through the essay funnel. Avoid using catchy lines that have little relation to your topic. Work to create hooks that appeal to the intelligence of your attended audience.

Review and Apply

Review and apply what you have learned about hooks, the thesis, and controlling ideas by completing Exercise 2 (at the end of this chapter).

Outlining

Making an outline will help you plan your paper before you write, like planning a trip before you leave home. The process of writing an outline can help you see where you have an excess of information or where you have a deficit. Any deficit will reveal where you need to do more research.

Directions: The sample scratch outline below is incomplete. Finish the outline, making sure that your additions are within, not outside of, the subtopic you are completing.

Main topic (the most general idea): *Inconsiderate, inattentive, and aggressive drivers are not only irritating, they are making Lower Mainland roads dangerous.*

I. Subtopic: General idea: *Inconsiderate drivers*

    A. Specific idea: *Stop in the street*
       1. Example: *(anecdote) I remember waiting for 15 minutes while a driver went in the bakery to get a loaf of bread.*
       2. *Example: (Research for a statistic. Does this cause accidents?)*

    B. Specific idea:
       1. Example:
       2. Example:
       3. Example:

II. Subtopic: General idea: *Inattentive drivers*

    A. Specific idea: *Talk on cell phones*
       1. Example: *(anecdote) I remember waiting for 30 minutes while a driver talked on a cell phone.*
       2. *Example: (Research for a statistic. Does this cause accidents?)*

    B. Specific idea:
       1. Example:
       2. Example:

III. Subtopic: General idea: *Aggressive drivers*

    A. Specific idea: *Tailgate*
       1. Example: *What defines tailgating*
       2. Example: *How often does tailgating result in accidents*
       3. Example: *Compare walking aggressively to driving aggressively*

    B. Specific idea:
       1. Example:
       2. Example:

Seven Elements of Paragraph Construction
Integrating source material into body paragraphs

Don't let the words and ideas of other people (quotes, paraphrases, and summaries) highjack your paper. Avoid plagiarism by integrating source material into the structure of a paragraph. Make sure your paragraphs are largely constructed with your own ideas and words. Below is a list to help you integrate your research with your words when constructing paragraphs. Notice only number 4 in the list is words from an outside source.

Directions: Read and define the seven elements below. Then, find the seven elements in the following sample paragraph from *Emotional Intelligence* by Daniel Goleman. Notice how the author doesn't drop his reader short and simply let the evidence stand for itself. Instead, he elaborates on the evidence by explaining it in his own words and with his own ideas.

1. Transition
2. Topic sentence
3. More specific statement, might introduce quote, paraphrase, or summary.
4. Quote, paraphrase, or summary
5. In-text citation
6. Your interpretation of the quote
7. Your illustration of the connection between the quote, paraphrase, or summary and the main topic or subtopic.

Excerpt from:

Goleman, D. (1995). *Emotional Intelligence: Why it can matter more than IQ.* New York: Bantam

. . . show that their common trait is the ability to motivate themselves to pursue relentless training routines.

To motivate yourself for any achievement requires clear goals and an optimistic, can-do attitude. Psychologist Martin Seligman of the University of Pennsylvania advised the MetLife insurance company to hire a special group of job applicants who tested high on optimism, although they had failed the normal aptitude test. Compared with salesmen who passed the aptitude test but scored high in pessimism, this group made 21 percent more sales in their first year and 57 percent more in their second (Goleman, 1995).

A pessimist is likely to interpret rejection as meaning *I'm a failure; I'll never make a sale.* Optimists tell themselves, *I'm using the wrong approach,* or *That customer was in a bad mood.* By blaming failure on the situation, not themselves, optimists are motivated to make the next call.

Your . . . positive or negative outlook may be inborn, but with effort and practice, pessimists can learn to think more hopefully. Psychologists have documented that if you can catch negative, self-defeating thoughts as they occur, you can reframe the situation in less catastrophic terms.

Referencing Source Material

Clear organization or structure is an essential element that builds clarity in your research paper. It lays a foundation for the content or the real meat of your paper. Because this is a RESEARCH paper, your ideas will be supported by source material. Together the two are the content and give strength to your argument. Remember to not overload your paragraphs with quotes or paraphrases. Integrate source material into YOUR words and ideas, not the other way around.

Referencing source material can be a difficult task because it takes clear note-taking and careful attention to details. We will cover the following things to improve your research writing skills:

- Tips for taking research notes
- Quoting
- Paraphrasing and summarizing
- Detecting and avoiding plagiarism
- Using and editing for APA style

Taking Research Notes

Sometimes it is the method students use for taking research notes that can get them into plagiarizing trouble. Below are some hints for taking good research notes that, if followed, may help you not plagiarize inadvertently.

1. Record the complete reference for any notes you take from a source.

2. Always put quote marks around any notes that are direct quotes.

3. Don't halfway paraphrase. Make a choice to paraphrase or quote from the source into your notes. If you get lazy and copy phrases from the source into a paraphrase, you may forget that the phrases are in fact little quotes.

4. Always record the source page number for any quote you record in your notes. Consider recording source page numbers for paraphrases and summaries as well. Page numbers allow you to quickly find the source, if your notes need clarification.

5. What other helpful hints can you add?

APA Style

Most college and university instructors require you to use a uniform style of referencing. In this course, you are required to write your research paper in APA style. The stylebook of the American Psychological Association (APA) provides guidelines that ensure accurate referencing of sources to prevent plagiarism.

In APA style, you will provide a short *in-text citation* every time you use the words or ideas of another author. The first word of the in-text citation corresponds to a complete reference supplied on the last page of your essay or the *References* list. This system allows people reading your paper to easily find the original source of any material you borrowed. When you are researching, you might try finding new source material by checking through the list of references provided at the end of any scholarly article or book.

Quoting

A quote is a copy of another person's words. The words are maintained exactly as they appeared in the original source. Quoting can seem like an easy task, simply extract a sentence or two from a source, throw quotes around it, and you have a quote. In fact, quoting is difficult, because it can be easy to lose the connotation of another author's words by removing them from context. Also, poorly cited and marked quotes result in plagiarism. It is essential to provide a complete source for every quote and to set the quote off using quote marks.

Misleading quotes

Watch out for quotes that don't represent the whole meaning, tone, or position of the article. After reading the "Self Esteem is earned, not learned" article, consider what is wrong with these quotes?

1. Schmoker (2000) encourages us to believe, "what is precious can be gotten cheaply" (p. 1).

2. In his article, "Self-esteem is earned, not learned," the author investigates the correlation between low self-esteem in students and lack of motivation to complete homework. Schmoker reports that teachers find, "a malaise among students, adding that only about half of their students will even do homework" (2000, p. 1). Students, who never complete their homework, never gain the self-esteem associated with completing a task and receiving a grade.

Possible ways of introducing quotes

As Bussey (2001) states, "Canadian food is more than just meat and potatoes" (2001, p. 27).

As a result, "what is served in our restaurants reflects the diversity of our country" (Nelson, 2001, p. 29).

According to Samson (1985), "We have one of the cleanest food supplies in the world" (p. 200).

Samson (1985) explains, "We have one of the cleanest food supplies in the world" (p. 200)

APA citation notes

1. Remember to provide the date of publication and page number in-text.

    Note: Page numbers are only required for quotes. When paraphrasing, page numbers are optional.

Example:
> Wang (1985) encourages his readers to reassess their definition of Canadian cuisine, "because Canada is a country of many ethnicities, Canadian cuisine spans the globe." (p. 24).

2. Remember to have a corresponding complete reference for every in-text citation. The in-text citation (e.g. Wang (1985)) should correspond with the first words of the complete reference.

> Wang, E.C. (1985). *Book Title*. City, Province: Publisher.

3. To make an in-text citation for a work with no author, cite the first two to four words of the title and the date.

Reference list entry:

A great dictionary of spoken language. (1999). City, Province: Publisher.

In-text citation example:

As language experts attest, "language is always changing." (*A great dictionary*, 1999, p. 100).

A great dictionary (1999) illustrates, "language is always changing" (p. 100).

4. If you begin your quote in the middle of the author's sentence, you don't have to use ellipsis points (...).

Wang (1985) shows his readers that "Canadian cuisine spans the globe" (p. 24).

Ellipsis marks are not necessary *(this example shows ellipsis marks)*
Wang (1985) shows his readers that " . . . Canadian cuisine spans the globe" (p. 24).

Activity 1: Quoting exercise

1. In pairs, find a quote from the *"Self-esteem is earned, not learned"* article or another article you have read for class.

2. Introduce and cite the quote as if you were including it in the body of your research paper.

3. Follow the quote with an interpretation in your own words. Watch out for changing the meaning of the quote by misinterpreting the overall meaning of the article.

4. Create a reference entry for the quote (what would appear in the final page of your research paper).

5. In groups of four, compare and check your quotes, citations, and reference entry.

Paraphrasing and Summarizing

In a paraphrase or summary only the meaning, not the words from a source, are transferred into your document. Writing a good paraphrase or summary is hard work because it is difficult to maintain an author's idea while changing the author's words. If it is difficult, why do you think authors use paraphrases and summaries at all in their writing? When might you choose to use a paraphrase or summary rather than a quote?

Possible ways to begin a paraphrase or summary

A recent British Columbia Labour Relations Board (2002) report found that . . .

A recent study by Statistics Canada (2001) . . .

Dahliwal, Davies, and Ding (2002) illustrate that . . .

In 2002, Statistics Canada studied . . .

A *New Art* magazine article ("Ceramics in a new century," 2001) reported that . . .

8: Writing a Research Paper

Notes about in-text citations for paraphrases and summaries

1. Don't forget to provide the date in parentheses after the author (or if there is no author, after the first words of reference entry).

2. Don't include paraphrases here and there in your paragraph and then add a citation to the end of the paragraph. You need to clearly mark every place where you used the ideas of another author.

Getting It Right: Paraphrasing

Activity 1: Unacceptable Paraphrasing

Read the following paragraph of raw data reference material.

> When teachers ask students to bring drafts to class, the students and teacher are assuming there is room for improvement, changing the function of correction. In the traditional classroom, teachers give writing assignments with a due date, expecting only to evaluate the final product. There is no class time devoted to the interim steps in writing the paper. Alternatively, in process writing, formative comments on drafts are emphasized and evaluative correction is de-emphasized. Teachers and peers provide feedback during the developmental stages of student papers. By working on drafts and receiving feedback and correction, students learn that writing includes revising and decision-making.

Directions: Consider why the following paraphrase of this excerpt is unacceptable.

1. Underline any words or phrases that are the same as the original reference* material.

2. Why is this paraphrase unacceptable?

A recent article in Journal of Successful Student Writing (2004) *explained that students and teachers are assuming there is room for improvement when teachers ask students to bring drafts to class. Many teachers expect only to see the final product of student essays. These teachers do not devote class time to helping students to write their papers. On the other hand, in process writing, teachers and fellow students give comments on drafts. When students work on drafts and receive feedback and correction, they learn to revise.*

Activity 2: Acceptable Paraphrase

Directions:

1. Now that you have examined an unacceptable paraphrase, make your own paraphrase of the original paragraph.

_____
_____
_____
_____
_____
_____
_____

2. Trade papers with another student.

3. On your classmate's paper, underline any words or phrases that are the same as the original paragraph.

4. Together, discuss the result of your underlining. Have you made an acceptable paraphrase?

Plagiarism

Plagiarism is a scary word, because if found plagiarizing, students can receive a failing grade on the paper or a failing grade in the class. In some cases, the penalty is worse. If you have questions regarding the plagiarism policy at your college, check the Academic Dishonesty policy posted on your college web page.

What Is Plagiarism?

Make a list of the things you can do to avoid plagiarizing:

1. Do not list extra references in your References page. The function of the reference page is to allow your readers to find the complete source for any in-text reference. If there are more entries in your references page than were cited in the text, your teacher will be left wondering where you used that material. Your teacher will also wonder if you have plagiarized by not giving proper in-text citation for those references.

2. Always include a complete reference in your references page for any in-text citation.

3. Avoid over use of any source. If you are finding yourself recounting paragraphs of information from one source into your paper, you are plagiarizing. Get help integrating your own ideas into your paper.

4. _____

5. _____

6. _____

Activity 1: Appropriate Referencing

Directions: The references for the following student paper are sloppy and will bring the student's mark down. Find the student's errors in APA style by completing the steps below.

1. Use an APA style guide to correct the mistakes in each reference listed on the "References" page.

2. The references should appear in alphabetical order. Number the references to show the order in which they should appear.

3. Use an APA style guide to check the in-text citations. Correct any that are done improperly.

4. Compare the references with the in-text citations. Are any references missing from the "References" page? Add the last name of the in-text citation to the "References" page.

5. Compare the references with the in-text citations. Are there any references that do not have corresponding in-text citations? Cross out any extra references from the references list.

6. Use "as cited in" when you have not gone to the original source but are citing one author's words as they appeared in a second author's article or book. Take care and use this method of citing minimally in your paper. "As cited in" reveals you are quoting from a secondary source, one author's impression of another author's ideas. Why might it be problematic to quote one author's impression of another author's ideas? How many times was "as cited in" used in *Re-Assessing the letter grading of assessment*?

Abstract

Assessing primary school students' learning by relying solely on letter grading is counterproductive and restrictive. Without incorporating into the assessment formula a compilation of indicators, highlighting a comprehensive showcase of student classroom learning, self-esteem, goal realization and keenness to learn, are shown to be effected adversely. With the aid of scholarly research, support is given favoring a move away from letter grading towards a more thorough assessment of achievement. Evidence presented from a current evaluation procedure along with professional observations, will point out the virtues of a 'well rounded' approach to primary student assessment. Finally, improvement for many students, particularly those whose hidden potential may require unconventional as well as compassionate exploration, emerges as the re-assessment of letter grading evolves and earns its success in the primary classroom.

Re-assessing the letter grading
of assessment for primary school students

Student Name
Student number
STSU 100-001
Teacher name
Date

Abstract

Assessing primary school students' learning by relying solely on letter grading is counterproductive and restrictive. Without incorporating into the assessment formula a compilation of indicators, highlighting a comprehensive showcase of student classroom learning, self-esteem, goal realization and keenness to learn, are shown to be effected adversely. With the aid of scholarly research, support is given favoring a move away from letter grading towards a more thorough assessment of achievement. Evidence presented from a current evaluation procedure along with professional observations, will point out the virtues of a 'well rounded' approach to primary student assessment. Finally, improvement for many students, particularly those whose hidden potential may require unconventional as well as compassionate exploration, emerges as the re-assessment of letter grading evolves and earns its success in the primary classroom.

Re-assessing the letter grading
of assessment for primary school students

A+ in one of your classes in grade 4, congratulations! You have obviously worked hard and succeeded at displaying the highest level of achievement within the pre-determined standards. This is undoubtedly an enviable accomplishment and one to be applauded and acknowledged. But what do you really know? Is there more here than first meets the eye? Certainly course requirements have been met and exceeded. But more importantly, has this knowledge been dispensed along with an equal dose of understanding as to its relevance and/or application? Or has this fundamental and critical cornerstone of learning been skimmed over and given a back seat in favor of grade recognition? With the emphasis on grade superiority "the tail of assessment thus comes to wag the educational dog" (Kohn, 1999, p. 3). Moving away from the weight given to letter grading towards a more complete method of assessment encompassing a broader range of classroom endeavors would result in clearer illumination of the extent to which learning by the primary student has been accomplished. The resurgence of a keenness to learn, self-esteem as well as goal realization, will benefit from improved assessment procedures and go a long way towards fueling the potential of elementary school students.

Today, the widely used method of attaching a letter grade to student performance has evolved from an application initiated during World War I. According to measurement expert Darrel Bock (1997) "the point system or 'Alpha Test' as it was known then, was developed in an attempt to evaluate, in a minimal amount of time, the abilities and suited tasks of military recruits. Moreover, the results of this testing was to allow for a judgment as to the potential for recruits becoming officers or remaining enlisted men" (as cited in Marzano, 2000, p. 44). In time educators began to recognize the potential possibilities this type of testing might provide them with. "From there it wasn't much of a step to assign points to assessments that could not be scored as correct or incorrect such as essay items and presentations and the like. Without realizing it, educators were soon entrenched in the point or percentage method" (Marzano, 2000, p. 47). Inevitably, the transformation to letter grading through its adaptation and application for the school room was welcomed and embraced. Its allure and propensity to condense as well as stream line the arduous task of determining achievement for a large student population has become a hallmark of the assessment formula.

In the primary classroom the weight and influence the teacher commands in assessing achievement is enormous. Accordingly, as the teacher strives to compel the young student to regurgitate the 'right answer,' opportunities for these learners to contribute thoughtful and insightful responses may be systematically passed by. Holt (1964) describes a case in point: "A math text book said that it took one and a half cans to paint the window trim in a house and asked how many half cans that was. When one of her students gave the answer one, she asked how he got that. He said there's one full can, and there's one half can. Nothing wrong with that; indeed it's what we would have seen in the real life situation. But too many teachers, and of course all machine scored tests, would have simply marked the answer wrong" (p. 244).

Furthermore, determining achievement by assigning a letter grade to the work of a primary student does little to promote their desire to learn. Consequently, the development of novel and creative approaches to problem solving may be inhibited. "There must be a better way to educate young children so that the great human qualities we know are in them may be developed. But we won't do it as long as we are obsessed with tests" (Holt, 1964, p. 241).

Primary teachers and students alike have too often succumbed to the expeditious attraction the letter grading offers. It is not surprising then, that the depth of learning that does take place is unfortunately quite frequently superficial. "If it's not going to be on the test, forget it!" (Sigelman, 1999, p. 222). This knowledge of how to 'pull the strings' of achievement speaks clearly that the reliance on letter grading has resulted regrettably, in less than desirable initiative to learn anything more than what is simply needed to 'make the grade.'

It begins to look as if the test examination marks business is a gigantic racket, the purpose of which is to enable students, teachers, and schools to take part in a joint pretence that students know everything they are supposed to know, when in fact they know only a small part of it—if any at all (Holt, 1964, p. 232).

Certainly, there is room for improvement in how testing is administered within the elementary school room. Grading and assessment can be adapted to encourage the attainment of knowledge. Additionally, with emphasis given to developing the strategies necessary to facilitate this undertaking, the foundation will have been laid to provide the confidence for primary students to engage in rewarding and meaningful life of learning. "If I can't give a child a better reason to learn than a grade on a report card I ought to lock my desk and go home and stay there" (De Zouche, 1945, as cited in Kohn, 1999, p. 5).

When primary students feel they are free to offer input without the fear of criticism that low letter grading may produce, they are likely to develop, and indeed increase their desire and interest to be part of the learning experience within the classroom. "Successful learners enjoy inquiring, solving problems, and making connections, both independently and with others" (National Research Council, 1999, as cited in The Primary Program, 2000, p. 25). In contrast, when an elementary school child feels apprehension and fear of being labeled a failure, precipitated by a poor letter grade, learning can be impeded. The possibility of eliciting from a young mind the interest and confidence to break new ground is diminished as his/her perception of available pathways to learning are overgrown with self-doubt and anxiety. "Included in the current reform rhetoric is the need to change the method we evaluate students' achievements. To do so will open gates of opportunity rather than close them off" (National Commission on

Testing and Public Policy, 1990, as cited in Jovanovic & Solano-Flores, 1994).

A critical role of the primary school environment is the development, encouragement, and promotion of self-esteem. Welcoming new challenges rather than being intimidated by them is to a significant extent, the flower that blooms in the garden of learning. As young students are encouraged to participate they also are prone to making errors. When mistakes are presented to classmates and teachers, these youngsters allow themselves to become vulnerable to possible misinterpretation and ridicule. Yet, part of the formula for appreciating success is the experiencing of failure. However, as educators learn to assess their young students in a more progressive manner and avoid attaching a letter grade to rather meaningless individual event, these young people will come to realize the value of their continued efforts and participation. Without the debilitating cloud of inaccurate assessment hanging over them, primary students are more likely motivated to confront and welcome increased challenges and therefore, increase their chances of success. When success can be viewed worthy of pursuing, the seeds of self-esteem have been sewn. As Mike Schmoker points out in his article *Self Esteem is Earned not Learned* "For our part, the best we can do is teach young people, in an atmosphere of compassion, that self-esteem is earned, often with considerable difficulty, and equip them to earn it" (no date for original, Adams and Patterson, 2001, p. 167)

Increasing numbers of school districts are experimenting with a novel method of assessment with an eye of moving from a "grade orientation to learning orientation" (Kohn, 1999, p. 30). Amanda Arnold Elementary in Manhattan, initiated a creative approach to assessment in 1993. According to Dismuke (1993) "the evaluation process revolves around an evaluation conference where students are asked to display their best work and then offer reasons for their choices. More students choose to display work that they thought reflected improvements and firmer grasp of material to be learned" (page 4-20). These children were obviously eager and excited to show off the results of their learning and encouraged to do so. Certainly then, this experiment indicates there are benefits to be gained for elementary school children from utilizing a method of assessment that encourages their participation and promotes variety in their efforts. Consequently, this strategy has yielded the Amanda Arnold school students improvements in their attitudes towards learning and themselves.

Anyone who has heard the term 'authentic assessment' knows that abolishing grades doesn't mean eliminating the process of gathering information about student performance and communicating that information to parents. Rather, abolishing grades opens up possibilities that are far more meaningful and constructive (Kohn, 1999, p. 6).

Presently, B.C. primary school teachers are incorporating an evaluation process that took shape in 1989 and forms the framework for a policy on assessment outlined in a Ministry of Education document entitled: *The Primary Program 2000*. The document outlines the rationale for a more thorough approach to assessment. Currently, in B.C. no letter grades are assigned to primary students. In a written statement Mandoli, Principal of Fairview Elementary in Maple Ridge, shares, "I believe the shift has been occurring over the past 20 years as we discover that we are educating the whole child and not just the areas reported on. As the assessment measures were not an exact science there were many discrepancies in the interpretation of marks" (personal communication, 2001). At present, primary school teachers are encouraged to employ a variety of assessment tools. By doing so, the intent is to minimize inaccurate determination of their students achievement and to cultivate within them an interest and excitement in learning within a nurturing, as well as stimulating learning environment. "Effective teachers look for patterns in the assessment evidence rather than making judgments about children's learning based on a single assessment" (Ministry of Education, 2000, p. 169).

At the centre of the current method of assessment in B.C. elementary schools, is the teacher's observation of and discussion with students. In addition, feedback provided students focusing on their progress and development, in the context of assessment, forms and integral part of this student to teacher interaction. As Mandoli (2000) states, "Students are measured against curricular standards to show growth in their class, but rather against widely held expectations for children of their age group." The message here is clear. By concentrating on interpreting accomplishments and improvements as well as determining what areas require further effort. Since students rarely perform equally in all areas of classroom activity, this 'hands on approach' is conducive to continued interest, effort, and personal development. According to Vygotsky (1978) (as cited in Segelman p. 89) "learning is most effective when children engage in appropriately challenging activities accompanied by support."

Educators are learning to understand that the method they employ to assess achievement had an enormous and long lasting impact on overall achievement and development of primary school children. The connotations many individuals take with them to adulthood concerning their experiences with letter grading are not always remembered fondly. The word "grading" is however, merely a word. Nevertheless, for many, this particular word possesses the powerful ability to immediately attract and maintain one's consideration and has been known to effect individuals in strange ways. In fact, as I write this paper my hand trembles as it once again finds its way to the chip bowl. However, many things change over time. Individual ideas and their perceptions of them are no exception. That is what, in part, contributes to the attraction that learning has to offer. As teachers and students converge on the appreciation of fair and inclusive assessment, both can partake in the benefits. "Grading can become a tool for all to use in pinpointing strengths and weaknesses in students' understanding. More important, a carefully developed grading system can help us improve student performance over time rather than simply label it at periodic intervals" (Marzano, p. 122).

With the growing emphasis on divergent, rather than superficial letter grading, approach to the assessment of primary school children, optimism for these young minds reaching their goals is apparent. By seeking out and looking favorably upon alternative, and often revealing interpretations from their students to issues within the classroom, educators set in motion a journey towards the accomplishment of understanding that will ignite and fan the fires of learning. According to Theorist Gardner (1983) (as cited in Sigelman, 1999, p. 238) "Instead of asking 'How smart are you?' we should be asking, 'How are you smart?" As confidence is gained to 'wade deeper' into more classroom activities, young students may find that their goals of being accepted by their peers as well as their teachers can be considered achievable.

Unfortunately, many young students must contend with less than stimulating home environment and as a result, arrive at school ill prepared and in many instances, with frequently damaged views of themselves. By employing properly calibrated yardstick of appraisal, these students can come to anticipate the excitement and intrigue their school day has in store. For them, the opportunity to 'belong' in school can become crucial as stabilizing force in their lives. In addition, 'fragile souls' will find increased numbers of teachers highly trained and prepared to appreciate their uniqueness. Moreover, these young learners will come to understand that they too are worthy of attention and nurturing in the primary classroom, within the broader context of assessment. As a result, by relinquishing the reliance on letter grading in the primary classroom, educators and succeeding as budding learners work towards and benefit from improvements in their goal realization, self-esteem, and interest in learning. To conclude Mandoli observes:

> Personally I feel we are doing a one hundred percent better job at teaching the students 'how they learn,' how to problem solve, how to be critical, how to be creative and how to determine what they need. I have also noticed that fewer children say they are 'dumb' and feel awful about being a learner. I think that fading the lines between the A's, B's, C's and dimming the expectation between grade 1, 2, etc. has also allowed children to learn to improve against themselves. A much better approach.

References

D.G. Bachor, and J.O. Anderson, (1994). *Elementary teachers' assessment practices as observed in the Province of British Columbia*. Assessment in education: Principles, policy, & practice, 1, (1), page 63 - 31. Retrieved November 16, 2001 from EBSCO (Academic Search Full Text Elite) on the World Wide Web: 9512190091.

Dismuke, D. (1993). Are report cards obsolete? *NEA Today, May-June 11*, (9), p. 12(2). from Infotrac, Expanded Academic Full Text ASAP. October 2, 2001, World Wide Web: *http://web3.infotrac.galegroup.ccm/itw/in*

Holt, J. *How children fail*. Dell Publishing: New York. (1964).

Adams, R.W. and Patterson, B. (2001). *Developing reading versatility*. Toronto, ON: Harcourt College Publishers.

Sigelman, C.K. (1999). *Lifespan human development*. (3rd Edition). Pacific Grove: Brooks/Cole.

Higgins, E.A., Rholes, W.E. and J.C. Nelson (1977). Category accessibility and impression formation. *Journal of Experimental Social Psychology 13(2)*, 141-145.

Kohn, A. (1999). Degrading to de-grading. *School District 10*, updated Friday, January 26, 2001. *http://www.district10.nbed.nb.ca/Reading/Grading.htm* retrieved October 24, 2001 on the World Wide Web:

Marzano, R.J. (2000). Transforming Classroom Grading. Alexandria: ASCD.

Ministry of Education, Province of British Columbia (2000). The primary program: A Framework for Teaching. Victoria, B.C.

F.F. Romeo. Child abuse and report cards. *Education, 120*, (3), p. 438. Retrieved October 10, 2001 from Expanded Academic Full Text ASAP) on the World Wide Web: *http://www.infotrac.galegroup.com*. (2000).

Jovanovic, J. & Solano-Flores, G. (1994). Performance-Based Assessments. *Education & Urban Society, 26* (4), Retrieved November 16, 2001, EBSCO (Academic Search Full Text Elite) on the World Wide Web: 9503100796. p. 352+.

Editing

Now that you have fixed the APA style in "Re-Assessing the letter grading of assessment for primary school students," reread the paper and complete the activities below.

Activity 1: Structure and Content

Breaking down the structure of a text by making a reverse outline is a good way to analyze content. After you isolate the thesis and identify the controlling ideas, you can investigate whether the paper has sufficient support and any possible instances of plagiarism. While you make the outline, look at the structure this student used and reflect on what you have learned about the structure of an essay.

1. Make an outline of the student paper, "Re-Assessing the letter grading of assessment for primary school students."

2. After you complete the outline, consider whether the student's assertions are sufficiently supported. Is there enough evidence from outside sources?

3. Remember that a research paper with too much support might be plagiarized. It is important when writing a research paper to use research to support your own words and ideas. Review the student's paper again. Where did the student do a good job of using research to support his own words, as opposed to solely recounting the research?

4. Discuss the grade you would assign this paper.

Activity 2: Mechanics

Don't lose points for simple mechanical errors. Punctuation, format, spelling and other such details can seem like unnecessary window dressing, but they are an essential part of writing. A missing comma can easily lead your reader astray and imply a connection between words where none was intended. Repeated mechanical errors frustrate and annoy readers, causing the content of your paper to become secondary. If your mechanical errors have brought your grade down in the past, consider doing one or all of the following things to help bring your writing standard up:

- Purchase and use a writer's handbook that details the mechanics of writing. You can use a handbook as a resource tool to answer questions ranging from comma placement to APA style.
- Find a friend who is good at reading for details and ask him or her to proofread your papers.
- Create an ongoing list of your mechanical errors. Include in the list an example and a correction and explanation. When you are proofreading your own paper refer to this list and look for similar errors.
- Take a Developmental Studies course in writing that includes a focus on mechanics.

Now, fix the following mechanical errors in the sample student paper, "Re-Assessing the letter grading."

1. Long quotes (quotes of 3 or more lines) should be indented. Scan through "Re-Assessing the letter grading of assessment for primary school students." Are all long quotes indented?

2. What voice was the student paper written in? Did the student ever switch from first to third person, making reading awkward?

Notes on pronoun use

Most academic essays are written in third person (he, she, it, they), not first person (I, we). Second person (you) gives the impression that you are intending to give advice. "One" is sometimes used in place of "I" or "you," but it can sound stuffy. Compare the two examples below. Notice that "one" is replaced with the subject "students." The subject "students" is concrete and gives your reader an image they can relate to. In making the subject "students" plural, the pronoun "they" and possessive pronoun "their" is used. Plural subjects allow writers to avoid the complication of deciding whether to use "he" or "she" with a singular subject.

Compare the different subject choices below. Which do you prefer "one" or "students?"

Example a: With practice and a guide, *one* will develop editing skills and transfer that knowledge to editing *one's* own work.

Example b: With practice and a guide, *students* will develop *their* editing skills and transfer that knowledge to editing *their* own work.

Peer Editing

Peer editing is a helpful learning process for both reader and writer. Peer editors will be able to point out the strengths and weaknesses in your writing. For example, when other students read your paper, they will have questions you need to clarify. These questions mean there are gaps in your writing, things that need more explanation. Readers will also point out parts of your paper that are clear and well supported. Knowing what you have communicated well can help you to build on your strengths by modeling the same in other parts of your paper. It is the more experienced writer, not the novice writer who is willing to revise and accept comments with the goal of improving.

Analyzing structure, content, and mechanics helps readers better understand these parts of writing. By consciously looking for the underpinnings of a text and questioning how well it is supported, you as a reader will build your abilities as a writer and your critical thinking skills. Your instructor will provide class time for a Peer Editing Workshop. Complete Exercise 3: Peer Editing Worksheet while peer editing.

As a peer editor, remember to be careful with your comments and give your fellow students the benefit of the doubt. Make your comments clear and validate them. Writing can seem like a very private and personal tool, but in research writing, remember you are not writing a journal. When another student or teacher questions your work, they are not criticizing you personally. Editing is meant to be a helpful tool and a method for learning to write.

Conventions for an Academic Paper

Before turning in the final draft of your paper, make sure you have checked your instructor's requirements regarding what the paper should look like and what style sheet you should use. Remember that your teachers will be reading many student papers, not resumes. You don't want your paper to stand out on pink paper in an enormous font, you want to let the content of your writing speak for itself. Below is a list of common conventions for paper format to use when your teacher has not provided requirements. Refer to the sample student paper "Re-Assessing the letter grading" as an example.

1. Provide a cover page with the title of your paper, your name, your student number, the course title and number, your teacher's name, and the date.

2. Set the margins for your essay at one-inch around.

3. Use a simple font in 12-point size, such as *Times New Roman*. Avoid large stylish fonts that may look interesting to you, but might tire your teacher's eyes.

4. Make a running "header" at the top right corner of your paper that provides your name or an abbreviated title of your paper and the page number.

5. The final page of an APA style paper is simply titled "References" with no fancy script, underlining, or bold type.

6. Alphabetize the References page by the first letters of the first words in the entry. Usually this is the last name of the author. If you have more than one article or book by the same author, list these references chronologically, with the most recent date last.

Summary

Which step are you on in writing your research paper? Have you been keeping up with your schedule? Organization and diligence are keys to becoming a good writer. As you have learned from reading this chapter, research writing is a difficult and time-consuming process. Always leave sufficient time for creating and revising your thesis, outlining, finding and integrating support, and giving proper sources and all other steps in between. Make time to write more than one draft and find someone to edit your work. Writing is difficult, but remember, it's a learning process. With each paper you write, you learn more and your writing skills improve.

Reflect and Apply

Consider what you have learned about citing sources and plagiarism. Refer to Exercise 4 and read the case study "This paper is plagiarized." The sources in this student paper are in a different style than APA. Therefore, your challenge is to review the paper and find just why the teacher is accusing the student of plagiarizing. You are not looking for poorly done APA style. Among other things, you are looking for whether the student gave a clear source for every use of another person's words.

Name: _____ Date: _____

Exercise 2: Hook, Argument, and Controlling Ideas

Directions: After reading each of the example paragraphs, answer the questions to find the hook, argument, and controlling ideas.

Example paragraph 1:

> Title: _____
>
> Over the past fifty years, women have staked their claim in the professional world, obtaining white-collar jobs that in the past were positions held mainly by men. However, even though women have infiltrated previously male-dominated professions, there are still many factors that prevent women from reaching the highest professional ranks. We used to say it was men who prevented women from realizing their full professional potential. It is not men, rather children that hold women back. The time women are away from work having and raising children, the difficulty of re-adapting to the work place after being away for great lengths of time, and the limited job choice due to family responsibilities all contribute to hindering women from advancing in the workplace.

1. What is the hook? _____

2. What is the argument? _____

3. What are the controlling ideas?

   1) _____

   2) _____

   3) _____

4. What title would you give to the above paragraph?

191

Example paragraph 2:

> Cartoons and what they teach our children
>
> Cartoons and the art of animation have been around for close to fifty years now. In that time, they have brought fantastical imagery, laughter, and entertainment first to the big screen and now into the home of almost every Canadian family. The capability, speed of production, and general quality of these pictures continues to grow. Technological advances, however, are not half as important as the content of what our children's minds are absorbing. Sadly enough, even many well-meaning parents seem unaware of what their children are watching and learning right under their noses. Today's cartoons, animated videos, and movies are rife with explicit violence, adult-oriented dialogue, and humour, implied sexuality and gender stereotyping. Though at first they seem to be targeted at the entertainment of the young, they are, in fact, not suitable for children, but more appropriate for adults.

1. What is the hook in paragraph 2? _____

2. What is the argument? _____

3. What are the controlling ideas?

    1) _____

    2) _____

    3) _____

Example paragraph 3

> ### Casino not the answer for ailing city
>
> In a bid to make downtown New Westminster more attractive to tourists and businesses, city council has gone through with its misguided plan of opening *another* casino in the city. In a city that already has a high rate of drug dealing, street fighting, and an increasing amount of prostitution, this plan seems destined to backfire. City council seems to think that by putting the gaming on the river and making it seem historical and very "Natchez under the Hill," this will entice people to come. Chances are, however, that with all of the bars in the area, this will encourage those leaving the bars, in an already clouded state of mind, to gamble away what money they have left. Furthermore, any jobs that are to be had from the Casino will quite possibly go to people outside the community due to the high rate of single parent, low-income families, and elderly retired people living in New Westminster. Increased gambling is clearly not a good thing for New Westminster.

1. What is the hook? _____

2. What is the argument? _____

3. What are the controlling ideas?

    1) _____

    2) _____

    3) _____

Essay writer's name: _____ Editor's name: _____

Exercise 3: Peer Editing Worksheet

I. Macro Reading:

In this phase of the editing process, you are reading for the general "sense" of the essay. Read at your regular speed. Where your interest seems to lag, put a pencil check in the margin. When you have finished reading the essay, elaborate

1. The strengths of the paper
2. What you perceive to be the general weaknesses of the paper (based on your check marks). Indicate clearly where the problems begin and end. You don't need to make suggestions for improvement. You only need to state the problem.
3. Erase your check marks so the next reader is not influenced.

Strengths:

_____
_____
_____
_____
_____
_____

Weaknesses:

_____
_____
_____
_____
_____
_____

II. Micro Reading

Please be thorough. For every "no" answer, elaborate or give an example. You are not expected to fix problems but to identify them.

Introduction

1. Is the title page in APA style? If not, what way does it not meet this format?

2. Is the abstract interesting? Is it written in past tense and does it accurately summarize the purpose, methodology and results of this research?

3. Does the outline follow a logical, academic outline format? Does it include the full thesis (argument plus controlling ideas), a skeleton of the main ideas and supporting details, and a shortened version of the conclusion?

4. Does the introduction have a good hook? Does it capture your attention? Do you like the tone the writer sets in the first paragraph?

5. Does the introduction give the reader a clear idea of how the paper will develop? Is the thesis clear and recognizable? Is the thesis posed as an argument with clearly identified controlling ideas? Does the argument appear to be sustainable?

Body Paragraphs

6. Does each paragraph have a clear main idea (topic sentence)? If not, which paragraphs don't seem to have topic sentences?

7. Do the topic sentences reflect **progress** in the essay? (Can you see the argument developing through a study of the topic sentences?) Are the paragraphs organized in a logical sequence?

8. As a reader, can you clearly understand what each paragraph is arguing? Does each paragraph have supporting evidence (from the author) or does it use supporting evidence from secondary sources?

9. Can you find any instances when the author does not use his or her own ideas for the topic sentences? (Uses a quote, paraphrase, or summary to introduce the topic sentences of the paragraph.) If so where?

10. Does the writer introduce quotes, paraphrases, and summaries in a way that clearly indicates where another writer's thoughts/concepts begin and end? If not, where?

11. When the writer uses quotes, paraphrases, or summaries, do these secondary sources overwhelm the paragraph, or does the writer take the time to explain the ideas in the secondary source and /or transition to his/her own ideas? If not, where?

12. Is there any section that appears to sound like someone else's voice, but which is not attributed (has no citation)? If so, where?

General Language/Writing

13. Does the writing contain serious sentence errors (fragments, run-ons, comma splices)? Are there spelling or usage problems? If yes, give examples and show location.

14. Does the writer show the relationship between sentences? (Consider use of transitional words such as *however, secondly, therefore,* and *by contrast*, etc.)

Conclusion

15. Does the conclusion restate the thesis and main ideas in new language?

Name: _____ Date: _____

Exercise 4: This Paper Is Plagarized: Case Study[1]

This Paper Is Plagiarized

This case depicts a freshman, Amy Sloan, being accused of plagiarism by her instructor. She is not sure how to respond. Her paper is included as an exhibit with this case.

Amy Sloan could not believe what she was hearing. Her instructor, John Bell, had asked her to see him after class and now, as she stood in front of him near the classroom door, he handed her the paper she had turned in last week. She flipped the pages quickly and saw no marks, not even a grade. When she looked up, she heard him say, "This paper is plagiarized."

This was Amy's first semester as a college freshman and it had not been an easy start to college. Her family lived in a rather small town nearly an hour and a half distant. Her leaving home for the first time had not been easy for her mother. As a matter of fact, her mother had called several times in a state of near hysteria and Amy had responded by driving home to be with her and to help reassure her that everything was alright at college; she was still alive and healthy.

By going home, Amy had missed five class meetings of her freshman seminar course. She did not want her frequent absences to be a problem for her, so she had met with Mr. Bell and confided that she had a personal problem at home and had to be there on several days which had caused her to miss class. She showed him her journal, which was required for the course, and let him see that she had faithfully continued to write her journal entries even though she had not been in class. He seemed to understand.

The assignment required that students pick a topic and write a research paper using at least four sources of reference. Each student was also to give an oral report to the class on the research paper they had done. Amy decided to write about schizophrenia since she had done a lot of reading about that subject and knew quite a bit about it.

This was Amy's first college paper, so she did not know exactly what to expect. She liked to write and had been encouraged by her high school teachers who often told her that she was a good writer. That encouragement had led her to experiment with her writing and she had done some poetry and short stories. She felt comfortable and successful with her writing and had chosen English as her major.

And now she listened in shock as Mr. Bell continued, "It's not a regular research paper, you couldn't have written it. No freshman could write this kind of paper!"

She looked back down at her paper (Exhibit 1), and, with a rising sense of panic, she searched for the right words with which to explain.

---

[1] From *First Time Around: Case Studies of the Freshman Year Experience* by Michael Welsh. Copyright © 1999 by Kendall/Hunt Publishing Company. Used by permission.

EXHIBIT 1

Schizophrenia: an overview of the disease
and one woman's struggle for sanity.
September 19, 1995

Lori Shiller was the perfect child in what seemed like the perfect family. She had loving parents and two brothers that looked up to her. She was a straight "A" student, was very involved with high school, and had a very bright future in front of her. The suburb she and her family lived in had an extremely high status and was very wealthy. At seventeen she was working as a camp counselor at Lincoln Farm Summer Camp. and it was there that she heard them for the first time. she heard something that no one else heard at the time and that no one would ever hear. "You must die! You must die! You will die!"

Not knowing what was wrong with her, she tried her hardest to keep it inside. but the rest of the camp staff started to notice a change in her always perky attitude. They noticed how spaced out she was and that she was extremely depressed. She was sent home. Her parents were on vacation at the time, so there would be no questions asked and she would have a few days to get herself together. She hid the screaming voices inside her head and went on with life as normal.

The next fall she began her college career at Tufts University. She shared an apartment with two of her closest friends. She tried to conceal the voices even though they became more frequent and sinister. Her mood changes became violent and threatened the lives of her roommates and herself. At twenty-three she made her first suicide attempt. The was the first warning of a secret disease taking root in her mind.

Her parents were shocked at the thought of Lori being mentally ill, and kept thinking that she was just depressed and that everything would work itself out. The staff at the Payne Whitney Clinic in New York had different ideas. Lori was breaking down. Almost every person she came into contact with was showered with the voices in Lori's mind. They shouted at her, threatened her, and gave her ideas of killing everyone. The voices not only talked to her and wouldn't let her sleep at night, they occupied her every moment. Then the hallucinations began. At some moments she would look at her hands and they would be splitting open oozing blood. This type of occurrence became a normality.

Even after the doctors diagnosed Lori with chronic Schizophrenia, she still thought nothing of her illness. She found the voices irritating, but had no idea of its seriousness. Lore couldn't believe that no one heard the voices she heard. She was self conscious around others because of it. She was discharged from the hospital with the idea that she would live at home under supervision. Lori convinced the doctors that she could do it on her own. This was her parents and her doctors first mistake.

On her own, Lori attended day classes at the hospital while her parents worked. But soon she found it easy to skip the classes and began hanging out with the wrong people. She started doing cocaine because it helped smother the voices, but her habit turned into something she could not handle. Her parents began to threaten her about ending her drug habit and she had a mental relapse. She tried to commit suicide again and was forcibly hospitalized.

Lori had gained almost fifty pounds by this point, weighing in at one hundred and seventy pounds which was far from her normal, slim physique. A lot of the weight gain came from heavy medication, but depression played a key role as well. Lori had been pulled into the mental health care system and eventually was hospitalized five different times. She had many relapses, two suicide attempts, and a screaming, full-blown schizophrenia that seemed beyond the reach of any cure.

Two women, and incredible staff, a loving family, a self-examination, and a newfound will to live pulled Lori out of madness and she began to cope. Lori co-wrote her book <u>The Quiet Room,</u> she has a job on weekends, and devotes a lot of her time to mental patients and their families. But there one thing in her past that will be with her forever . . . The voices. (Bennett, Shiller, The Quiet Room)

Schizophrenia in a literal sense means "split mind", but the disease does not imply a split personality. It is not someone acting like two different people. Schizophrenia was not distinguished from other forms of psychosis until the twentieth century. (Achernect, 92)

Schizophrenia almost always develops before middle age. The first episode normally takes place sometime during adolescence or young adulthood and is followed by other increasingly detrimental episodes. The disease causes deterioration in a person's work, social relationships, and ability to look after himself or herself. (Wolman, 195)

The symptoms of schizophrenia are not routine and are not the same for every individual. Some common symptoms include isolation from family and friends, hallucinations, perpetual problems, sudden disturbances in movement, and odd speech and behavior. (Wolman, 198) "Being unable to control one's own thoughts, being isolated by a vision of reality all one' own, being commanded to act by disembodied voices-these are the experiences that make schizophrenia such a frightening experience." (Shiller, 278)

Scientists agree that schizophrenia has not single cause. It is the product of an interplay of biology, psychology, and culture. The disease does tend to be genetically inherited. It is more likely to affect someone that is a close relative to a schizophrenic than the population at large. Whereas only one or two out of every one-hundred people become schizophrenic over a life time, about ten out of every one hundred children who have one schizophrenic parent eventually will develop the disorder. (Wender, 115)

Whether schizophrenia is caused by a biochemical abnormality, a neurological defect, or a bad enzyme is still open to question. Most scientists believe that the strength and severeness of the disease varies from one individual to another. (Brunner, 177)

Research has led to some breakthroughs linking a number of environmental factors to schizophrenia. For example, unclear communication within families is one potential condition, although scientists are still unsure whether miscommunication in the family is a cause of schizophrenia or an after effect. Poverty has also been associated with the disease. (Brunner, 181)

The most powerful treatment for alleviating schizophrenic symptoms is antipsychotic medication. (Horwitz, 54) These drugs have for the first time enabled patients to function without breakdowns or unpleasant symptoms. They are used to hault episodes of schizophrenia and also to prevent future problems. These drugs, however, do have drawbacks. They can produce minor side effects such as drowsiness and dry mouth and can also have long term consequences. Some patients that use the drugs for a long period of time develop a condition known as tardive dyskinesia. This disease is characterized by abnormal movements of the mouth and tongue. This is especially serious because tardive dyskinesia has no known cure and may not disappear once the patient stops using the drug. Not every patient benefits from antipsychotic drugs, and some seem not to need them at all. Some forms of psychotherapy are also used to treat schizophrenic patients. It is also used to help patients who do not receive medication. (Maisto, 97-9)

Schizophrenia is a dangerous disease that often times causes its victims to totally withdraw from society and from their normal routines. Even though in the past it was thought as only as "abnormal." or "weird", the disease known as schizophrenia is now taken seriously, and continual breakthroughs are being made to help it's victim. The disease still has not cure-only ways to lesson the symptoms and the voices. "The voices taught me about a hell that was beyond all religious beliefs, It was beyond all imagining, beyond all human hope. The voices that spoke to me were as clear and as real as any voices around me. In fact, they were more real, because they were both inside me and outside me.

"Come to me," they crooned. "Come to hell with me."

I didn't want to listen. I didn't want to hear. But I had no choice. Where would I go?" L. Shiller

Bibliography

Ackernecht, E. H. *A Short History of Psychiatry.* Hafner, 2d ed., rev., 1970.

A Casebook in Psychiatric Ethics. Brunner/Mazell, 1990.

Bennett, Amanda and Shiller, Lori. *The Quiet Room:* A Journey Out of the Torment of Madness.

Horwitz, Elinor Lander. *Madness, Magic, and Medicine:* the Treatment and Mistreatment of the Mentally Ill. Lippincott, 1977.

Maisto, Stephen A. and others. *Drug Use and Misuse.* Holt, Rinehart, and Winston, 1991.

Wender, Paul H. and Klein, Donald F. *Mind, Mood, and Medicine:* A guide to the New Biopsychiatry. Farrar, 1981.

Wolman, Benjamin B., ed. *International Encyclopedia of Psychiatry, Psychoanalysis, and Neurology.* 12v. Van Nostrand, 1977.

This Paper Is Plagiarized

What is this case about? Immerse yourself in this case by reading the paper that Amy Sloan turned in only to have her instructor say it was plagiarized. If this was your paper, how would you respond?

Get the facts. List the facts that you know about Amy and her situation:

1. _____
2. _____
3. _____
4. _____
5. _____

State the problem, issue or question that needs to be resolved.

_____

_____

List several ways that the problem might be resolved.

1. _____
2. _____
3. _____

Write down the best way to solve the problem and why you would solve it that way.

_____

_____

_____

CHAPTER 9
Preparing for and Taking Tests

In your college career, you will likely spend from 25 to 40 percent of your time preparing for or taking tests. Test-taking and test-preparation skills are crucial to your success in college. Your grade point average is affected more by your testing abilities than any other factor, a truth that causes anxiety for many students. This chapter will introduce you to a variety of different types of tests, as well as the best test-preparation and test-taking strategies for each of these tests.

What Could Take the Trauma out of Test-Taking?[1]

In the first place, we expect too much out of our memories! Due to the myth that cramming is effective, too many students believe that the best way to study for a test is to cram all the information possible into your mind the night before the test. That way all the information will be fresh! In no other area of life would we expect so much out of our abilities. Would you ever consider that you were physically fit for life because you had worked out at the gym last night? Or would you ever take a bath and feel that you had completed that task and would never have to do it again? Of course, these examples are obvious, but until we get in our minds the idea that information must be reviewed consistently to be remembered, test scores will consistently point out that we have not quite mastered the material. Many students make the mistake of trying to "view" the material the night before rather than "review." Information is retained by systematic, spaced overlearning. There is no other effective means. Cramming MAY give you a passing grade, but it will not show much practical benefit as far as retaining the material—and isn't that why you are in college?

Before the Test: Three Rules for True Test Preparation

Three basic rules—plus omitting the word cramming from your vocabulary—will make a great difference in your view of test-taking preparation (and the possible trauma it creates).

Rule 1: Start studying for each test the first day of class. Do not feel that you do not need to study biology today since you just had a test last Thursday. The way you study

---

[1]From *Practical Approaches for Building Study Skills and Vocabulary, Second Edition* by Funk et al. © 1996 by Kendall/Hunt Publishing Company. Used by permission.

the material being learned this week will determine your test grade just as much as the way you study the night before the test.

Rule 2: Don't get behind on assignments! Finish each day's work on that day, if at all possible. Stay caught up on reading assignments and text-note taking, revising lecture notes, and extra assignments. Don't procrastinate or your grade will reflect it.

Rule 3: Incorporate the use of three ZAPS in your study schedule—daily, weekly, and test-taking. EACH DAY spend a few minutes revising your lecture notes from that day and reviewing them. Read your text assignment, take notes, and review them. Do this for each class taken on that day. Sometime during the week, you need to go back and review all the PAST lecture and text notes from the current semester. Don't wait until test-time! Now is the time to start preparing. Think of what a difference you will feel if you have already reviewed each set of notes four or five times BEFORE you start to study for the test! Two or three nights before the actual test you can do an IN-DEPTH REVIEW of all the material, but it won't be cramming filled with panic and pressure. You will have built a solid foundation on which to study for the test.

Bloom's Taxonomy for Test Preparation and Test-Taking[2]

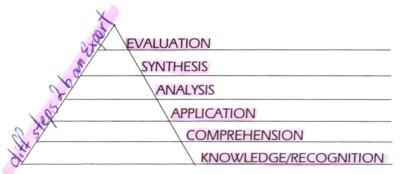

Figure 1.

BLOOM'S TAXONOMY. Luckily, you already know how to think and are aware that different tasks require different degrees of thinking. The thinking you do when you remember a phone number differs from the thinking you do to solve a math story problem. If you can identify the level of thinking you already do, the level you may need to achieve, then you can apply this knowledge to areas involved in studying coursework. Figure 1 shows the levels of thinking according to a system called **Bloom's Taxonomy**. Each level builds on the previous level. That is, a student cannot speak and comprehend a foreign language until they have memorized the basic vocabulary. Effective students are aware of learning strategies that incorporate the level of thinking required for success in each course.

Knowledge and **recognition** of information are the first level and form the basis of understanding. It requires you to remember what you heard or read, but not necessarily to understand it. It is as simple as remembering the name of the person you just met or what you need at the grocery store. In course work, this level is necessary to build information for any subject. Many general education courses you select will require you to learn the basic vocabulary and principles of the course. Memorization can achieve this, but this is not meaningful learning, which requires understanding of the material. A student operating at the recognition/knowledge level may memorize the name of "Köppen" and the contribution that he made to science. Possibly, you will form a study group for the course. When you compare your notes for the course, each of you list Köppen as an important person. You practice asking each other key names and other definitions from that chapter. The test for this chapter asks you to apply his classification system to describe a particular type of climate. To answer this question the study group needed to do more processing of information. Simply memorizing the conditions and episodes was not sufficient.

---

[2]From *Your Utah State Experience: Strategies for Success, Fourth Edition* by Utah State University Academic Support Services. © 1998 by Utah State University Academic Support Services. Used by permission of Kendall/Hunt Publishing Company.

Comprehension level emphasizes studying for an understanding of the material you are trying to learn. In this level of Bloom's Taxonomy, you become more focused on what the material is trying to explain to you. During your geography study group time, you may explain to each other the characteristics of each type of climate. Then you can answer the essay question that asks you to describe the different climatic types. At this level, you can explain information to someone else. You can share the plot of a movie or a novel, report the homework assignment to a roommate who missed class, or explain the course syllabus.

The third level in Bloom's Taxonomy is **application**. When you apply what you understand, you begin to link the information you gained to examples in your own life. After seeing a movie or reading a novel, you connect with similar personal experiences. Your ability to see a parallel between the example in the text and the experience in your own life is the thinking skill of application. At this level, math courses require students to solve word problems or solve problems different from those previously seen. You are asked to compare and contrast information on an essay test question. Many courses will ask you to provide examples in your own life of the information you study, determine causes and effects, or draw analogies. The more ways you apply the information, the longer you will retain the concepts.

Analysis requires you to break apart and examine the components of a concept in depth. Depth is the key element that true analysis demands. If when discussing a movie or novel with a friend, you discuss the main theme and what made the leading character so evil, then you are using analytical thinking skills. If your friend disagrees with your analysis and questions your theory, the friendly debate that may follow requires additional analytic thinking.

Synthesis is the creative level of thinking. You combine different ideas to create a new whole. When you synthesize you combine your current understanding of concepts with new information that you create. Many instructors assign group projects where students must design, create, or propose a solution to a problem. The instructor may require that you work in a group to generate solutions to farming problems that have developed because of global warming. Examples that require that you operate at a synthesizing level are using music or art to express yourself, developing a topic for a research paper, or answering essay questions that ask you to "tie together" all the information you have learned to solve a problem.

Evaluation forms the highest level of thinking in Bloom's Taxonomy. At this level you must use your personal judgment regarding an issue's relevance, depth, value, or other qualities. To do this you would review all the relevant "facts" and review sources for their contribution to the topic under discussion. You often use evaluation to make judgments and decisions in your personal life. Choosing to attend college, whether to live on or off campus, or how many hours you can work and still do well in school require evaluation. Course work may ask you to evaluate decisions in court cases or whether a social policy is adequate in providing aid and assistance to poor people. Geography classes may require you to judge what types of vegetation could adapt to climatic changes.

Although this text describes the levels of Bloom's Taxonomy separately, few learning situations depend solely on one level or another. Generally, as the information increases in complexity, the effort needed to learn also increases. Your classes will increase in complexity as will the levels of thinking required as you specialize in a content area. This information will help you as a learner continually decide what you know, what you still need to learn, and the ways in which you must learn.

Different Types of Tests

There are really just three types of tests—**objective**, **subjective**, and a **combination of the two.**

a. **Objective tests** include multiple choice, true-false, and matching items. These questions have only one right answer because the grader is looking for a specific letter or word. These items are all recognition items, because the choices are spelled out for you. You may choose true or false, or you may choose from a list of two or more possible answers.

b. **Subjective** tests are also called essay tests. The question will call for a very broad answer, and the correct answer depends on the "subject" who is grading it. What one grader might call an acceptable and complete answer could be viewed as incomplete, or even completely wrong, to another grader.

c. **A combination of subjective and objective** characteristics could involve sentence completion items (or fill-in-the-blank, as they are commonly called) or short answer items. These are more of a combination of objective and subjective traits because, even though one basic idea is being asked for, more than one specific word or concept could be the correct answer. Therefore, a little bit of subjectivity is being used.

Advantages of Each Type

Objective tests are probably used more often than subjective tests for several reasons. An instructor can test over a lot of material in a very short amount of time with this approach. They are easy and fast to grade, and a student worker could help the instructor in the grading if time is a priority. Many instructors like to use these tests because they are less subjective and involve less decision-making when grading. No matter who grades the test, or when it is graded, the credit will be the same. So it may appear that this type of testing is a little more fair to all. But, as we all know, objective items can be worded in such a way that they may not appear "fair." Even so, ease in grading and equality in fairness are two definite advantages of objective tests. Also, since the student is not required to write long answers on objective tests, many instructors feel that these tests do not let a student's writing ability interfere with the test score. Poor writing ability does not hurt the grade; neither can a good writer cover up for lack of knowledge with outstanding writing ability. So in several ways the objective test may appear more fair.

On the other hand, subjective tests really do what a test is supposed to do—show what you really know. When you have to write out detailed answers on a topic, it quickly becomes obvious if you really LEARNED the material! Subjective tests force recall learning, and that's the best kind! Subjective tests are also much easier and faster for the professor to compose than objective tests.

Disadvantages of Each Type

Even though there are advantages to either of these two major types of tests, there are also disadvantages that make the choice hard for instructors to make. Objective tests may end up only testing "test-awareness," or the ability to play the game of test-taking. Many students become good guessers, and they are able to recognize enough and bluff enough to make the grade. But the test has not accomplished its purpose—that of trying to show true knowledge learned. As mentioned previously, good objective items are fairly difficult and time consuming to write. Questions may end up being tricky or testing for details only.

Perhaps the main disadvantage of subjective tests is that they are very difficult to grade. This difficulty involves two aspects—time and fairness. It does take an enormous amount of time to grade essay tests. So if an instructor has several sections of one class, time factors make these tests a real trial to grade. This time and pressure factor may influence how fairly each test is graded. It may be all too true that one essay test could receive many different scores, based on the person who grades the test, the time of day it was graded, and even the order in which it was graded. Fatigue plays a role in fairness, time limits add to the problem, and personality factors of the grader complicate the matter. A student's writing ability may also influence the grader. Neat handwriting, correct spelling and grammar, a "way with words," and overall neatness of the paper may sway the judgment of the grader. Unfortunately, the opposite kind of paper may do the same thing—only in the opposite direction!

Causes of Poor Test Performance

Even though the most obvious answer as to why students might not perform well on a test would be INADEQUATE KNOWLEDGE, this is certainly not the only answer. Part of the purpose of this chapter is to help you to analyze your typical test behavior and sort out the hindrances to your success. It is true that many students do not perform well on a test simply due to the fact that they did not study enough—or in the proper way. It is vital that you understand that it is not how MANY hours you study for a test that makes the difference. It is the QUALITY of those hours and the way they are DISTRIBUTED that spell out your success rate. Weekly reviews based on questions and recited answers over thorough lecture and text notes are the secrets to mastery. Intense cramming sessions the night before the test will not assure you that the information will be there when needed.

LANGUAGE-RELATED PROBLEMS can also affect your performance on tests. If you read the textbook but do not comprehend it, you will not perform to the best of your ability. If you have trouble understanding the test items, or knowing specifically what the question is asking for, your answer cannot be top-notch. Therefore, reading problems do influence many students' test grades.

Also, many students simply do not know how to take a test. Even though they may have taken hundreds in their lifetime, INEFFECTIVE EXAM-TAKING SKILLS may still be hindering their performance. Test-taking is a game one must learn to play—a skill that can be learned with practice. Certain rules must be learned and adhered to or the results will not please you. We will cover these "rules" in the next several sections.

Finally, TEST ANXIETY can cripple your test scores. You may have studied adequately, and you may feel you really do know the information, but if you panic during the test, your memory will not cooperate. Take a minute now to TEST YOUR TESTING SKILLS. Complete the inventory that follows to see if exam anxiety is a problem for you, or if you suffer from other "testing deficiencies."

Name: _____ Date: _____

Exercise 1: Test Your Test-Taking Skills

Answer yes or no to the following questions to check up on your ability to play the testing game.

Before a Test, I

	Yes	No
1. usually wait until a test is announced before reading text assignments or reviewing lecture notes.	____	____
2. often think of tests as trials that can't be escaped and must be endured.	____	____
3. often do not read my textbook because the instructor will cover it if it's important.	____	____
4. feel that I have a good memory, so I do not usually take notes over lectures.	____	____
5. sometimes have to memorize formulas, definitions, or rules that I simply do not understand.	____	____
6. generally have trouble deciding what I really need to study.	____	____
7. depend mainly on last-minute cramming to prepare for the test so that it will be fresh in my mind.	____	____

During a Test, I

	Yes	No
8. am sometimes unable to finish answering all the test items within the allotted time.	____	____
9. sometimes am forced to leave an item blank because I cannot decide on the correct answer.	____	____
10. often find I cannot decide what the question is really asking for in an answer.	____	____
11. frequently feel that I have not studied enough, or that I have not studied the correct information.	____	____
12. start with the first item and answer each question in its correct order, regardless of difficulty.	____	____
13. catch myself thinking about how much smarter other students are than myself.	____	____
14. worry about what will happen if I flunk the test.	____	____
15. get so nervous that I feel sick to my stomach and have trouble remembering what I studied.	____	____
16. often think, "The more I study, the less I remember!"	____	____
17. then realize I would much rather write two essays than take one test!	____	____

After a Test, I

		Yes	No
18.	almost always feel that I could have done better.	___	___
19.	often find that I have made careless mistakes or left unintentional blank answers.	___	___
20.	find that I should have changed an answer, but I did not because I felt my first answer is usually best.	___	___
21.	try to forget about the test as soon as possible so that I can start fresh on new material.	___	___
22.	only look over my mistakes, because the rest of the questions were correct and therefore do not need to be analyzed.	___	___

SCORING: Count up your yes responses. As in the game of golf, the lower your score, the better you play the game of test-taking. If you answered yes to three or more of questions 13–18, you have some problems with test anxiety also. What's a GOOD score for this test on test-taking? If you scored higher than a 7, practicing the suggestions from this chapter could completely change the way you feel about tests!

Physical, Emotional and Intellectual Preparation

We have already discussed the problem of test-smartness, but the goal is to be test-wise—to know how to play the game of taking tests successfully. Three main areas of test preparation need to be considered: physical, emotional, and intellectual preparation.

Be Physically Prepared

You need to be in top physical condition to do your very best in a test situation. We don't mean you need to be able to run a marathon, but on the other hand, don't handicap yourself by not being physically prepared. Although you would not do this purposefully, you are in effect handicapping yourself if you do not accomplish these physical tasks before a test:

a. *Attend class*—each and every one. The worst class to skip is the one before the test. Never skip class in order to study more. Important reviews may take place right before the test session, so don't miss them!

b. *Ask questions*—These questions may include the type of test (objective or subjective), length of exam, time allowed, material covered, possible points and percentage of total grade, examples of test questions, and if any aids are allowed, such as pocket dictionary, calculator, etc. These answers may influence the way that you will study.

c. *Eat properly*—Don't skip breakfast, and try to include some protein in the meal before your test. Give yourself "brain fuel!"

d. *Sleep properly*—Don't skip study time to sleep, and don't skip sleep time to study. Schedule each for its proper time. Don't plan all night studying sessions. Sleeping seems to "cement" learning, or help your memory to consolidate what you have studied. If you do not get an adequate amount of sleep, your spontaneity and originality may be hurt, and your level of anxiety may be heightened. Also, the worst time to "party hardy" is the night before the test! You need a clear head and quick thinking ability to do your best on the test, and drinking will not help you in either of those areas!

e. *Study in a simulated test-taking atmosphere*—Try to make your study sessions like the real thing! Set time limits, sit at a desk, don't allow interruptions, and don't peek! Anxiety may be increased in a testing situation simply because it is so different than what you are used to.

f. *Use a multi-sensory approach to studying*—Cross all three learning styles when preparing. Remember to use your eyes to see, but also your voice to recite, your ears to listen, and your hands to write the information you need to learn. The more ways you put the information in your mind, the better chance you have of it sticking!

Be Emotionally Prepared

Now that you've mastered the physical aspects of test-preparation, consider these emotional aspects:

a. *Think positively!*—Push for success, not just to avoid failure. Too many of us think as the little boy who reluctantly told his father, *"Dad, I'm afraid I flunked that math exam."*
   "Son, that's negative thinking!" admonished his father. *"Think positive!"*
   "Then, Dad, I'm positive I flunked that test!" the son replied.

Understanding Test Words

Learn the meanings of these testing words because they are usually not interchangeable! You must know what the instructor is asking you to do before you can do it!

1. COMPARE—bring out points of similarity AND points of differences
2. CONTRAST—show differences when placed side by side
3. CRITICIZE—give YOUR judgment of; approve OR disapprove; give *good* and *bad* points
4. DEFINE—give the meaning of, explain the nature of
5. DESCRIBE—tell about, give a word picture which characterizes; do not just name or label
6. DIAGRAM—make a drawing, chart, or graph, and usually add labels; possibly add a brief explanation
7. DISCUSS—examine, analyze carefully, and give reasons pro and con; be complete and give details
8. ENUMERATE—give a numbered list; name over one by one
9. EVALUATE—cite both advantages and disadvantages; include appraisal of authorities and your own appraisal
10. EXPLAIN—make clear, interpret, make plain
11. IDENTIFY—name, label, classify, or characterize
12. ILLUSTRATE—make clear by stories, examples, or diagrams
13. INTERPRET—translate, give examples, give your judgment
14. JUSTIFY—prove your point, give your argument; discuss bad and good points and conclude with it good
15. LIST—write a numbered list
16. OUTLINE—give the main ideas in organized arrangement; use headings and subheadings to give a well-ordered list
17. PROVE—establish that something is true by citing facts or giving logical reasons
18. RELATE—stress associations or connections between ideas
19. REVIEW—analyze a subject critically
20. STATE—present the main points briefly
21. SUMMARIZE—give the main points briefly
22. TRACE—give a description of progress in a definite order; follow the trail of

---

Don't dwell on the past or even what the future will bring. Think only on the OPPORTUNITY of this one test. A test is not a trial, but a chance to show what you know, and learn what you've missed. Use it to its full advantage!

b. *Visualize a good grade*—Although this is similar to the suggestion above, it is so helpful that we want to include it separately. See an A+ paper in your mind. Tell yourself, "It will be just like me to ace this test!" Instead of putting yourself or your ability down, pump yourself up! These "coping statements" will make a big difference in your attitude and confidence!

c. *Tie main ideas in with your life*—Try to apply the big ideas of what you have studied to your own situation. The more applicable you can make the information, the more apt you are to remember and benefit from it.

d. *Avoid pre-test hall chatter*—Have you ever noticed the typical statements of students before they go in to take a test? You hear things such as, "I didn't study at all for this test! Did you?" or "I hope to goodness I don't flunk this thing!" You don't need this type of talk! Whether you have studied enough or not, don't erode what you do have!

e. *Remember that some anxiety is helpful*—Although you can suffer from too much test anxiety, a little bit of nervousness will keep you alert and on top of things. Accept this as natural and helpful!

Be Intellectually Prepared

Intellectual preparation for testing is the ONLY area that many students feel has to be dealt with, but as we have discussed, physical and emotional preparation are essential also. However, this area of being intellectually ready for the test is obviously crucial. Consider these vital components of being intellectually prepared:

a. *Review lecture and text notes weekly*—This vital weekly review has already been emphasized, but it cannot be stressed too much. This one step will make an enormous difference in how ready you *feel* for a test—and how prepared you REALLY are! Also remember to study handouts, past assignments, previous tests, and make use of study guides if they are provided. As much as possible, try to make your study notes manageable with mnemonic systems, questions, highlighted vocabulary, etc.

b. *Always study as for essay tests*—Many students tend to worry more about essay tests than objective tests. They feel that essay tests are harder, and in some respects they are because recall is necessary—not just recognition. Therefore, you should study for ALL tests as if they were essay, whether they are or not. Think in terms of main ideas, and recite questions and answers aloud. Force learning by recall, and all tests—whether essay or objective—will be easier and more beneficial.

c. *Get old tests and talk to "old" students*—If your instructor has old tests in his or her files, ask to see them or have a copy of them. Your library may even keep a "test bank" of past tests for you to look through. Former students of your current class are excellent resources. Ask them questions about what they remember of the tests, and see if they possibly still have their old tests. Is this cheating? No! You are studying the instructor's format of testing, and you are also studying in the best possible way—with questions and answers.

d. *Anticipate test questions*—Some ways to do this have already been mentioned in the previous paragraph, but also think about some other clues for your instructor's possible test questions. Information that was written on the board is usually a good resource. The teacher may have even told you during lecture that certain information was important, or asked you to particularly note that section. You should have emphasized this in your notes in some way (such as a star, or a box). Information that is mentioned in both text and lecture would be good test questions. Don't forget vocabulary words that are often in italics or boldface print! They make excellent matching questions. Review questions at the beginning or the end of the chapter are also an easy way for your teacher to get a question. Don't omit any of these clues to help you to anticipate test questions.

e. *Understand question words*—This suggestion is especially crucial for success with essay tests. To be asked to diagram a concept is not the same as to explain it. To summarize does not mean to criticize. You cannot get full credit for an answer if you do not answer the question! Study the "Understanding Test Words" chart to ensure you know what your instructor is asking you to do.

What should I do the week before a test to get prepared?

Remember that to best prepare for a test, you need to begin your semester with good study habits. In the week before a test, you should have read and reviewed all of the assigned material. In the last week before a test spend your time doing a last review then synthesise your notes and other course materials. Focus more time on applying what you've learned by answering sample test questions and posing questions in a study group. Complete Exercise 2: Preparing for exams case study. Consider the different needs of the students in the study. One student has been keeping up with class and studying regularly, the other student hasn't. Help each student make a detailed study plan for the week prior to the test.

Test Anxiety[3]

In the TEST YOUR TEST-TAKING SKILLS worksheet, you may have been able to see if test anxiety is a problem for you. Many things can cause this problem, but you can help yourself by deciding to eliminate the following characteristics if they describe you during testing.

Test anxiety may strike if you:

- focus on yourself rather than the task at hand.
- associate a test score with your self-worth.
- allow negative self images.
- compare your performance with others around you.
- continually rethink an answer.
- allow panicky self-talk.
- begin to feel out of control.

You must stay in control and take care of your job one step at a time. Recognizing what causes test anxiety is the first step toward solving the problem.

What's the Cure for Test Anxiety?

The real cure for panicking during a test is over-preparation BEFORE the test! Better planning will replace panic with confidence. Then when you get into the testing situation, do not focus on yourself OR on what others are doing. Focus only on the task in front of you. If that scares you, focus on some other object for a minute, such as your shoe! Regroup your thoughts and talk positively and confidently to yourself. Remind yourself that you are competent and in control. Then start to work on the test. Only think of that one task. Don't allow negative thoughts to enter into your thinking. Plan to arrive a little earlier on test day so you won't be rushed. Then you could do some relaxation techniques (as discussed in the chapter on stress) to help you to relax. Always start with the easier questions on the test to build your confidence, and keep encouraging yourself with positive self-talk. Perhaps the best strategy is simply to realize that test anxiety is a learned set of responses that are only detrimental to your performance and that can be changed. Focus on changing them!

---

[3]From *The Community College: A New Beginning, Second Edition* by Aguilar et al. © 1998 by Kendall/Hunt Publishing Company. Used by permission.

Name: _____ Date: _____

■ Exercise 2: Preparing for Exams, A Case Study Activity

Directions:

You are a *Learning Centre* tutor. Give advice and plan what students Randy and Linda will each do to prepare for an upcoming history exam. Make a plan for each student that:

- maximizes study time
- meets the test type
- falls within time limits
- gives sufficient details and pointers to really help a student who is out of practice at studying and test-taking.

Scenario

Today is Friday and Randy and Linda have a history final exam next Friday. Their instructor said the exam will be multiple choice, short answer, and essay.

Randy

Randy plans to spend about 5 to 6 hours studying for the exam. He worries that this won't be enough time, but he hopes to use his time well.

Randy loves history and would like to major in it eventually. He spends a lot of time each week reading both the texts and additional readings. He makes summary notes as he reads and is confident of having a good grasp of the major topics for this test.

Linda

Linda has to study for the test, but she also has to work and write a paper. She figures she can donate about 8 hours to studying this week.

Linda has been swamped this last month with two major assignments. Last week she was sick for three days and missed several classes, including history. She likes the subject but hasn't put in much time studying or reading the assigned material. She is worried about the test.

Make a study schedule for each, for example:

Day and amount of time for this activity	Detail of what student should do during this study time	Goal of doing this study activity

During the Test: Some General Test-Taking Strategies

1. Avoid rushing. Get to the test early. Think calmly and act calmly.

2. Pick a good spot to sit and recite notes calmly. The best spot is usually your normal seat, because you will feel more comfortable there. But the best spot is also usually away from distractions and close to the front. That's why it's important to pick the right spot the FIRST day of class and stick with it. It is a good idea to study up to the last minute, as long as you can do so calmly.

3. Get rid of undue anxiety by relaxation techniques, positive self-talk, and focusing only on the task at hand.

4. Wait for oral instructions. Do NOT begin the test as soon as you receive it. After you put your name on the paper, WAIT. You may miss vital information or clues if you do not listen to instructions.

5. Jot down memory clues before you begin. If there are dates, names, or mnemonic strategies you are afraid you may forget, jot these down on the back of the test. This may relieve some stress immediately!

6. Skim the entire exam, reading directions carefully. This is a crucial step that is often overlooked. As you quickly look over the test, look for:

    a. point allotment—All questions are not created equal, and you should spend the most time on items worth the most points.

    b. type of questions—Which will take more time for you? What order would be best to answer the questions?

    c. clues—Often, test questions may have clues farther on in the test, or perhaps you may even find the answer!

    Although reading the directions is not a difficult step, it is one to which you should learn to give strong emphasis!

7. Ask specific questions if needed. Notice that you wait until the instructor has had time to explain, AND until you have had time to skim the test! Many questions can be answered by these two steps. If you still have questions, ask pointed, specific questions.

8. Do the easy ones first. This suggestion will make a big difference in your confidence level. It will also help you with the time problem, because you will make sure you complete the ones you know quickly, and you will have the rest of the time to concentrate on the harder ones.

9. Skip the harder ones, mark them so you will remember to come back to them, and return to them after you complete the easy ones and have warmed-up. A little mark beside the more difficult ones will also make sure you note these as you get your test returned after grading. Of course, you will notice it if you miss it! But if you get it correct, you may not remember the correct answer two weeks later unless you take special note of it.

10. Do all tests four times. Most of us hate the thought of doing a test once, but you need to go through four steps to do your best. First, skim the test as stated. Then do the easier ones while you mark and skip the harder ones. Return to do the harder ones, and finally, look over the entire test to check that you have answered all questions.

11. **Change your answer if needed.** Although this policy has been hotly debated, recent research seems to point out that when an answer is changed, more often than not it is changed from a wrong answer to a right one. But you also need to analyze your pattern. What usually happens for you? If the answer was clearly just a guess, perhaps your first guess IS your best answer. But, if after second thought you feel the need to change the answer, do so!

12. **Budget your time.** Do this before you start by considering the point value of the question. Also, make sure you allow enough time to complete the whole test with time to double-check.

13. **Never leave blanks!** A guess is better than a miss, so don't guarantee an error by leaving a blank. You may luck out. Usually a middle answer in multiple choice questions or true answers in true-false questions are more apt to be correct.

14. **Write answers clearly.** Do not try to fool the instructor by making your T also resemble an F in true-false items. Don't try to make the "a" also pass for a "c" in multiple-choice items. All you will probably succeed in doing is aggravating the grader who may check the item wrong with a flourish.

15. **Make the test serve you after it's over.** You have paid for it, so get your money's worth. Don't purposely try to put it out of your mind. Talk about strategies with other students. Look up the ones you weren't certain about. (You will remember the answer much longer than any other question if you do!) When you get the test back, check errors and also guesses that turned out to be correct. If you have marked the difficult ones, this will be easier. Analyze why you missed the question. Learn for the next test—and there's ALWAYS a next one! Make the doing of the test in itself beneficial.

Now that you have reviewed helpful strategies for test-taking in general, check your TEST-TAKING IQ!

Complete Exercise 3: "What's Your Testing IQ?" to measure your objective test-taking skills. After the test, read the correct answers and learn simple hints that can improve your test-taking IQ.

Specific Strategies for Taking Objective Tests

If you want to "show all you know," there are specific suggestions you should follow for each type of objective test. Remember to put into practice the general suggestions that have been given for all tests, and then study the specific suggestions that follow. Look back at your WHAT'S YOUR TESTING IQ? answers to see how these strategies work. We have included the reasons for the answers after each item.

True-False Tests

1. Watch for qualifiers. These include words that are absolutes or limiting words, and those that are tentatives.
   a. Absolute or limiting words indicate a false statement. These include: always, every, all, no, never, none, only, entirely, invariably, guaranteed, great, or much. They leave very little room for exceptions, and sentences containing these words would seldom be true.
   b. Tentative words leave room for exceptions and would tend to indicate true statements. These words include: seldom, sometimes, some, often, most, many, few, usually, generally, frequently, or ordinarily.

This suggestion explains why question 1 is false (always, each, every), and question 2 is true (frequently).

2. **Remember, if any part is false, the whole thing is FALSE!** Every word must be true before you would answer the statement as true. As some great test-taker has said, "Whatever is almost true is quite false." Question 3 is false because we cannot say that NO ONE studies as much as they should.

3. **Watch for negatives or negative prefixes.** Words such as not, none, no, or except often confuse you as to what the question is really asking. Negative prefixes, such as il-, im-, ir-, dis-, un-, non-, or a- may do the same thing. It is suggested that you circle or underline these negatives so that you do not disregard them, as test-takers are prone to do. Question 4 would be made less confusing by omitting the word **not**, deciding the answer is false, putting the word back in, and reversing the answer to true.

4. **Don't read more into the statement than is actually there.** Look for qualifiers, but then read the statement as it is. In the statement, "Hunger leads to decreased concentration and increased apathy" (Question 5), the word is hunger—not extreme hunger or starvation. This kind of statement would probably be false, in most cases.

5. **Guess true if you have to guess.** Teachers usually dislike writing false statements for two reasons—they are afraid you will believe the false item, and good false statements are difficult to write. They either wind up being obviously false (and a little bit stupid) or being tricky because they are so near the truth. For this reason, you will usually find more true statements than false. So if you didn't know the answer to question 6, you should have guessed true.

6. **If you have to guess, consider a possible pattern.** Don't count on it, but consider it. True-False tests are difficult to grade because the grader can easily get confused. Therefore, some teachers incorporate a pattern. Check it out. (Notice the T-F-T-F-T-F pattern of the True-False section of the test.)

Multiple Choice Tests

1. **Read the directions carefully.** How many correct answers are possible? Do the directions say choose the correct answer, the correct answers, or the BEST answer? Ask for clarification if you are not sure.

2. **Read the question and each option separately,** making sure you consider all options. If you consider each as a true or false statement and mark it to the side accordingly, you will help yourself immensely by ruling out distractors, as in question 7. Watch for grammatical matches that might give you hints, as shown in question 8. Option **a** did not fit with the question grammatically, so this is a clue that it is not the correct choice. Usually your professor would have pointed out the mistake if it was a correct answer.

3. **Don't choose unfamiliar or foolish options**—as in question 7 (option a) or question 8 (option c or d). If you've never heard the word before or never heard the idea mentioned in class, chances are THAT is not the correct answer.

4. **Be suspicious of negatives and absolutes.** Circle or underline these to make sure you are aware of them. Question 9 could be tricky if you do not take out the negative and decide without it. Option b implies that ALL students do not study enough, and we cannot say this is true. Option d has the absolute word "never," so we can rule it out as a distractor.

5. Consider carefully similar options, opposite answers, longer answers, more general, or more inclusive options. Usually, one of these will tend to be the correct answer. Options c and e of question 10 illustrate opposites and longer answers.

6. Number answers tend to be in the middle range of options. Question 11 shows that you could rule out the second option because it is the only one that is in kilometers. Why would the right answer be so obviously different? You then have a range of 500 to 10,000 miles. Consider only the options that are in the middle range, and you have narrowed your odds considerably!

7. Try to answer before you look at the options to lessen your confusion. The distractors will be more obvious if you have already formulated an approximate answer.

8. Consider "all of the above" carefully, especially if it is not used very often. All you have to do is find two answers that are correct. As question 12 demonstrates, even if you do not know about the third option, it must be true IF you can only choose one answer and IF there are no options like "answers a and b."

Matching Questions

1. As always, read the directions carefully, and ask questions if necessary. Since our test said to write the correct *answer*, we assume only one will be possible. But we would need to ask if options could be used more than once to know what to do with questions 13 and 15. If we can use an option twice, option d could be the answer to both. If we can't, option b **or** c might answer number 15.

2. Get an overview of number comparisons before you start.
    a. If you have equal numbers of questions and options, it will be easier to eliminate distractors, so be sure and do so systematically.
    b. If the numbers are not equal, start with the *longer* column and look down the shorter column for matches, even if it is the option side. It is important to consider each option each time.

3. Always answer the easier ones first to better your odds!

4. Consider grammatical clues. Are you trying to match up nouns, adjectives, events, dates, etc.? Question 17 is an adjective, so look for an option that describes an adjective, not one that describes a noun.

5. Guess if necessary, but only as a last resort! Work mainly with eliminating distractors.

Sentence Completion or Fill-in-the-Blank

1. Reword the question so the blank is at the end, if possible. Use all the words in the question as your best clues. (See question 18.)

2. Watch carefully for grammatical clues. Question 19 gives you a clue that the blank must start with a consonant due to the word "a," so you have a good guess that the animal must be a whale instead of an elephant. Check to make sure that there will be subject/verb agreement with your answer. Is the blank calling for a name, date, event, noun, verb, adjective, or what?

3. Check to see if length or number of lines indicates a clue, as in question 20.

4. Ask very specific questions if needed. If you tell your instructor that you are not sure what should go in question 21, you will probably hear, "I'm sorry, but I cannot help you." But if you ask for clarification on whether the question is asking for a country or a continent, you will probably get an answer, and a very good clue

at the same time. If you are completely off track, you will also probably get a clue about that too!

5. Never leave blanks! Consider every possible clue and then guess, and you might be amazed at the partial credit you may receive!

Short Answer Questions

1. Think before you write, and then start off by restating the key words of the question in your answer.
2. Watch for the key question words (describe, evaluate) to make sure you do what it says.
3. Give direct, concise answers.

Suggestions for Subjective Tests

Many students may give an unconscious shudder at the sound of the words "essay test." Why do we fear them so much? Maybe because we feel in these tests we really have to KNOW what we're being tested over! The word recall is the key word again. But another major problem with subjective tests is that HOW you answer is almost as important—if not more so—than WHAT you answer. Organization, relevancy, writing ability, and even neatness all enter in as a vital part of your grade. Students typically do two things wrong with essays: they write everything they can think of about the topic (whether it is relevant or not!), or they write only their feelings to fill up space, rather than the facts that were asked for in the question.

The Lab B$_2$owl System

Critical Thinking

It may be an error in judgment to assume that most students do not score their best on tests because they do not know the material. Look back at one of your past tests and analyze your errors. Were they due to lack of knowledge, or was it possibly lack of reading skills, lack of exam skills, or exam anxiety? Before you can correct your test-taking errors, you have to know what is causing them. Then you can decide what steps to take to correct them.

L—ook over the entire exam before you begin. Read the directions carefully, and underline the testing words (verbs) that are crucial to your answer. As you answer, it is a good idea to come back and check off each verb to make sure you have done what the question asked.

A—sk for point allotment if it is not given. Don't assume all of the questions have equal value, and don't spend the same amount of time on each question.

B—udget your time based on the point allotment. Make a tentative time schedule before you begin to make sure you allow enough time to finish the test, and to make sure you spend the most time on the questions that are worth the most points. (But you know the most information about the question that's only worth three points? That's the way it usually goes, but you had better come up with more information for that 30-pointer!)

B—egin with the easiest question. This is an important practice in all testing, but especially when you have to write essays! This will increase your confidence, get you warmed-up, and get a large portion of the test done quickly. If you start each answer on a separate page, the order that you answer will not matter. You can then put the answers in the correct order before you turn in the test. You also have a way to add more information to a question later in the test if you allow this space.

B—egin each answer with a thesis or topic sentence. One way to quickly create a thesis is to restate the essay question in a statement. Opening with a clear statement of your main topic will not only help you focus on your intended answer, it will show your instructor that you understood the question.

O—utline each question before you begin on a pre-essay page. This page will be a thinking page to help you get started. Your time schedule could be figured out here, along with the order that you will answer the questions. You might want to copy the testing words here to make sure you answer in the correct way. Make an outline of each answer before you start to write, and the writing will be much easier and faster. Label this page Pre-essay Page and you will really impress your professor! As you try to outline question 4, you may remember something else you needed to add to question 2, and you can jot that down on this thinking page. Don't spend TOO much time here. You still have to write, so include this thinking time in your time schedule.

W—atch those key testing words! As mentioned before, to diagram does not mean the same as to discuss. Be very aware that you do what you are supposed to do!

L—ook over the exam again before you turn it in to correct errors or omissions. Teachers sometimes seem to make snap judgments on your grade based on the way your paper looks, so make it look good!

How Can I Raise My B's to A's on Essay Exams?

Because HOW you answer is just as crucial as WHAT you say in an essay, there are a few impressive things that you can do to make your test give a good impression, and hopefully add points to your score. Your instructor may not consciously give you more points, but there **is** a natural tendency! So consider these steps to add the "icing to the cake":

1. Write in essay form. This means use paragraphs, topic sentences, transition words between paragraphs, complete sentences, etc. Also, repeat part of the question (usually the testing word) in the first sentence of each portion of the essay.
2. Be accurate grammatically and with spelling. You may want to bring a pocket dictionary with you to the test. It will pay off!
3. Start each answer on a new page and number the answers correctly.
4. Neatness is vital! So:
   a. Write in pen.
   b. Write on one side of the paper only.
   c. Remember to leave margins—side, top, and bottom.
   d. Use unlined paper with a line guide underneath if you really want to impress!
   e. Put your name on each page and staple all pages together.
5. If you run out of time because you did not budget correctly, outline your answer. You may get partial credit.

Summary

This semester, when you approach test time, consider not only what you will do to study, but how best to study for the test type. Ask your teacher whether your test will be objective, subjective, or a combination of the two. This information will help you make your study plan and study tools. The best way to learn good test-taking preparation and skills is to learn from every test you prepare for and every test you take. After each test, consider what you did well. Remember your strengths and build on them to become even better at taking and preparing for tests. Use what you learned from this chapter to evaluate your skills and make a change. When you enter the next semester, think about your study habits from the semester before. Did you study enough each week? Had you kept up in class enough to be ready when test time approached? If you felt anxious about taking a test, what were the causes of your anxiety?

Reflect and Apply

1. Review the chapter and make a list of at least three test-taking or test preparation tips you want to implement for your next test. Make an effort to apply these skills and reflect on whether they were useful.

2. You've spent many years of your life as a student. What was your most successful test? Write a paragraph about the test you did best on. Why do you think you did well? Did the subject interest you or not?

Name: _____   Date: _____

Exercise 3: What's Your Testing IQ?

Answer these questions to the best of your ability. Use every test-taking strategy that you know.

A. True-False

Answer + for each true statement and − for each false statement. Each item is worth 1 point.

1. _____ Smart students always study 2–3 hours each day for every class.
2. _____ Frequently, students leave too much studying to do until finals week.
3. _____ Some students study a lot, but no one studies as much as they should.
4. _____ The way to learn the most efficiently is not to succumb to distractions.
5. _____ Hunger leads to decreased concentration and increased apathy when studying.
6. _____ According to the textbook, most students study at a 1-1 ratio of hours studied versus hours in class.

B. Multiple Choice

Write the letter of the correct choices for each item in the blank. 4 points each.

7. _____ Test-taking can cause:
    a. hardening of the arteries.
    b. students to study harder.
    c. professors to have papers to grade.
    d. late night studying.
    e. all of the above
    f. answers b, c, & d
    g. answers b and d
    h. none of the above

8. _____ Students go to class because
    a. since it is necessary.
    b. information is being taught.
    c. it is the most fun way to spend the day.
    d. the law of xfghot recommends it.

9. _____ Which statement(s) is(are) not correct?
    a. Students often study in the library.
    b. Students do not study enough.
    c. Most students should try to study more.
    d. Professors should never give essay tests.

10. _____ Colleges often
    a. blow up.
    b. get torn down.
    c. try to educate students in the best possible manner with the least amount of expense.
    d. change their names.
    e. try to educate students in the worst possible manner with the greatest amount of expense.

229

11. _____ The distance from Paris to New York is approximately
    a. 3000–4000 miles.
    b. 10–20 kilometers.
    c. 9000–10,000 miles.
    d. 500–1000 miles.
12. _____ Mass hysteria can result when large numbers of people
    a. believe something that is not true.
    b. fear an invasion.
    c. share delusory perceptions.
    d. all of the above

C. Matching

Write the letter of the correct answer in the blank. 2 points each.

13. _____ preview
14. _____ test-taking
15. _____ survey
16. _____ time schedules
17. _____ quixotic

a. a writing system
b. to manipulate data
c. used for evaluation
d. getting an overview of a chapter
e. used for efficient studying
f. idealistic, but impractical
g. determines the appropriateness of using a dictionary

D. Sentence Completion

Write the missing word in the blanks. 10 points each.

18. _____ is the process for becoming a citizen.
19. The largest animal in the world is a _____ .
20. _____ is the collective name of Superior, Huron, Erie, Ontario, and Michigan.
21. Lions are most likely to be found in _____ .

E. Short Answer

Answer concisely but completely. 1 point each.

22. Describe the best way to make a time schedule.

_____

_____

23. Evaluate the practice of previewing in studying a chapter.

_____

_____

F. Essay Question

24. Trace the history of your immediate family. Enumerate how many people are included, list their occupations and ages, and discuss their personalities. State if you care for them or not, and make a decision as to their honesty when considered as a group.

Answers for "What's Your Test-Taking IQ?" Worksheet

Before you started taking the test, you should have skimmed over the entire exam to see the type of questions and to budget your time according to point value. Notice that you could have missed ALL of the True-False questions and only have done the damage of missing three Matching questions. Missing all of the Matching questions would have been the same as missing ONE Sentence Completion question. Also notice that the Short Answer questions were only worth one point. Therefore, it was not worth your time or effort to spend a lot of time on these answers. Examine the point value carefully before you take a test, and spend more time on the most points! Below are the correct answers. If there was a "clue word" in the sentence, it is given also.

A. TRUE-FALSE
   If you did not answer with a "+" or a "–", you missed all six questions. You must follow the directions to get the credit!
   1. – (always, each, every)
   2. + (Frequently)
   3. – (no one)
   4. + (not)
   5. – (Hunger)
   6. + (According to the textbook)

B. MULTIPLE CHOICE
   Notice that the directions said you might have more than one answer (the word was CHOICES).
   7. f
   8. b
   9. b, d
   10. c
   11. a (kilometers)
   12. d

C. MATCHING
   Note that the directions clued you in to the fact that you would only have one answer for each question, but it did not say that you could not use the same option more than once! If this had been a real test, you may have needed to clarify these points.
   13. d
   14. c
   15. d
   16. e
   17. f

D. SENTENCE COMPLETION
   18. Naturalization
   19. whale (a)
   20. The Great Lakes (3 blank spaces)
   21. Africa

E. SHORT ANSWER

22. Possible answer—Denote class time, work time, and other necessary time by the hour and plan the best times to study and take care of other responsibilities.

23. Possible answer—Experts say previewing is crucial to effective studying of a chapter because it increases concentration and comprehension, and I would agree.

F. ESSAY

24. (If you were REALLY bored enough to answer this monster of a question, you should have first shown some type of a chronological review of your family history. This would be followed by a numbered list of the job and age of each person in your immediate family, and a brief description of their personalities. You should have stated your feelings for each one, and finally stated an opinion as to whether your family could be considered honest or not. This question really involved seven questions—trace, enumerate, list jobs and ages, discuss, state, and decide—and would have best been answered in six or seven paragraphs with the key word repeated in the topic sentence of each.)

By the way, how many points was this awful essay question worth, or does it matter? Would it make any difference how long you spent on it if it was worth *10* points rather than *100* points? Of course it would—or should! You need to ask, if point values are not given, and then write accordingly. If the essay is worth 100 points and you don't have anything to say, you had better come up with something! If it is only worth 10 points, don't spend three pages answering the question. BUDGET TIME BY POINTS AND DIFFICULTY!

Did You Follow Directions?

What is your testing IQ? Points excluding the essay question add up to 82, so let's say the essay question was worth a meager 18 points to make it a nice, even 100 points. But let's also say that you got all 18 points on that essay! What is your test score? Add up your points and judge yourself on this scale, and then read ahead to find out how you might have done better, or, more importantly, how you may do better on the next REAL test!

95–100 points	A	Hey, you've got a good handle on this test-taking game!
90–94 points	B	Not bad!
85–89 points	C	Look forward to improving!
84 points or less		Have we got some great tips for you! Read on!

Name: _____ Date: _____

■ Exercise 4: Can You Follow Directions? YES YES YES

This is a test to see how well you read and understand test directions. You should do this test as quickly as possible. First, read through the entire test. Then go back and do what the items instruct you to do.

1. Write your name in the upper right corner of this paper.
2. Circle the word name in the first sentence.
3. Draw five small squares in the lower left-hand corner of this page.
4. Put an X in each square mentioned in Number 3.
5. Put a circle around each square.
6. After the title, write "YES, YES, YES."
7. At the bottom of this page, add 1991 to 2397.
8. Stand, turn around, and whisper, "I am a leader in following directions."
9. Working from top to bottom along the left margin, count by 2s from two to 32.
10. Across the bottom of this page, list your favorite four friends.
11. Recite "O Canada" to yourself and write the twelfth word in the song on this line.
    _____
12. Put a box around all of the words that start with a "b" on this page.
13. Write the name of the Prime Minister of Canada in the exact middle of the right side of this page.
14. Complete step one and six, disregard everything else and stop.

Name: _____ Date: _____

Exercise 5: What Makes a Good Essay Answer?

Decide the answer to this question by taking the role of teacher and grading the sample essay answers below.

Directions: You are the teacher, reading and marking student answers to an essay test.

1. Read the test question and underline any key words. Consider what the question is asking for.
2. Then, read each student answer and note what the student did well and didn't do well. Consider whether the student fully answered the test question.
3. Assign each answer a grade of A, B, C, D, or F. Be ready to justify your grade choice.
4. Discuss your ideas and grade choice with a small group and with the class.

Test Question: How did geometry and studies of anatomy affect the painting style of Italian Renaissance artists?

Answer #1

Geometry and mathematics both affected art and architecture during the Italian Renaissance. You can see geometrical shapes in many buildings and paintings. The buildings and paintings made during this period were also very ordered. Leonardo da Vinci was interested in geometry. You can see this in his sketchbooks and many of his paintings. It was similar with mathematics. It was important to many Italian painters, because they studied math and put elements of math into their art.

Answer #2

Anatomical studies didn't affect Italian Renaissance painting as much as geometry did. Many artists studied geometry and integrated what they learned into their painting and architecture. In his painting *School of Athens,* Raphael used one-point perspective to create the illusion of a window into a wide-open courtyard. All lines lead from the outer edges of the painting into the centre and creating a never-ending background. This method of using geometry in the form of perspective makes objects and people in the painting appear to overlap each other rather than stand above each other to show what is closer and what is further away. Leonardo da Vinci often used geometry to create order in and bring meaning to his paintings. In *The Last Supper*, da Vinci set the figures in groups of three, each group arranged under a square window. The three groups and three windows, represent the Christian trinity. Geometry was pervasive in many Renaissance paintings, because it was considered a new and exciting study for artists.

237

Answer #3

Italian Renaissance artists were the first Italian artists to expand their studies beyond the craft of art. As a result, what they learned about geometry and anatomy affected their painting style. Both geometry and knowledge of anatomy were essential to bringing a new realism to Renaissance paintings. For example, in Raphael's *School of Athens*, the artist used geometry to create an architectural setting that made the illusion of depth. By using one-point perspective, Raphael reduced the size of figures and structures to make them seem to move farther into the background. Another essential addition to create realism in *School of Athens* is the illusion of weight in the figures. Each person seems to literally stand on a ground. This illusion was created by adding light and shadow to musculature and below figures. Understanding where to place shadow to reveal musculature comes from studies in anatomy. By studying anatomy, artists such as Raphael were able to better understand how muscles and bone interact to reveal turns or twists of the figure and to show the way muscles sit at rest versus when a figure is standing on a ground. This understanding of anatomy, combined with the use of geometry, affected the art of many Renaissance painters in a similar way. These studies increased the realism that was in Renaissance paintings.

CHAPTER 10
Teamwork

Why teamwork? Many students find group projects to be a nuisance at best and a disaster at worst. Things take longer when you work as a group. You don't have total control over the quality of the project. What about incompetents who pull the group's performance down? Or slackers who contribute nothing, but still expect the same grade that the other members earned? Isn't a camel a horse designed by a committee? Why teamwork, indeed?

The answer is that the benefits to teamwork outweigh the costs. Yes, working collaboratively with others poses special challenges, but effective teams get better results than individuals. The world of sports provides many examples of groups whose performance exceeds the sum of the individual players' abilities. On paper, Team A should dominate Team B, but they don't. Team B doesn't have the athletes or the individual skills to win, but they do. They win because they pull together, back each other up, and sacrifice for the good of the team.

Teamwork makes as much difference outside the sports world. As you will see in the chapter on leadership, teamwork helped Ford Motor Company become the most profitable American car manufacturer. Whether you plan to work in business or industry, education or medicine, the military or scientific research—teamwork makes a big difference. For this reason, people who recruit graduating seniors want to hire people who have demonstrated the ability to perform effectively in a team setting. In fact, a 1999 survey of 120 corporate recruiters conducted by Georgia Tech Career Services revealed that communication skills and teamwork were the two top qualities sought by employers. It should be apparent that the same corporations and organizations who prize teamwork in full-time employees will want team players to fill their co-op and internship positions. Moreover, your ability to function in a student organization, to live in a residence hall, and to get the most out of your college experience rests to a considerable degree upon your ability to work effectively with others in a group setting.

Signs of Effective Team Functioning

Parker observes in *Team Players and Teamwork* that "You get a certain feeling when you are part of a solid team. You enjoy being around the people, you look forward to all meetings, you learn new things, you laugh more, you find yourself putting the team's

---

From *Building Success* by Bill Osher and Joann Ward. Copyright © 2000 by Osher and Ward. Used by permission of Kendall/Hunt Publishing Company.

assignments ahead of other work, and you feel a real sense of progress and accomplishment." He elaborates by identifying twelve characteristics of effective teams:

1. **Clear Purpose**. Every member of the team knows the mission of the team and is committed to it.
2. **Informality**. There is typically a comfortable atmosphere, relatively free of tension or boredom.
3. **Participation**. All members contribute.
4. **Listening**. Members listen *actively* to what each other says. They attend to the meanings and feelings behind the words and demonstrate this by means of eye contact, verbal acknowledgement, mirroring, and asking encouraging questions.
5. **Civilized Disagreement**. It may surprise you to learn that good teams do not lack for conflict. The conflict is out in the open, however, and relatively free of personal attack. Moreover effective members work to resolve differences.
6. **Consensus Decisions**. Out of open, spirited discussion of differences emerges agreements that members can stand behind.
7. **Open Communication**. There are no hidden agendas because members feel free to express themselves candidly.
8. **Clear Roles and Work Assignments**. Members know their jobs and what is expected of them.
9. **Shared Leadership**. While there may be a titular leader, all members "own" the group and help facilitate the way the group functions.
10. **External Relations**. The group devotes some of its energies to maintaining useful contacts and resources outside of the group.
11. **Style Diversity**. There are a variety of types of team players represented. They perform different functions to promote team effectiveness.
12. **Team-Assessment**. The team is capable of examining itself, its processes, and how to improve its effectiveness.

It is very satisfying to work on a good team, but the purpose of the team is not to provide satisfaction. Nor is the purpose of the team to be a team. Effective teamwork is rather a necessary means to reaching an end. Katzenbach and Smith, in *The Wisdom of Teams*, are very clear on this point. The power of teams is exploited when the team is challenged to produce, when performance standards are high, and when the team and its members are held accountable for meeting those standards. Larson and LaFasto, in *TeamWork*, note that effective teams always have a goal that is both clear and elevating. Ineffective teams lose their focus on the goal. They worry more about power, who gets the credit, or what others will think.

Improving Team Skills

By developing team skills, you'll become a more effective student while in college. You'll also be investing in your future. If you can demonstrate that you're a team player, you'll be a more marketable job candidate. You will almost certainly be asked about your experience as a member of a team when you are interviewed for jobs as you approach graduation. And if you can play team ball on the job, you'll get better results leading to higher raises and more promotions. There are some obvious ways to operate when you find yourself in a task-oriented group—listen well, speak your mind, respect others' viewpoints, do your share of the work, help keep the group on task. It should be obvious that time and data management, important skills for individual success, are even more important for effective team performance.

Glenn has found that there are four roles within an effectively functioning team. Each role is necessary for a team to perform at maximum efficiency. While anyone can perform any of the four roles, you will probably gravitate toward the role most congruent with your own personality. As described in *Team Players and Teamwork,* here are the four roles:

- A **Contributor** is task oriented, provides solid technical information, does what is assigned, and insists on high standards.
- A **Collaborator** is highly goal-directed, is motivated by the mission of the team, is flexible, is receptive to new ideas. Sees the Big Picture.
- A **Communicator** is attentive to how the team is functioning, is a good listener, and encourages other members of the team.
- A **Challenger** questions goals, strategies, techniques, and ethics. Will confront authority. Willing to take risks.

While all roles are present in a strong team, any one of them can be counterproductive when taken to extremes. For example, the Challenger can intimidate others and demoralize the group if too critical or overly aggressive.

The roles within a team invariably support two separate, but equally crucial, functions: **person** and **task**. The person is any member of the team. Each member must be encouraged, supported, challenged, and heard. While every team member can support every other, typically some members are more adept at communication and encouragement. They listen actively and demonstrate their attention to the rest of the team by means of body language and eye contact. They nod their heads when others speak and mirror key words and phrases that capture a speaker's meaning. They ask others to elaborate on the point. They verbalize support and enthusiasm. They make sure that communication is open, disagreements are above board, and everyone contributes. The task is what the team is trying to accomplish—its very reason for being. For a team to be successful, it must stay on task. While every team member can be task oriented, there are usually some whose skills are especially strong in this area. They may have technical expertise or an especially clear picture of the mission. Their contribution is to keep the group on task, ensure that deadlines are met, and that the best methods and resources are used.

Every effective team is focused on its task. Every effective team supports and draws on each team member. Reflect on teams of which you've been a member. Who served these functions on the effective teams? How was one or the other function neglected on ineffective teams?

Stages of Team Development

Even as individuals develop over time, so do teams. In an important 1965 article, B.W. Tuckman identifies four developmental phases:

- Forming
- Storming
- Norming
- Performing

He compares group development to individual development. The first stage, **forming**, he likens to the dependency associated with infants and toddlers. Members are trying to figure out what the rules are and what the objective "really" is. Out of their confusion, they look to each other and the leader to try to make sense of their team and its mission.

The **storming** stage is likened to a rebellious child who fights parents and teachers. Hostility may occur and resistance to the task may be prevalent. If disagreements are suppressed, they may still emerge in covert ways: members not completing their tasks, the formation of factions, and straying from the task.

The **norming** phase is compared with an older child who begins to accept societal values and thinks beyond his or her own selfish wants. Informal rules are accepted and practiced. Commitments are made to accomplish the task around which the team is built. There is more open communication and cooperation.

The **performing** stage is likened to the healthy, productive functioning of a mature adult. Each team member is committed to the mission of the team and works collaboratively to accomplish that mission. Members work together by communicating openly and contributing willingly from their own resources.

So What?

What does all this have to do with you? Nothing—if you plan to be a hermit. If, however, you want to get the most out of college and enjoy a successful career, your mastery of team skills and understanding of group dynamics will be very useful. While you're in school you'll be expected to perform in groups, both within the classroom and as a member of campus organizations. In the workplace, outstanding team players are probably even more highly prized than they are on a college campus. Your ability to perform as a team player will mean greater opportunity, bigger raises, and more promotions.

Practical Steps in Working on a Team

Developing outstanding team skills can be a tall order because teamwork requires a collaborative spirit that doesn't come easily for everyone. Remember, however, that different personalities can contribute in different ways to team performance. You almost surely possess some characteristics which will help the teams of which you are a member. Here are some practical steps you can take to build on what you already have developed.

Habits to Cultivate

- Initiate discussions
- Solicit information and opinions
- Listen actively
- Express differences candidly
- Suggest techniques and strategies for fulfilling mission
- Clarify ideas
- Summarize
- Seek consensus
- Help team stay focused on task

Tactics for Running Effective Meetings

- Use an agenda and follow it
- Have a facilitator who promotes communication and keeps team on task
- Take minutes
- Draft next agenda
- Evaluate the meeting

Problem Areas

Dealing with Ineffective Members. Our students tell us this is one of the biggest challenges they confront as members of teams. Students may find their term grade is in jeopardy because some members aren't pulling their weight on a group project. While there are no foolproof remedies for this problem (If you invent a more foolproof system, someone will invent a bigger fool!), here are some things you can do to protect your grade and improve team performance.

1. Analyze the stage of group development. Your group may not have progressed past the forming and storming stages. Several members are inherently conscientious and quietly go about doing all the work. Group norms have not been established.
2. Confront the non-contributor. This is hard, but consider the alternative—more work for everyone else and maybe a poor grade. Speak to the other person(s) candidly, but diplomatically. Maintain eye contact, but don't glower. Don't attack the person, but rather state that the person's behavior is threatening everyone's grade.
3. Give the person a chance to explain what's going on. Maybe sickness or other obligations are factors.
4. Come up with a new understanding and a new deadline.
5. If all else fails, discuss your dilemma with your professor who may have some useful suggestions for solving the problem. Alternatively, many professors will not permit a slacker to ride the coat tails of more productive members. They may reorganize the team or take points off of the less productive member's grade.

Teamwork and Ethics. Chances are you'll be assigned to contribute to a group project before you graduate. You might not prefer the assignment. You might not like your team mates. No matter, you are ethically bound to contribute your fair share. Even as your grade is affected by the performance of others, so is theirs affected by yours. If you have special circumstances such as illness or a demanding work schedule, let the other members know right away. Try to find a way to do your part. It is neither professional nor honorable to accept a grade for work that you haven't done.

CHAPTER 11
Communication

Communication for Success

Developing your communication skills will further enhance your ability to work well in a team. To be an effective communicator, it is important to be a good listener and speaker. Practice the techniques of good listening and use language that helps you enhance your success and establish good relationships. First consider the factors that can inhibit clear communication. Then, learn the keys to being a good listener. When communicating, it is essential to consider how your word choice controls the self-image you present to others and yourself.

To be an effective communicator, it is important to be a good listener and speaker. Practice the techniques of good listening and use language that helps you enhance your success and establish good relationships.

Problems in Effective Communication

Effective communication involves a loop in which a sender sends a message and a receiver receives the message. Communications are disrupted when:

- The receiver doesn't receive the message.
- The receiver hears the wrong message.
- The receiver doesn't care about the message.
- The receiver is more interested in talking than listening.
- The receiver only hears part of the message.
- The receiver only hears what she or he wants to hear.
- The receiver feels threatened by the sender.
- The sender didn't send the message correctly.
- The sender left out part of the message.
- The sender talks so much that nobody listens.
- The sender is not someone you want to hear.
- The sender is annoying.
- The sender was upset and did not mean to send the message.
- The sender assumes that you should know the message already.

From *College and Career Success* by Marsha Finley Fralick. Copyright © 2000 by Kendall/Hunt Publishing Company. Used by permission.

There is a joke circulating on the Internet:

> *A man is driving up a steep, narrow mountain road. A woman is driving down the same road. As they pass each other, the woman leans out the window and yells, "Pig!" The man replies by calling the woman a name. They each continue on their way; and as the man rounds the next corner, he crashes into a pig in the middle of the road. If only people would listen!*

As you can see, there are many ways to disrupt communication. Just because a message was sent, does not mean that it was received. The first step in communication is to be a good listener. Many factors interfere with good listening. Do you recognize some of these reasons for not listening?

Message Overload. There is so much communication going on today that it is difficult to keep up with it all. There are stacks of paper, multiple e-mail messages, voice mail, television, radio, and people who want to talk to you. Introverts may find this overwhelming, while extroverts may find it exciting. Both find it challenging to keep up with all these communications and to keep attention focused on the communication.

Worries and Anxiety. It is difficult to listen to other people when you are preoccupied with your own thoughts. You may be thinking about that upcoming test or paper that is due or worried about a personal relationship. While others are talking, you are thinking about something else of more immediate concern to yourself.

Rapid Thought. People think faster than they speak. They are capable of understanding speech at about 600 words per minute, and most people talk at 100 to 150 words per minute.[1] They use the spare time to become distracted. They daydream, think about what they will do next or think about their reply.

Listening is Hard Work. It takes effort to listen. It requires paying attention and striving to understand. People can't listen effectively if they are tired, overloaded or distracted.

Noise and Hearing Problems. Our world is becoming noisier. As people get older, many suffer from hearing losses. Younger persons are suffering hearing losses from listening to loud music. It is more difficult to get your message across when people can't hear everything you are saying.

Faulty Assumptions. There are many faulty assumptions. People assume that other people also know the information, and therefore they do not communicate. People listening may assume that they know the information already or that the information is easy, so it is not necessary for them to pay attention. They may assume the material is too difficult to understand and block it out.

Talking Too Much. Since listening involves effort, people consider what they have to gain before they invest the effort in listening. They might think that there is more to gain in speaking rather than listening. They may be trying to persuade or gain control. The speaker feels that he or she has control. You might feel that in speaking you gain the attention or admiration of others. If you are speaking or telling a joke and everyone is listening, you feel important. Also through speaking people release their frustration and think about their problems. They need to stop speaking in order to listen.

---

[1] A. Wolvin and C.G. Coakley *Listening,* Third Edition (Dubuque, Iowa: W.C. Brown, 1988), p. 208.

How to Be a Good Listener

Being a good listener takes practice and effort. Here are some tips on becoming a good listener:

Talk Less. It does no good to talk if no one is listening, if no one understands your message or if your message is irrelevant to the situation. In order to have a better chance of communicating your message, it is important first to listen to gain an understanding of the other person and then to speak. In marriage counseling, a common technique is to have one person talk and express his or her point of view. Before the other person can talk, he or she has to accurately summarize what the previous person said. Too often people do not really listen; instead they are composing their own message in their head. It is a Native American custom that when members of the group assemble to talk about an important issue, a talking stick is used. Persons can only talk when they have the talking stick. When the person holding the talking stick is finished, it is passed to the next person who wants to talk. In this way only one person can talk at a time, and the others listen.

Minimize Distractions. For important conversations, turn off the TV and the music. Find quiet time to focus on the communication. Manage your internal distractions as well. Focus your attention on listening first and then speaking.

Don't Judge Too Soon. Try to understand first and then evaluate. If you judge too soon, you may not have the correct information and might make a mistake. People are especially vulnerable to this problem when their ideas do not agree with those of the speaker. They try to defend their positions without really hearing the other point of view. People may need to put aside their mindsets in order to hear and understand.

Look for the Main Point. You may become distracted or impatient with people who talk too much. Try to be patient and look for the main points. In a lecture, write these points down.

Ask Questions. You will need to ask questions to make sure that you understand. Each person looks at the world in a different way. The picture in my mind will not match the picture in your mind. We have a better idea of each other's pictures if we ask for more information.

Feed Back Meaning. It is common for speakers to:

- Say one thing and mean something else.
- Say something and not mean it, especially if emotions are involved.
- Speak in a way that causes confusion.

Feeding back meaning means to restate the speaker's ideas in your own words to check the meaning. Feeding back meaning has two important benefits. It helps speakers to clarify their thoughts. It helps listeners make sure that they have received the correct message. Here are several ways to feed back meaning:

1. **Restate what has been said.** Sometimes this is called parroting. It is useful to clarify information, but sometimes it annoys people if you use it too much.

    Statement: Turn right at the light.
    Feedback: Okay. So you want me to turn right at the light?

2. **Ask for clarification.**

Statement:	Take the next exit on the freeway.
Feedback:	Do you mean this exit coming up now or the next one?
Statement:	(Referring to the joke about the man and woman on the mountain road): Pig!
Feedback:	What do you mean by "pig"?
Statement:	Be careful. There is a pig in the road ahead.

3. **Reword the message to check your understanding.** First restate what you have heard and then ask for clarification. This is called active listening.

Statement:	Turn in the draft of your paper next week.
Feedback:	You want the draft next week. Does this include the outline, the draft of the entire paper and the bibliography? Should it be typed, or is handwriting okay?
Statement:	Don't worry about your grade on this quiz.
Feedback:	You said not to worry about my grade on this quiz. Does that mean that the grade won't count or that I can make up the quiz?
Statement:	I need this project completed by Friday.
Feedback:	So this project needs to be done by Friday. What parts do you want included and how would you like me to do it?

4. **Listen for feelings.** Feelings get in the way of clear thinking. A person may say one thing and mean something else.

Statement:	Just forget about it!
Feedback:	I'm confused. You ask me to forget about it, but you sound angry.

5. **Use your own words to restate what the speaker has said.** In this way, you help the speaker to clarify thoughts and hopefully to come up with some solutions.

Statement:	I wish I didn't have to work so much. I'm getting behind in school, but I have bills to pay. I have to work.
Feedback:	You seem to be caught in a bind between school and work.
Statement:	That's right. I just can't keep working so much. Maybe I should go check out financial aid and scholarships.

Be Careful About Giving Advice. Whenever possible, listen closely and be an active listener. In this way, the person speaking to you has a way to clarify his or her thoughts and think about alternatives. When you listen, it is tempting to offer advice because you may have had similar experiences. You can share your experiences and offer suggestions, but beware of giving advice for these reasons:

- If you give advice and it turns out badly, you may be blamed.
- If you give advice and it turns out right, the person may become dependent on you.
- People are unique individuals with unique life situations. Something that works for one person may not work for another person at all.

How to Be Helpful. Most people have been in a situation where their friends or family are in distress or crisis, and they become listeners with a desire to help. If you become aware of a dangerous or critical situation, look for professional help. Go to your college Counseling Center, community organizations, your doctor or religious leader for help. Here are some general ideas for being a helpful listener.

- Let the person talk. Talking helps to clarify thinking.
- Paraphrase or feedback meaning.
- Avoid being critical. Comments such as "You asked for it" or "I told you so" do not help. They just make the person angry.

- Help the person analyze the situation and come up with alternatives for how to solve their own problem.
- Share your experiences but resist giving advice.
- Ask questions to clarify the situation.
- Offer to be supportive. Say, "I'm here if you need me," or "I care about you."
- Let people express their feelings. It is not helpful to say, "Don't feel sad," for example. A person may need to feel sad and deal with the situation. The emotion can be a motivation for change.
- Don't minimize the situation. Saying, "It's only a _____ (grade, job, promotion),"minimizes the situation. It might not be important to the listener, but it is causing pain for the speaker. Give him or her time to gain a perspective on the problem.
- Replace pity with understanding. It is not helpful to say, "You poor ____."

The following anonymous poem,[2] helps to summarize some ideas on how to be a helpful listener:

*When I ask you to listen to me
and you give me advice
you have not done what I asked.*

*When I ask you to listen to me
and you begin to tell me why I shouldn't feel that way,
you are trampling on my feelings.*

*When I ask you to listen to me
and you feel you have to do something to solve my problem,
you have failed me, strange as that may seem.*

*Listen! All I asked was that you listen.
   Not talk or do—just hear me.
Advice is cheap: 50 cents will get you both Dear Abby and
   Billy Graham in the same newspaper.
And I can do for myself; I'm not helpless.
   Maybe discouraged and faltering, but not helpless.*

*When you do something for me that I can and need to do
for myself, you contribute to my fear and weakness.*

*But, when you accept as a simple fact that I do feel what I feel,
no matter how irrational, then I can quit trying to convince
you and can get about the business of understanding what's
behind this irrational feeling.
   And when that's clear, the answers are obvious and I
   don't need advice.*

*Irrational feelings make sense when we understand what's
behind them.*

*Perhaps that's why prayer works, sometimes, for some people
because God is sometimes mute and doesn't give advice or
try to fix things. He often listens and lets you
work it out for yourself.*

*So please listen and hear me. And, if you want to
talk, wait a minute for your turn; and, I'll listen to you.*

---

[2] Found in *Care of the Mentally Ill*, 1977, F.A. Davis Publishing Company.

The Language of Responsibility

The way we use language reflects our willingness to take responsibility for ourselves and affects our relationships with others. Knowing about "I" and "You" messages, as well as how we choose certain words, can help us to improve communications. We can become aware of how our thoughts influence our behavior and communication. We can choose to use cooperation in dealing with conflicts.

"I" and "You" Statements

In communications, watch how you use the pronouns "I" and "You." For example, if you walk in and find your apartment a mess, you might say to your roommate, "Just look at this mess! You are a slob!" Your roommate will probably be angry and reply by calling you an equally offensive name. You have accomplished nothing except becoming angry and irritating your roommate. Using the pronoun "you" and calling a person a name implies that you are qualified to make a judgment about another person. Even if this is true, you will not make any friends or communicate effectively.

"You" statements label and blame. They demand a rebuttal. They cause negative emotions and escalate the situation. How would you react to these statements?

    You must be crazy.
    You make me mad.

When you use an "I" message, you accept responsibility for yourself. You might say something like this:

    I don't understand.
    I feel angry.

There are many ways to make an "I" statement. Instead of calling your roommate a slob, you could:

1. **Make an observation.** Describe the behavior:
   Your things are all over the floor.
2. **State your feelings.** Tell how you feel about the behavior:
   I get angry when I have step over your things on the floor.
3. **Share your thoughts.** Say what you think about the situation. Beware of the disguised "I" message which is, "I think you are a slob."
   I think it is time to clean up.
4. **Say what you want:**
   Please pick up your things.
5. **State your intentions.** Say what you are going to do:
   If you do not pick up your things, I will put them in your room.

A complete "I" message describes the other person's behavior, states your feelings and the consequences the other's behavior has on you. For example, when your things are all over the floor (behavior), I feel angry (feeling) because I have to pick up after you (how it affects me).

A variation on the "I" message is the "We" message. The "we" statement assumes that both persons need to work on the problem.

> We need to work on this problem so that we don't have to argue.

Practice changing "you" messages to "I" messages using the Communications Worksheet at the end of this chapter.

Words are Powerful

The words that we choose have a powerful influence on behavior. One of the least powerful words is the word "should." The word "should" is used frequently on college campuses.

> I should do my homework.
> I should go to class.
> I should get started on my term paper.

The problem with the word "should" is that it usually does not lead to action and may cause people to feel guilty. If you say, "I should get started on my term paper," the chances are that you will not start on it.

If you say, "I might get started on my term paper," at least you begin to start thinking about possibilities. It is possible that you might actually get started on your term paper. If you say, "I want to get started on my term paper," the chances are getting better that you will get started. You are making a choice. If you say, "I intend to get started on my term paper," you have at least made some good intentions. The best way to get started is to make a promise to yourself that you will get started. The following words—should, might, want, intend and promise—form what is called the ladder of powerful speaking. As you move up the ladder, you are more likely to accomplish what you say you will do. This ladder of powerful speaking moves intention from obligation (should) to promise (a personal choice to act). The ladder of powerful speaking looks like this:

The Ladder of Powerful Speaking

I promise

I intend to

I want to

I might

I should

Next time you hear yourself saying that you "should" do something, move one more step up the ladder. Move from obligation to making a personal decision to do what is important to you. If a friend asks to borrow money from you, ask, "Do you plan to pay the money back?" You would most likely be repaid by a friend who makes which of the following answers?

- I really should pay the money back.
- Well, I might pay the money back.
- I really want to pay the money back.
- I intend to pay the money back.
- I promise to pay the money back.

Be Aware of Negative Self-Talk

Self-talk is what you say to yourself. It is the stream of consciousness or the little voice in your head. This self-talk affects how you communicate with others. If your self-talk is negative, you will have debilitating feelings that interfere with communication. There are some common irrational beliefs that lead to negative self-talk. Becoming aware of some common irrational beliefs can help you to avoid them.

- **I have to be perfect.**
  If you believe this idea, you will think that you have to be a perfect communicator and deliver flawless speeches. Since this goal is unattainable, it causes stress and anxiety in attempting. If you believe in this idea, you may try to pretend or act as if you were perfect. This takes up a lot of energy and keeps others from liking you. Everyone makes mistakes. No one is perfect. When people stop trying to be perfect and accept themselves as they are, they can begin to relax and work on the areas needing improvement. They can write papers and make speeches knowing that they will probably make mistakes just like the rest of the human population.
- **I need the approval of everyone.**
  A person who believes this idea finds it necessary to have the approval of almost everyone. Much energy is spent in gaining approval from others. If approval is not obtained, the person may feel nervous, embarrassed or apologetic. It is not possible to win the approval of everyone because each individual is unique. Those who constantly seek approval will sacrifice their own values and what they think is right just to please others.
- **That's always the way it is.**
  People who believe this statement overgeneralize. They take a few events and use them to predict the future or exaggerate their shortcomings. Here are some examples:
    - I'm not a technical person. I can't install my computer.
    - I'm not good at numbers. I'll never to able to pass algebra.
    - Some husband/wife I am! I forgot our anniversary.
    - You never listen to me.

  Notice the absolute part of these statements. Absolute statements are almost always false and lead to anger and negative thinking. Remember that with a positive attitude, things can change in the future. Just because it was that way in the past, it does not have to be the same in the future. Beware of the "always" and "never" statements.
- **You made me feel that way.**
  Your own self-talk, rather than the actions of others, causes emotions. No one can make you feel sad or happy. You feel sad or happy based on how you react to others and what you say to yourself about it. If someone makes a negative

comment to you, you can say to yourself that it is only the other person's opinion and choose how you react. Your reactions and emotions depend on how much importance you decide to attach to the event. You tend to react strongly to the comment if it is from someone you care about.

People also do not cause the emotions of others. Some people do not communicate honestly with others because they are afraid of causing negative emotions in the other person. They may hesitate in telling people how they really feel. This lack of honesty leads to increasing hostility over time and difficulties in communication.

- **I'm helpless.**

  If you believe that what happens to you is beyond your control, you do nothing to make the situation better. Here are some examples:
  - I'm a shy person. It is hard for me to talk to people.
  - I won't consider that career. Women are always discriminated against in that field.
  - It's difficult for me to meet people.

  With these statements, the shy person doesn't attempt to talk to others, women limit their career options and people give up trying to make friends. Believe that there is a way to change and make your life better.

- **If something bad can happen, it will happen.**

  If you expect the worst, you will take actions to make it happen. If you expect that your speech will be a disaster, you will not prepare or you may forget your notes or props. If you believe that you will not pass the interview and that you will never get hired, you may not even apply for the job or attempt the interview. If you believe that your personal relationships will not get better, you will not invest the effort to make things better. There will be times when you make a poor speech, get turned down for a job or have relationships that fail. Learn from these mistakes and do better next time.

Some Barriers to Effective Communication

We all want to communicate effectively and to get along with people that we care about. We want to get along with our families, be a good parent, have friends at school and get along with the boss and our co-workers on the job. Life is just more enjoyable when we have good communication with others. Watch for these barriers to effective communication.[3]

- **Criticizing**

  Making a negative evaluation of others by saying, "It's your fault," or, "I told you so," causes anger, which gets in the way of communication.

- **Name-calling and Labeling**

  If you call someone a name or put a label on them, they will attack you rather than communicate with you in any meaningful way.

- **Giving Advice**

  Giving advice is often viewed as talking down to a person. They may resent your advice and you as well.

- **Ordering or Commanding**

  If you order someone to do something, they are likely to sabotage your request.

- **Threatening**

  Trying to control by making threats causes resentment.

---

[3] T. Gordon, *Parent Effectiveness Training*, (New York: McGraw-Hill, 1970).

- **Moralizing**
  Preaching about what a person should or should not do doesn't work because it causes resentment.
- **Diverting**
  Changing the subject to talk about your own problems tells the person that you do not care about them.
- **Logical Arguing**
  Trying to use facts to convince without taking feelings into account is a barrier to communication. Present your facts and state your point of view, but respect the other person's feelings and different point of view.

Practice the Win-Win Approach

There are several ways to approach a conflict. The Win-Win approach is a way of looking at conflict and using an approach where both parties win by having their goals met. Another approach is the traditional one called Win-Lose because one person wins and the other loses. This is the opposite of the Win-Win approach. Look at the barriers to effective communication listed above. Many of these approaches are an attempt at using the Win-Lose approach. The big disadvantage of this Win-Lose approach is that the loser becomes angry and often tries to get back at the winner. The conflict continues. Let's look at these approaches in more detail.

- **Win-Lose**
  Using this approach to conflict management, one person wins and the other loses. Many games and sports use this approach. One team wins and the other loses. Competition is part of the win-lose approach. In competition, power is important. In sports, the best and most powerful team wins.

  There are many kinds of power. There is power based on authority. Examples include your boss at work, your teacher or even your parents. Another kind of power is mental power or cleverness. Sometimes battles are not won by the most powerful, but by the most clever person. Another kind of power is majority rule. In a democratic society, the person with the most votes wins.

  At times, there is no choice other than to use the Win-Lose approach. Only one team can win, only one person can get the job and only one person can marry another. In some circumstances the other person does not want to cooperate but wants to compete. You have no choice but to compete.

  The problem with this approach is that there is only one winner. What happens to the loser? The loser can feel bad, resent the winner, give up or try again for victory. These are not always the best alternatives.
- **Lose-Lose**
  The lose-lose is another option for resolving conflicts. Both parties lose. Both parties strive to be winners, but the struggle causes both to lose. It is fighting to the death. Wars are often examples of lose-lose situations. Dropping an atomic bomb caused the surrender of Japan, but it polluted the environment with radioactive material and made atomic war a dangerous precedent. Recently Russia was able to stop a civil war by destroying Grozny, the capital of Chechnya. The city was so destroyed that it became uninhabitable. Everyone lost. On the interpersonal level, divorce can be an example of a lose-lose situation. The struggle becomes so destructive that everyone loses.
- **Compromise**
  Another approach to solving conflict is the compromise, where both parties to the conflict have some of their needs met. Both make some sacrifice in order to resolve the situation. For example, the buyer and seller of a used car may agree

on a price somewhere between what the seller wants to get and the buyer wants to pay. As long as both parties are satisfied with the outcome, the results are satisfactory. Difficulties arise when people are asked to compromise their values. If they compromise on something that is truly important, they may be dissatisfied with the outcome.

- **Win-Win**

In a win-win approach, both parties work together to find a solution that meets everyone's needs. There is no loser. In order reach a win-win solution, competition needs to be set aside and replaced with cooperation. This is often difficult to do because emotions are involved in the competition. These emotions need to be put aside for the benefit of both parties. This approach can be impossible when one person wants to cooperate and the other person wants to win. The steps in the win-win approach are as follows:

1. **Identify the problem.** Identify the problem as your own. If your roommate is having a party and you cannot study, it is your problem. You need to find a quiet place to study.

2. **Set a good time to discuss the issue.** While you are angry is probably not a good time to discuss issues. Set a time when both parties can focus on the problem.

3. **Describe your problem and needs.** Use "I" messages. Resist the temptation to label and call names. Goodwill is important.

4. **Look at the other point of view.** Understand the other person's needs, and make sure the other person understands your needs.

5. **Look for alternatives that work for both parties.**

6. **Decide on the best alternative**

7. **Take action to implement the solution.**

The win-win approach is a good tool for effective communication

Summary

Use the power of words to increase your ability to communicate effectively. Remember that barriers to effective communication can be lifted by increasing your listening skills and by asking for clarification before responding. Show yourself and others that you have confidence by avoiding negative self-talk. Instead, tell yourself to focus on positive statements and encouragements that you will complete tasks. Communication is a skill. How you develop the skill is up to you.

Reflect and Apply

1. Think of a time when you had a poor communication with a friend, family member, or acquaintance. Rather than focusing on who was at fault, think of what you might have done to turn the communication in a positive direction.

2. Review the "Words are Powerful" section. Envision a task you need to complete or a goal you want to reach. Avoid telling yourself what you "should do" and think of what you will and can do to complete the task or reach the goal. Below, write three statements clearly stating what you will do.

CHAPTER 12
Identifying and Dealing with Stress

Although you probably know how it feels to be "stressed out," you may not understand what happens to your body when it experiences stress. You also may not realize how many of your personal habits are motivated by the need to counteract the physical and psychological effects of stress. In this chapter, you'll learn how your mind and body respond to stressful situations and then you'll have the opportunity to discover how you currently cope with the stress in your life.

What Is Stress?[1]

Although there is no commonly accepted definition of stress, researchers have identified a series of physiological and psychological reactions called the *General Adaptation Syndrome* that occur when you feel stressed (see Figure 1). This syndrome can be divided into five phases:

- Phase 1: The Onset of Stress
- Phase 2: The Perception of Stress
- Phase 3: Preparing to Fight or Flee Stress
- Phase 4: Reacting to Stress
- Phase 5A: Exhausting Stress Adaptation Energy
  Or
- Phase 5B: Coping with Stress

Internal Stressors
- Emotional Arousal
- Effort
- Fatigue
- Concentration

External Stressors
- Pain
- Fear
- Humiliation
- Loss of Blood
- Great Success

Each phase of the syndrome is discussed in more detail below.

Phase 1: The Onset of Stress

You may encounter several potentially stressful events during the course of each day. Perhaps an unexpected traffic jam causes you to be late for work or the neighbor's barking dog disturbs your peaceful night's sleep. An important business meeting may cause you to worry more than usual and think

---

[1]From *Creating Connections: A Four-Step Program for Managing Stress* by Bobby Pfau and Mary Ellen Litzinger. © 1996 by Kendall/Hunt Publishing Company. Used by permission.

anxious thoughts, while an argument with a coworker can negatively affect an otherwise positive attitude about your job. These incidents, or "stressors," that trigger such reactions are classified in two categories:

1. *Internal Stressors:* Internal stressors are the thoughts and negative attitudes that cause you to worry and fret about a particular situation. These stressors occur within you and are not necessarily precipitated by the occurrence of an event. For example, you may worry about something that occurred fifteen years ago.

2. *External Stressors:* External stressors are specific events or conditions that trigger a specific response. Some external stressors originate in the environment (that traffic jam, for example), while others have their basis in interpersonal relations (an argument with a spouse or child). Sometimes you provide your own external stressor by overindulging at a party and waking up with a headache and heartburn.

Phase 2: The Perception of Stress

An internal or external stressor induces a stressful response in proportion to your perception of that stressor. You may experience stress in several ways. Sometimes you might feel fear (when you suddenly lose control of your car), and at other times you may feel excitement (when you've just won the lottery). Perhaps your jaw muscle will tighten or your stomach might become queasy. You might feel "jumpy" or have trouble sleeping at night. These conditions occur because your body experiences very specific physical reactions when you're presented with a stressor. However, you can positively influence these physiological stress reactions by developing specific coping strategies, such as focused breathing exercises, that mitigate the harmful physiological effects of stress.

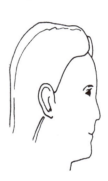

Phase 3: Preparing to Fight or Flee Stress

When you are confronted with a stressor, *the fight or flight syndrome is activated.* This process allows your body to protect itself from stress by either fighting its cause or running from it. A part of your central nervous system called the *autonomic nervous system* swings into action. This system controls the basic physiological processes such as hormone balance, metabolism, and vascular (blood vessel) activity. The activities of the autonomic nervous system are regulated by the *hypothalamus*, a collection of nerve cells located at the base of the brain. The hypothalamus prepares you to deal with stress by shifting blood to your heart so it can beat faster and help you flee from danger. The hypothalmus also prepares you to defend yourself by releasing hormones into your system so you can think and act more quickly than usual. A specific part of the autonomic nervous system called the *sympathetic nervous system* carries these hormones to various parts of the body so you can respond more effectively to your stressor. The pituitary gland and the adrenal glands also produce the hormones *noradrenaline* and *adrenaline*, which prepare the body to respond physiologically to the presence of stress.

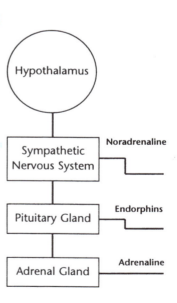

12: Identifying and Dealing with Stress

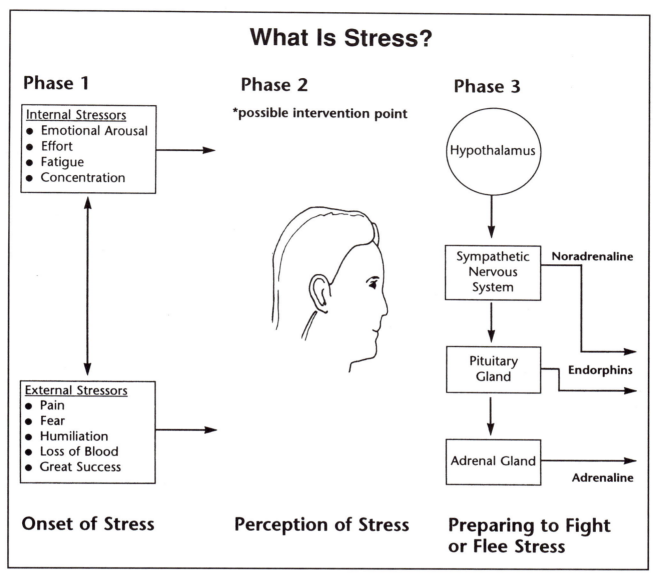

Figure 1 ■ What Is Stress?

Phase 4: Adapting to or Resisting Stress

Once the hypothalamus sounds the fight or flight alarm, your body begins to make a number of physiological changes which help it respond to or *adapt* to stress. These changes include increased heart rate and blood pressure, rapid breathing, enhanced muscular functioning, the rapid release of blood cells to essential areas of the body such as the heart, and the diversion of blood away from other metabolic activity such as digestion. If you've noticed that you feel queasy after an argument at the family dinner table, you're probably feeling one of the effects of the "fight or flight" response. Blood from your stomach moves to your heart so it can deal with the stress of the argument. Once the stressor has been removed (by settling the argument, for example), then the body returns to its original state and resumes its normal activity (like digesting your food).

Adaptive Processes:
Sympathetic Nervous System
- Increased papillary activity
- Increased lachrymal gland activity
- Increased salivary flow
- Decreased stomach motility
- Decreased intestinal motility

OR

Coping Processes:
Parasympathetic Nervous System
- Decreased papillary activity
- Decreased lachrymal gland activity
- Decreased salivary flow
- Increased stomach motility
- Increased intestinal motility

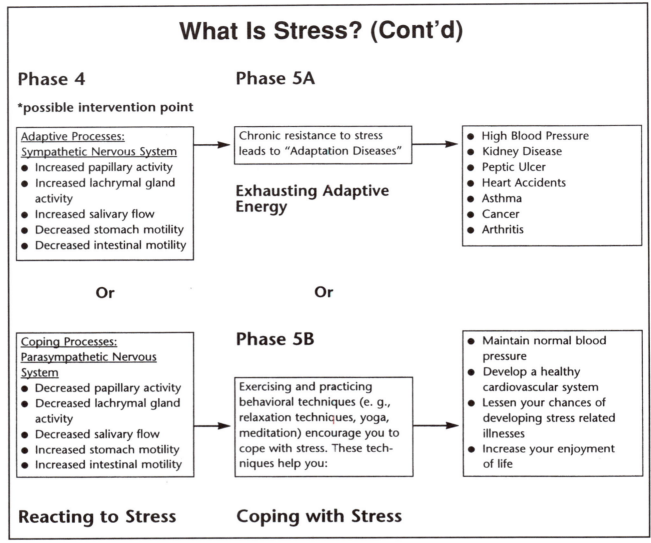

Figure 1 ■ What Is Stress? (cont'd)

Phase 5A: Exhausting Adaptive Energy

Should a stressful situation continue, one of the behavioral options available to the body is to continue mobilizing itself for *adaptive action*. Your heart will continue to beat more rapidly than normal, your blood pressure will continue to rise, your muscles will remain more tense than usual,

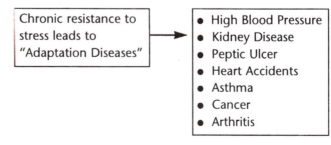

and metabolic processes such as digestion will still be ignored. Your body has only a finite amount of adaptive energy to use, however, and eventually it will exhaust itself fighting the various stressors with which it is presented. Bodies under chronic pressure from internal and external stressors eventually give way to a variety of *adaptive diseases* such as hypertension, peptic ulcers, kidney disease, arthritis, and asthma. Physical energy is lowered and mental clarity and creativity are decreased. This is often what you feel when you are "stressed out."

12: Identifying and Dealing with Stress

An important point to remember, however, is that not everyone has the same amount of adaptive energy. Some individuals have developed attitudes and beliefs that allow them to feel a sense of control over all aspects of their lives. These individuals possess a certain psychological hardiness that allows them to thrive in very stressful situations. These people can withstand stress longer than many of their peers, although eventually their ability to adapt will also falter. Unfortunately, there are no specific tests to absolutely determine who has the best chances of thriving in stressful situations.

Phase 5B: Coping with Stress

Exercising and practicing behavioral techniques (i.e., relaxation techniques, yoga, meditation) encourage you to cope with stress. These techniques help you . . .	• Maintain normal blood pressure • Develop a healthy cardiovascular system • Lessen your chances of developing stress related illnesses • Increase your enjoyment of life

In contrast to exhausting your adaptive energy, you can instead learn to cope with stress. Coping is the a process of identifying various stressors in your life and developing more effective ways of dealing with them. There are several medical and nonmedical interventions that encourage coping with stressors rather than adapting to them. Treatments such as tranquilizers, psychotherapeutic chemicals, and anti-ulcer drugs can mitigate the physical effects of stress on either a short-term or long-term basis. Other techniques that have proven useful in coping with stress include relaxation training, yoga (especially using yogic breathing patterns to control respiratory responses to stress), meditation, prayer, biofeedback, and physical exercise.

While almost anyone can withstand an occasional jolt of adaptive energy, a successful long-term program of stress management requires that you learn to cope with stress rather than exhausting yourself adapting to it.

Can You Relax When You're Under Stress?

No matter how much we might wish otherwise, stress is a constant presence in our lives. Is it possible to relax enough to mitigate the harmful effects of stress? The answer is definitely yes! You can even think of stress as an ally that encourages you to perform activities you thought were impossible, and allows you to increase your energy in the process.

One of the key factors in learning how to relax is to understand the relationship between your stress level and your energy level. Simply put, the General Adaptation Syndrome needs energy to sustain itself. All the metabolic and emotional changes that occur during a typical stress reaction are fueled by energy that you would otherwise use to participate in enjoyable activities—walking the dog, playing with your children, or reading a book, for example. The longer you are under stress, the less energy you will have to enjoy the pleasurable things in your life.

Your body instinctively understands the equation between stress and energy, and strives to maintain a constant internal balance in spite of changes in its external environment. This instinct to maintain a "steady state" of energy balance, which some researchers call "homeostasis," may also unconsciously drive many of your behavior choices. You gather energy from one activity and expend it on another so that you can maintain your body's homeostatic state.

Sometimes the energy choices you make are positive ones. To gather energy to write a report, you might take a walk outside to "clear your head" and organize your thoughts. You return to your desk refreshed with more energy to spend on your task. On other occasions, your choices may not be so positive. Suppose it's 11 p.m. and you have a paper due at 8 a.m. the next morning. You've only begun to write the paper, so you increase your energy by drinking three cups of coffee and eating a candy bar. While you may have a momentary burst of energy from the caffeine, in a few hours you'll probably feel exhausted since caffeine ultimately robs the body of its natural energy.

If you can develop a positive relationship between the level of stress in your life and the amount of energy you have to cope with that stress, you will learn how to relax when stressed, and to store energy to cope with future stressful situations. In the next two sections of this chapter, you will participate in exercises that help you determine which areas of your life are especially important to you and therefore deserve to be the focus of your energies. You'll also have the opportunity to discover how you currently maintain the homeostasis between external stress and internal energy balance. Finally, you'll identify specific behaviors that you're currently using to cope with stressful situations. Armed with this information, you'll be able to develop a stress management program that provides you with enough energy to accomplish what you "should" while still leaving you with enough energy to do what you enjoy.

How Do You Spend Your Time?

Part of successful stress management is understanding how you spend your time. Many people feel that time is their most valuable resource, yet many of us are unaware of where our time "goes" or why we choose to participate in one activity rather than another. The following exercises will help you determine how you currently spend your time and how you use personal habits, such as smoking or drinking, to deal with the effects of stress.

How Do I Spend My Time?: The Circle of Life

Part 1: Thinking About the Last 24 Hours

Look at your watch and see what time of day it is right now. Write that time down in this space __21:00__. Now consider what happened to you in the last twenty-four hours. For example, if you answered "12:00 p.m. Thursday" in the space above, think about what you did from 12:00 p.m. on Wednesday to 12:00 p.m. on Thursday. Use the questions below to help you account for your activities. Record your answers in the spaces provided.

- The amount of time you slept yesterday. __9 hrs__
- The number of times you ate a meal or snack yesterday __3__ and the times that you ate each meal or snack. _____
- The number of hours you spent at work. __9__
- The activities that you performed to help someone else yesterday. __took bro to school__

- The activities that you performed just for you (i.e., something that was self-enhancing). __went to school, finished paper, went to post office__

- The number of hours or minutes you spent exercising (i.e., walking, jogging, playing basketball). __0__

12: Identifying and Dealing with Stress

- The amount of time you spent participating in an activity that provided you with the opportunity to quietly think or contemplate (i.e., meditation, a long walk in the woods). _0_

- The amount of time you spent playing. (Notice how you define "play.") _0_

- The amount of time you spent engaged in intellectually stimulating activities. Also write down one thing that you learned in the last twenty-four hours. _5 hrs, most likely will die of stress related thing_

- The amount of time you spent with someone that you love. _hr_

- The amount of time you spent completely alone (i.e., time you spent without having to do anything for anybody else or without anyone else). _2 hrs_

Part 2: Completing the Inside of Your Circle

1. Write down the time of day at the top of your circle and then divide your clock into four six-hour intervals. Your clock should look similar to the clock shown below:

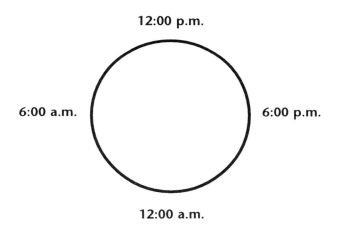

2. Now divide your circle into a pie chart that represents how you spent your time yesterday. First, record the amount of time that you slept. If you slept for eight hours, you would mark off approximately one-third of your circle to represent the time that you slept (since eight hours is one-third of a 24-hour day). Label this section of your circle "Sleep."

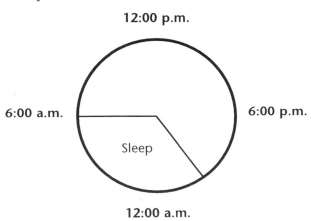

3. Now indicate the number of hours that you spent at work or attending class. Let's say that you worked for 8 hours yesterday. Mark the appropriate segments on your circle.

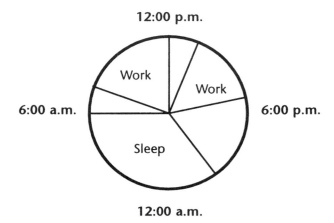

4. Using the remaining information you collected at the beginning of this exercise, complete your circle. When you're finished, your circle should look something like the Circle of Life pictured in Figure 3.
5. Now take a few moments to reflect on this activity. Were there any surprises? Anything that you really had trouble recalling? Were your last 24-hours unusual for you? Would you consider this to be your normal routine?

Part 3: Completing the Outside of the Circle

Now we'll examine the legal substances that you may have consciously or unconsciously used to energize or relax yourself during the past 24-hours. We'll be using the "Circle of Life" again to determine how often and at what time of day you used caffeine, alcohol, and nicotine.

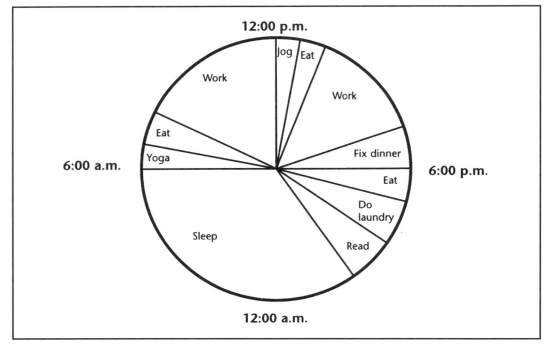

Figure 3 ■ How Do You Spend Your Time?: The Circle of Life: Example 1

Caffeine

Place the letters "CA" around each point in the circle when you used caffeine during the last 24-hours (see Figure 4). Notice when you used caffeine. Perhaps you drank four cups of coffee in the morning to feel more alert. Or perhaps you needed to keep a steady flow of caffeine in your body during the day to maintain the energy necessary to do your job or attend your classes.

Nicotine

Now consider your consumption of nicotine. If you smoked cigarettes or used nicotine in any form, mark the letters "CI" around the edge of the circle at the appropriate points (see Figure 4). Notice if you smoked cigarettes continuously throughout entire day or if there were certain periods of time where you smoked more frequently than others.

Alcohol

Finally, examine your consumption of alcohol. If you used alcohol during the last 24-hours, then mark "AL" at appropriate points around the circle (see Figure 4).

Note: If you haven't used nicotine, caffeine or alcohol in the last 24-hours, there will be no letters around the outside of your circle.

Part 4: Taking a Closer Look at the "Inside" Circle

Let's examine the inside of your Circle of Life in more detail. Try to identify specific behavioral patterns that may be sapping your energy reserves (are you getting enough rest, for example?) and determine how you might modify these habits to increase your energy level.

Eating

You should be eating meals that are spaced evenly within two to three hours of each other for optimal nutritional efficiency and energy. If you ate six evenly spaced meals

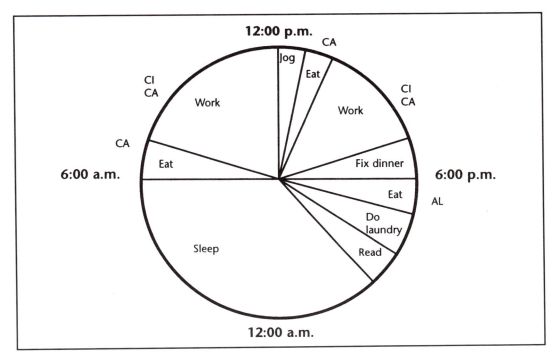

Figure 4 ■ How Do You Spend Your Time?: The Circle of Life: Example 2

throughout your day, you probably noticed that you had more energy than if you tried to eat all of your food at one or two meals. Starting out the day with breakfast is important in maintaining a high level of physical and mental energy. It's the meal that "breaks the fast" you endured while you were sleeping. Examine your circle. If your pattern differs significantly from the "six small meal" standard, try to remember if you felt tired at certain points during the day and recall how long it had been since you provided your body with nourishment.

Sleeping

Examine your sleep pattern. We know that Americans tend to get less sleep now than they did 50 years ago, even though the standard advice to "get at least eight hours of sleep" is still physiologically and psychologically sound. Eight hours of sleep each night is probably more helpful to your physical and mental health than even seven and a half hours of sleep. When you regularly reduce your sleep time by even 30 to 60 minutes, your stress levels will rise proportionately and your immune system becomes suppressed, making you more susceptible to viral and bacterial infections. Think of a time when you have been deprived of sleep and remember if your stress levels rose significantly. Any sudden noise or movement was probably very irritating to you! Since sleep is so important to your physical and mental well-being, notice how much sleep you received in the last 24 hours. Did you manage to catch any "cat naps?" Some people function more efficiently when they rest for short periods during the day. That rest may consist of sleep, but it may also include the time you spent meditating or participating in a self-nourishing activity like reading.

Time Alone

Notice the amount of time you spent alone yesterday. In our culture, we spend most of our time with others and we're often considered unusual if we want to spend time alone. There is a great deal of difference between being alone and being lonely, however. Being alone can be a positive activity because it provides an opportunity to tune into your body, mind, and breathing. Experiencing silence may be difficult for you, but some solitary activity is important in counteracting the effects of stress.

Time with Those You Love

Look at your circle and notice how much time you spent with those you love. Researchers now think that the quality of your life is directly related to the support you receive from your friends and family. By surrounding yourself with those you love, you are contributing to your longevity. People who are alone or have a small circle of friends tend to die earlier than those who have extensive support systems.

Time Spent Doing Something for "Others"

In our culture, it's often a temptation to do errands for others rather than ourselves. For example, females are often the caregivers for aging parents and relatives, and they tend to spend more time nourishing others rather than themselves. Notice how much of your time yesterday was spent taking care of and nurturing others. Is this a typical day for you? Are you happy about this pattern?

Exercise

Exercise is a self-enhancing behavior as well as a great stress reducer. The more you participate in and enjoy it, the less likely you are to develop heart disease, cancer or any other life-threatening illnesses. Notice the amount of exercise you were able to fit into your life yesterday and determine if this is a typical pattern for you.

Play

Now look at how many moments you spent playing yesterday. What does the concept of "play" mean for you? Is it an activity that allows you to smile and have fun? Is it an activity that is done for sheer pleasure? Do you regularly set aside time in your schedule for play?

Part 5: Taking a Closer Look at the "Outside" Circle

Now let's examine the outside of your circle more closely. Before you begin this analysis, you should understand that this activity is designed for stress management purposes only. It is not intended to imply that you should or should not drink alcohol, smoke cigarettes, or consume caffeine.

Nicotine

Note the number of times you've used cigarettes in the last 24 hours. Cigarettes act as a stimulant to the body's systems. You may be attempting to raise your energy and lower your stress if you're regularly smoking cigarettes or consuming nicotine in some other way. Most people who smoke admit that they use their cigarettes as a stress-reducer. If you picture yourself smoking a cigarette, you'll realize you're taking a nice, long deep breath every time you drag on the cigarette. These long breaths function as stress-reducers.

When do you smoke cigarettes? Do you smoke before you go to work in the morning and remain smoke-free while you work or attend class? Do you make up for this abstinence when you get home? Nicotine needs to be replaced in the system every 17 to 18 minutes in order to keep the body from experiencing symptoms of drug withdrawal. If you're not able to replace nicotine according to this schedule, then the withdrawal symptoms will also deplete your body of energy.

Alcohol

Notice how much alcohol you consumed in the last 24 hours and when you had a drink (or drinks). Did you drink because you believed that you would feel more relaxed if you consumed an alcoholic beverage? Although alcohol is classified as a depressant, it acts as a stimulant when consumed in small quantities, raising your sense of well being and allowing you to feel more calm and relaxed. Our culture celebrates this aspect of alcohol consumption by creating rituals like TGIF (Thank Goodness It's Friday).

Caffeine

Did you start your day with a few cups of coffee? Are you trying to drink less coffee because it makes you jittery when you consume too much? Then you're probably aware that caffeine is a stimulant. It is found in a wide variety of beverages and also in a multitude of over-the-counter drugs. For example, a cup of caffeinated drip coffee contains 150 milligrams of caffeine, and one tablet of aspirin can contain from 32 to 65 milligrams of caffeine.

Caffeine is very popular in our culture because it serves us so well. If we need a small "pick-me-up," nothing works quite as well. If you use caffeine as an energy enhancer, realize that you will develop a need to replace this drug on a regular basis throughout the day. If you plan to eliminate your daily consumption of caffeine, you should do so slowly over time. Your body quickly begins to depend on caffeine as an energizer, and some people will experience caffeine withdrawal symptoms that include excessive sleepiness, lack of concentration, and painful headaches.

You should now have a more accurate idea of which activities account for your daily expenditure of energy. You should also understand more clearly how you use alcohol, nicotine, and caffeine to restore some of your energy and manage your stress.

Stress Management[2]

Several years ago there was a television commercial that showed a harried mom whose houseful of bratty kids were running and screaming all around her. Just then the dog starts barking, as the male voice-over says in increasingly frantic tones, "You've had a bad day, . . . the kids!, . . . the dog!, . . . the phone!, . . . the doorbell! . . ." By that time the poor woman is pulling on her hair yelling for her favorite brand of bubble bath to take her away from it all.

There are times in all of our lives when we feel just like that mom. Sure we each have different stresses, but what made that commercial so successful is that it touched on a common thread. We've probably all wished for a magic potion that could just take us away from it all.

As college students, you are likely to have more roles than the average person. Most of you probably work full or part time. Some of you might be married, might be parents, and might be active in your community, religious, or social organizations. Others might be encountering pressures to choose a career, might be looking for or trying to maintain a meaningful relationship, or might be struggling to gain independence from your parents. Some of you may still be in high school trying to get a jump start on your education. Now, you've added the pressure and time commitment of attending classes and studying to your already full life. How are you managing so far? Do you feel comfortable and in control, or do you feel like a juggler frantically throwing one ball up in the air so you'll have a free hand to catch the ones that are falling around you? At this point in the semester you may be facing midterm exams. Papers and projects are due along with the usual quizzes and assignments. If you're feeling like the juggler, you need to read this chapter. If you are calm and controlled, read it anyway. You may find some great pointers to share with your more stressed-out classmates.

Stress

Let's talk for a moment about stress. Stress is the body's *reaction* to an occurrence or an event. It can be the result of either positive or negative, short or long-term events in our lives. A wedding or graduation is positive, unemployment or illness is negative; a math quiz is short-term, a cancer treatment is long-term. The event itself is not the stressor; the event is neutral. It is how we view the event, or how we react to it that causes stress. People have different ways of handling a situation. What is distressful to one person may be a challenge to another. Our own reactions come from a variety of sources: the importance we place on the event, our habits and our beliefs, our past experience of responding to stress, our own health and well-being, our perception of our own self-worth, and our ability to handle adverse consequences.

Stress is unavoidable and affects everyone in its own unique and personal way. In other words, everyone has stress in their lives. When stress is not handled properly, though, it can become destructive. Some forms of stress cause acute anxiety. When your reaction to an event is negative and you dread the event or its consequences, you may develop physical symptoms of discomfort and illness. Before we talk about that, though, let's take a look at the causes of stress and the anxiety it can produce.

Stress and anxiety come in many forms and manifest themselves in different ways. Stressors come from all aspects of our lives. Some of the most common are the conditions and circumstances that surround our family, friends, money, health, and relationships

---

[2]From *The Community College: A New Beginning, Second Edition* by Aguilar et al. © 1998 by Kendall/Hunt Publishing Company. Used by permission.

at home, work and school. All of these can contribute to our mental and physical feelings of stress and anxiety. Major life changes, conflict, frustration, everyday hassles, and overextension of ourselves in all of these areas are responsible for much of our stress. Too many changes and too much responsibility at once can overload our ability to adapt.

Stress can also be self-imposed. Sometimes we set unrealistic goals for ourselves or set our standards too high. When we expect too much of ourselves by overrating our abilities, we may fail to reach our goals or fail to make satisfactory progress toward them. Failure also causes us to be stressed. It can produce a state of depression where we are no longer able to function effectively.

Another cause of stress is a conflict in our values. When we are in situations where we act contrary to our core beliefs and values, we feel the pressure of being phoney. Time constraint, a feeling that we are continually overloaded, is one of the biggest stressors today. When we lack the proper support and resources, or feel that the school/job demands interfere with our personal activities we may exhaust our abilities for reducing and resisting stress.

Some anxiety and stress are normal, but extremes are damaging. Your body can tolerate high levels of stress, but only to a point. When you are in a constant state of overload, reactions to stress can actually cause chemical wear and tear on the body, resulting in physical, emotional, or behavioral problems.

Stress Reduction

Take a moment now to look at Activities 1 and 2. You will learn some of the physical, emotional and behavioral symptoms of stress. As you go through these lists, you might discover that you have a lot of the symptoms. You may already know that you're under a great deal of stress without the checklists. The big question is, what are you going to do about it?

We cannot control all of life's stressors, but we can control how we react to the stress and the degree of anxiety that the stress places in our lives. Learn how to reduce stress by starting a stress management program and tailor the program to your individual needs. If you alter your beliefs and your way of thinking, you can reduce the amount of anxiety that results from stress. You can also condition your body to resist any ill effects from the stress that remains. Stress is manageable. Let's examine some of the ways people have successfully dealt with the stress in their lives.

1. **LOOK FOR STRESS SYMPTOMS.** Be aware of the symptoms of stress. Awareness is always the first step in solving any problem. Recognize the symptoms and don't deny that you have them.

2. **IDENTIFY STRESSFUL TIMES/SITUATIONS/PEOPLE.** Identify the times and places when stress strikes you. No single aspect of your life is responsible for all of your anxiety. Rather, it is a combination of factors that puts you into stress overload. Learn how to recognize those stressful events and elements. Keep a journal or diary to pinpoint periods of heavy stress. This forces you to think about what is happening. You will learn the major causes of stress in your life. Record the different stressors and your ways of reacting. Then list the kinds of things that were successful in relieving the stress. Review the diary to see what works best for you. Also record in your diary any relaxation sessions. Mark the technique used to relax. You may see your stress lowered. Also, don't let conflict with your significant others become a way of life. It's too exhausting, frustrating and stressful! Learn skills (such as assertive communication) to improve and soften all of your relationships.

3. **ELIMINATE UNNECESSARY STRESS.** Whenever possible eliminate the causes of unnecessary stress. From your journal you might have noticed a pattern of things/people that always stress you. When you come to that situation/person again, think ahead. Try to anticipate what will happen. Then, avoid those stressful situations. Not so easy, you say. Yes, some events in our lives are unavoidable. In those cases you may have to develop a tolerance for what you cannot control. The key is to get better organized and plan for those stressful times. Sometimes people take advantage of us because we're not with it. Be proactive (that means take action first, don't wait and react to a situation) and make appropriate adjustments. For example, if spending Christmas Day with both sets of parents who live 200 miles apart leaves your family frazzled and ruins the holiday every year, decide what **you** would really prefer to do next Christmas. Announce your change of plans early (like before July) so no one can lay a guilt trip on you about how they went to *so much trouble, and now you won't be here, sob!* Don't accept false guilt! You would be amazed how much stress that will take off you. People who try to control you with guilt are thinking only of their own interests, not yours. Take direct action, and have confidence in yourself. On the other hand, there will be times when even advance planning won't get you out of a stressful situation. Adopt the philosophy that you will change what you can, and accept what you cannot. The best way to do that is to KEEP YOUR PERSPECTIVE. Think about it. Just how important is this situation? Will you even remember it next week? Next month? If not, why get upset about it? Keep stress at a minimum level. Don't overreact.

4. **UNDERSTAND YOURSELF.** Examine your value system. Earlier I mentioned that values conflicts can cause serious stress. If you are not sure of your values you won't be able to act consistently. Spend some time thinking through what you really believe and why you believe it. Often college is the first time people are really challenged about their beliefs and values. The diversity in the student body and faculty bring in many new or different perspectives you may not have considered before. In addition, college is supposed to teach you to think critically. Many impressionable young people have become very disillusioned after being challenged to defend their values. Students who don't know what they believe are often easily swayed by someone else's opinion. They swing back and forth depending on who they're with at the time. Stressful? You bet!

Learn to set realistic goals. If your goals are not realistic, you may become depressed when you fail to achieve them. Goals should energize you because they help you focus on what is most important. Be sure that they are clear, so you know exactly what you plan to accomplish, and review them from time to time. Monitor your self-expectations and change them whenever necessary.

Another way to reduce stress through self understanding is to know your personal strengths and find strategies to compensate for your weaknesses. It is stressful when you feel inferior or incompetent in any area of life. We all need to accept the truth that no one (alas, not even you) is perfect. You will never be perfect. But you can change and improve. Start by recognizing your unproductive habits and eliminating your self defeating behaviors. Then, look for ways to overcome your weaknesses or at least get around them.

Become aware of minor tensions and know your stress levels. Daily hassles such as traffic jams and ringing phones can produce significant stress. Find ways to make them less annoying and more productive. Use your time in that traffic jam to listen to a book on tape, the class notes that you've recorded for review, or even just to relax with some music. If you don't have a tape recorder in your car, mentally review your notes, memorize vocabulary words, go over your list of things to do, plan an upcoming event, sing. . . . You know what I mean. Be creative in using that time to get something done or try some deep breathing exercises. Don't let the traffic get you uptight. You're not going to get there any faster by clenching the wheel, swearing at other drivers, or saying negative things to yourself. Remember, stress is caused by your **reaction** to what's going on. The same goes for the ringing phone or any of those other annoyances. Don't let them control you. Identify the cues that signal stress so you can bounce back.

Learn decision-making and problem-solving skills. This will help you feel more in control of your life, and less like a helpless victim of circumstances.

5. **TRY CHANGING YOUR BEHAVIORS.** Behavior modification is a powerful tool that can enable you to change or modify stressful behavior. We won't launch into a whole psychology lecture here, but if you have a serious problem with stress, seek the help of one of the counselors in the counseling center or get professional therapy.

There are some other ways to change your behavior to reduce the amount of stress in your life. One is to seek alternative solutions to problems. Be creative rather than locked into a single method for doing things (especially if your way is causing stress!). Break big problems into smaller ones. Often the whole thing seems unmanageable in its entirety. But the first step isn't so bad.

Here's a big stress reducer: try cooperation rather than confrontation! Learn how to compromise and work out conflict rather than avoid it. Use conflict as a powerful catalyst for positive change.

6. **ESTABLISH SUPPORT SYSTEMS.** Develop a good support system and spend quality time with family and friends. Everyone needs nurturing and satisfying relationships. Maintain the positive, supportive friendships you already have and build new ones. Feeling isolated increases stress. Join clubs or organizations with others who have similar interests or needs. Ask for help when you really need it. It's okay to acknowledge that you can't do everything on your own. We all need assistance from time to time. Involve others when the stress in your life becomes too much to bear alone. Having someone you trust with whom you can share your troubles makes them more tolerable. In addition, don't overlook the resources available through the helping professions and your community. The college, area hospitals, social service agencies, civic groups, and churches often have support groups or classes to meet a variety of needs.

7. **ENJOY LEISURE ACTIVITIES.** Reward yourself for your accomplishments. Give yourself a break and combat built up tension. A few quiet minutes can provide a change of pace from daily routines that produce anxiety. Music can soothe tension: soft, gentle music, the sound of waves lapping the shoreline, birds chirping in the sunlight all help you relax. It is difficult for your body to be uptight and fearful when your mind and heart are singing. Take time out for yourself to play, have fun, and recharge. Make time for hobbies, sports, interests, and activities you love. Read a novel, go to the movies, learn to do something new. Start small, vary your activities, and be flexible. It is not always possible to stick to a regular schedule. Remember to enjoy some free time alone. You're worth it!

8. **MAINTAIN A HEALTHY LIFESTYLE.** Take care of yourself. Good nutrition and diet are always important in managing stress, anxiety, and tension. Eat balanced meals each day (as opposed to a day full of junk food or waiting until late at night to pig out). You've probably heard all of this advice a million times, but just in case someone reading this book has been in outer space lately or has ignored all of the experts, we'll repeat it again. Restrict your intake of sodium, sugar, fats, caffeine and other things you know are not healthy. Stop smoking. Never rely on illegal drugs, nicotine, or alcohol to help resolve your problems. Drugs do not remove the stressful conditions. Alcohol and nicotine are depressants that decrease your energy and make you feel down. So, even though these (and other) drugs

may seem to mask the symptoms for a while, they are actually making the problem worse. All of these may become habit forming and create their own stress and anxiety. Be cautious with prescription drugs and do not self-medicate.

Get more sleep. People who are under a great deal of stress need more (not less) sleep, just as they do when they have a physical illness. When your body is sleeping, it is able to repair damaged cells and heal itself. Researchers have found that the typical college student does not get enough sleep. You probably could have told them that without the scientific study! There never seems to be enough time to do everything, so we stay up late trying to cram one more thing (usually homework) into the day. Or, do you ever spend time watching dumb shows on TV when you really should be sleeping because you're just too tired to get up off the couch and go to bed? That's another one of those self-defeating behaviors we keep telling you about. If you are emotionally and physically drained, one of your best defenses is to get more sleep. The other is to get plenty of exercise. Invest 20 to 30 minutes two or three times a week in any number of activities that will provide you with the physical exercise sometimes necessary to work off tension. An aerobic workout reduces your anxiety, and regular exercise improves your overall health. When you are healthier, you are better able to cope.

9. **PRACTICE EMOTIONAL CONTROL.** This one probably should be at the top of the list. Emotional stress is so commonplace. We live in an angry, violent society today. The current trend is for everyone to feel victimized by some form of unfairness. Many people go around with a huge chip on their shoulders just daring others to try and knock it off. They find such freedom when they learn to let go of their pent up anger and hostility! Forgiveness releases you. A very wise teacher gave instructions to his students that one of their first priorities should be to make things right with anyone who had a grievance with them. He told them that one of the keys to a truly successful life is to live in peace with all people. We know it isn't possible to control the attitudes and behaviors of others, but you can be at peace within yourself. You can control your emotions. Many counselors advise couples or parents and children in therapy not to go to bed angry with each other. Keep anger from controlling your life. Let go of rage and resentment. I like the title of the book by Dr. Tim LaHaye, *Anger is a Choice*. That means you can choose not to be angry. If anger is a problem for you, try to develop techniques for anger management.

Another emotion to gain control over is self pity. Have you ever known someone who is always feeling sorry for him or herself? It's hard to be around all that negativism. If you're the one who is suffering from an overdose of self pity, you're likely to feel stressed more often. Get rid of those self defeating, negative thoughts. Sure, you may have it bad, but someone else is in a worse situation than yours. It's all a matter of perspective. There's a poem that begins with the line, "I felt bad because I had no shoes until I met a man who had no feet." I think you get the message. Remember, self pity never solves the problem, it just makes things worse.

Banish negative stressors and consciously replace negative thoughts with positive ones. Negative thinking only increases stress. You begin to overreact, lose control, and exhibit inappropriate behavior which takes away from your ability to reduce stress. Use past, successful experiences to deal with present situations. We'll talk about this in more detail in the next chapter.

10. **LEARN TO COMMUNICATE EFFECTIVELY.** Being able to express yourself is such an important concept we're going to devote an entire chapter to it. Pent up feelings eat away at oneself and increase stress. You need to be able to let people know how you feel. I'm sure at some time in your life you've experienced the frustration of being misunderstood. If that's an everyday experience, though, it

has probably become a source of continual stress. Try to improve your situation by becoming more assertive. Respect yourself and others. Be more honest about your feelings. Remember that there are indirect as well as direct methods of communication. Don't say one thing with your mouth, but the opposite with the rest of your body. Also, learn active listening skills. Never assume you know what the other person is thinking or what he or she will say. You may reach the wrong conclusion and create a misunderstanding.

11. **MANAGE YOUR TIME.** In the age of fax machines, e-mail, high speed transportation, fast food, automated express lanes, and instant everything, it is easy to feel like your world is out of control. You can reduce stress when you simplify your life and modify your routines. Develop good time management habits. Maintaining balance and moderation are keys to good stress management. Don't push beyond your limits. Practice saying "no" without guilt. Eliminate the unnecessary drains on your time made by others, and do not overextend yourself. There are only 24 hours in a day, and you are only one person. Prioritize. Keep tasks in perspective, and keep a check-off list.

Manage your schedule. Concentrate on getting good grades in a few classes rather than poor grades in a lot of classes. It may seem like it will take you longer to graduate if you take fewer classes each semester. But, in the end, it will be a lot less stressful, less expensive, and might even take less time than repeating courses that you failed or dropped because you were trying to do too much at once.

12. **USE HUMOR.** Lighten your emotional load. A good sense of humor and laughter always puts things into a positive perspective. Someone once said that laughter is the best medicine. In his writings Norman Cousins, author of *Internal Jogging*, discusses the positive benefits of laughter. It exercises the lungs, relaxes the diaphragm, increases the oxygen level in your blood, and tones the entire cardiovascular system. The relaxation response after a good laugh has been measured as lasting as long as 45 minutes. Smile more, too. It brings out the best in other people as well.

13. **CRY/SCREAM/VENT.** Crying is a healthy way to relieve anxiety. It could prevent a headache or other more serious symptoms of stress. Socially, it may be embarrassing or it may not be the macho thing to do; but psychologically, it is a proper response to overwhelming stress. It is cleansing, healing, and effective. Screaming and venting your frustrations also produce feelings of relief. Just be sure you do it when you're by yourself, not in a crowded room or at another person.

14. **ACCEPT CHANGE.** Accept change with a positive attitude. Change is an inevitable part of life and not always a negative experience. Allow yourself time to adjust. Fighting change causes additional stress. In the 21st century, we are faced with many challenges as a result of increasing technology and fewer support systems.

15. **LEARN NEW SKILLS.** Look toward a bright future. Develop a happier, more motivated self. One of the most effective ways to combat depression is to learn something new. It energizes and revitalizes your spirits. Improved skills that increase productivity will help you feel you are accomplishing more in the same amount of time and with the same effort. Learning how to cope with a crisis makes you feel more competent and in control. If you see the problem that used to cause anxiety as an opportunity for growth, you can change that deficit into an asset. Become a lifelong learner.

16. **MASSAGE THERAPY WORKS WONDERS.** No longer a luxury reserved for the rich and famous, massages are now affordable and as convenient as a local hair/tanning salon. Devices designed to massage your neck, feet, or back are available at most retail stores. Many colleges offer classes in massage therapy. Check

the personal interest, non-credit or continuing education section of the schedule. If that's too much trouble, treat yourself with a hot bath, like the mom in the TV commercial. It sure worked for her! Anything relaxing reduces your stress level and contributes to your general well being.

Relaxation Techniques

It is difficult to eliminate all the stress in your life, but you can learn to cope by practicing relaxation exercises. If you always think of the correct answers after you turn in your test and walk out of the room, it is because your tension has been released. By learning how to release that tension during the exam, you will be able to concentrate properly and come up with the correct answers when you need them. Balance your stress with periods of relaxation. It is not important how you relax, but rather that you do relax. Use one or more of the following relaxation techniques whenever you feel yourself becoming anxious, to help you sleep the night before a test, or as a stress reducer between study sessions.

Deep Breathing

Shallow, rapid breathing occurs when one is stressed. Deep, slow breathing can reduce stress and help you relax. Oxygen is the body's natural stress reducer. By increasing your intake of oxygen you relieve tension. Begin by closing your eyes. Exhale slowly and clear the air from your lungs. Then inhale deeply through your nose and hold your breath for the count of five. When taking a deep breath your stomach should be expanded. Slowly exhale using your lips to control the rate of air that you move out of your lungs. Begin the cycle again. Repeat this several times whenever you feel tension building. You can do this anywhere and any time you feel stressed, even while you are taking an exam.

Deep Muscle Relaxation

One of the most common reactions to stress is muscle tension. Deep and progressive muscle relaxation will help you to relax your entire body from head to toe by first tensing, then relaxing various muscle groups. The whole process takes about 20 minutes and can be done almost anywhere. Find a comfortable position either sitting or lying down. Loosen any tight clothing. Close your eyes. Begin with the head and facial muscles—scalp, brow, eyes, lips, jaw, etc. Tighten the muscles and hold tense for ten seconds, then relax. Continue contracting and relaxing the muscles by moving through the neck, shoulder, back, and chest areas. Keep doing this through every major muscle group. Concentrate on arms, elbows, fists, abdomen, hips, legs and feet while concentrating on your breathing. When you have completed all the muscle groups you will feel refreshed and relaxed and your tension will have disappeared. This type of relaxation will also help you sleep better.

Autogenic Exercises

Another way to control your stress is to use conscious thoughts to influence the way your body functions. With intense concentration you can focus on any part of yourself that you feel is tense in order to develop a more relaxed and tranquil frame of mind and body. This technique requires total concentration, so begin by lying down in a darkened room. Begin with deep breathing, then slow your breathing to its most relaxing pace. Focus your thoughts on the part of your body that you wish to relax. Repeat each statement several times "My head is heavy, my mind is calm." "My body is heavy and relaxed." "My breathing is calm and regular." "My body is warm and comfortable." "My head is quiet and relaxed." Focus on any one part of your body or move through your all your muscle groups individually as you did with Progressive Muscle Relaxation.

Meditation

Meditation is one of the oldest techniques which helps you clear stressful thoughts from your mind, but it will take time to learn. Find a location where you won't be disturbed (your bedroom, couch, hot tub, etc.) and get comfortable. Close your eyes and focus on a peaceful word or image. You are trying to find a quiet place and a peaceful state of mind. Concentrate on something calming and do not let any other thoughts enter your mind. Return to the one image or word you have selected, clearing your mind of any stress and allowing yourself a peaceful break. Breathe deeply.

Guided Imagery

Guided imagery is another type of mental exercise. It is like taking a mini vacation, but in actuality it is nothing more than daydreaming. You achieve the same feeling of tranquility that you achieve with meditation, but the technique is different. Rather than concentrating on a single thought, you create an entirely relaxing, though imaginary, place of your own to which you can escape. Once again, close your eyes to visualize a totally relaxed state. You can build confidence by visualizing the accomplishment of a goal or building your own little world.

Biofeedback

Biofeedback shows the body's reaction to stress. It helps you to focus on the physical symptoms of stress. The biofeedback machine measures the physical changes in your body when different stress management techniques are used. This is a practice used by some mental health professionals.

Stress is manageable, but each person is unique and must find his/her own way to cope. No one method will work for everyone. Choose the technique or techniques that best fit your individual needs to bring about the calming effects you desire. Remember, though, that it takes commitment. You are not necessarily going to do them perfectly or achieve immediate results the first time you try. You must take the time to practice. In the end you will feel better, be a happier person, be able to deal with stress, and look forward to all of life's challenges. It is simply a question of mind over matter. Decide to do it now.

Summary

We need to acquire the skills necessary to eliminate and control excessive stress in our lives. A number of strategies to help you identify stress and develop your own stress management program were covered in this chapter. Practicing a healthy lifestyle, developing and using support systems, and learning to use relaxation techniques are especially effective. If you have very high stress levels that have lasted for long periods of time, seek professional help. Remember that you can reduce many of your life stressors by identifying the people and events that cause you stress; yet, work to recognise the things you have control over and can change. Avoid focusing on changing things that are out of your control.

Reflect and Apply

1. Think about a stressful situation you're currently facing. Explain why you are feeling stressed. Make self-confident statements about your ability to cope with the situation. For example, you might say, "This isn't so hard" or "Relax, I can handle it." Then explain the steps you will take to reduce your stress level.

2. Complete Inventory 1 and Inventory 2 on the next pages to make an informal measure of your stress level and find out whether stress is negatively affecting your life. Then review the chapter to better understand any symptoms of stress you may be experiencing. Adopt at least one relaxation technique and try using it regularly to relieve stress or anxiety.

Name: _____ Date: _____

■ Inventory 1: Physical Symptoms[3]

How many of the following symptoms have you experienced in the last six months? Is your body trying to tell you something? Are you at risk? Go over this list and rate yourself on each item using a scale of 1 to 5, with 1 being "not a problem" and 5 being "I experience this all the time."

__2__ 1. Tension or migraine headaches

__3__ 2. Back, shoulder, neck, or joint pain

__3__ 3. Excessive tiredness and chronic fatigue

__1__ 4. White knuckles or cold, clammy hands

__3__ 5. Grinding teeth, jaw ache, or pain

__1__ 6. Rapid or irregular heartbeat, tightness of chest, or chest pain

__1__ 7. Shallow breathing, shortness of breath, hyperventilation, or asthma attacks

__1__ 8. Excessive perspiration or changes in body temperature

__1__ 9. Digestive disturbances such as abdominal pain, nausea, upset stomach, diarrhea, frequent urination, or constipation

__1__ 10. Trembling, nervous tics, shaking hands, or voice tremor

__2__ 11. Increased blood pressure or increased adrenaline flow

__2__ 12. Acne, psoriasis, dermatitis, hives, rashes, allergies, and other skin problems

__1__ 13. Frequent colds, cough, or flu

__1__ 14. Weakness, dizziness, or blurry vision

__3__ 15. Excessive thirst

__1__ 16. Choking sensations

__2__ 17. Change in appetite or weight gains or losses

__2__ 18. Impotence, decreased sex drive, or infertility

__1__ 19. Menstrual problems

__1__ 20. Loss of consciousness

__34__ **Physical Symptoms Subscore**

---

[3]From *The Community College: A New Beginning, Second Edition* by Aguilar et al. © 1998 by Kendall/Hunt Publishing Company. Used by permission.

Emotional or Psychological Symptoms[4]

How many times in the last six months have you had these feelings? Review this list and rate yourself on the same 1 to 5 scale with 1 being "never feel this way" and 5 being "feel this way all the time."

__1__ 1. Depression
__1__ 2. Hopelessness
__2__ 3. Mood swings
__3__ 4. Loss of interest
__2__ 5. Dissatisfaction
__3__ 6. Feelings of guilt
__2__ 7. Preoccupation
__3__ 8. Mental distraction
__3__ 9. Boredom
__2__ 10. Sadness
__1__ 11. Loneliness
__1__ 12. Fear
__2__ 13. Worry
__2__ 14. Feeling overwhelmed
__2__ 15. Frustration
__1__ 16. Confusion
__5__ 17. Forgetfulness
__3__ 18. Burnout
__1__ 19. Panic
__1__ 20. Suicidal feelings
__42__ **Emotional or Psychological Symptoms Subscore**

---

[4]From *The Community College: A New Beginning, Second Edition* by Aguilar et al. © 1998 by Kendall/Hunt Publishing Company. Used by permission.

■ Behavioral Changes[5]

Have you noticed any of these kinds of changes in your behavior in the last six months? What about the last semester? Review this list and rate yourself on the same 1 to 5 scale. Do you see yourself? Now go back and total all your numbers. How do you rate?

__2__ 1. Overeating or undereating

__1__ 2. Increased use of alcohol or tobacco

__4__ 3. Sleeping too much or insomnia

__1__ 4. Nightmares

__1__ 5. Overspending

__1__ 6. Increased reliance on prescription or non-prescription drugs

__2__ 7. Impulsive behavior

__4__ 8. Inability to concentrate or poor memory

__2__ 9. Accident proneness

__3__ 10. Compulsive or repetitive behavior

__1__ 11. Excessive anger or aggressive behavior

__1__ 12. Increase in risk-taking behaviors—e.g., speeding

__3__ 13. Difficulty in making decisions or poor judgement

__2__ 14. Stuttering or other speech difficulties

__3__ 15. Loss of productivity

__2__ 16. Mood swings or irritability

__1__ 17. Nervous laughter

__3__ 18. Restlessness

__2__ 19. Apathy, loss of interest or withdrawal

__1__ 20. Self-mutilation

__40__ **Behavioral Symptoms Subscore**

---

[5]From *The Community College: A New Beginning, Second Edition* by Aguilar et al. © 1998 by Kendall/Hunt Publishing Company. Used by permission.

Look at the inventory you have just completed. Write your subscores for each scale on the lines below.

Physical Symptoms   34

Emotional/Psychological Symptoms   42

Behavioral Symptoms   40

TOTAL SCORE   106

If your total score is below 100, you are probably able to manage the stressors in your life.

If your total score is 100–200, you should try to reduce your stress as quickly as possible.

If your score is over 200, get help now; you are at risk for a stress-related illness.

Name: _____   Date: _____

Inventory 2: College Student Stressors[6]

Mark each of the common stressors with 0 (never), 1 (rarely), 2 (sometimes), or 3 (often) to show how frequently they bother you.

__2__ 1. Placement tests

__2__ 2. Registration for classes

__0__ 3. Beginning a new semester

__1__ 4. Adjustment to college

__2__ 5. Tuition costs

__2__ 6. Organizing time

__0__ 7. New social interactions

__1__ 8. Acceptance by other students

__2__ 9. Concern over academic performance

__2__ 10. Academic workload

__2__ 11. Homework/Assignments

__1__ 12. Being unprepared for class

__1__ 13. Class participation

__2__ 14. Falling behind in coursework

__2__ 15. Examinations/tests

__1__ 16. Final exams

__0__ 17. Grades

__0__ 18. Financial aid applications

__3__ 19. Lack of spending money

__2__ 20. Fear of failure

__1__ 21. Being late for classes

__0__ 22. Missing a class

__2__ 23. Making up missed classwork

__2__ 24. Writing a term paper

__0__ 25. Group class projects

__1__ 26. Oral reports/class presentations/speeches

__0__ 27. Finding one's way around the library

__0__ 28. Meeting with advisors/counselors

__2__ 29. Career decisions

__1__ 30. Competition

__0__ 31. Transportation/commuting

__0__ 32. Study techniques

__0__ 33. Meeting with a tutor

__0__ 34. Study groups

__0__ 35. Child care

__0__ 36. Relationships with instructors/professors

__0__ 37. Talking to instructors/professors

__2__ 38. Balancing home/school/work issues

__0__ 39. Lack of support at home

---

[6]From *The Community College: A New Beginning, Second Edition* by Aguilar et al. © 1998 by Kendall/Hunt Publishing Company. Used by permission.

__1__ 40. Low self-concept/lack of confidence
__0__ 41. Concerns about intelligence
__2__ 42. Health
__1__ 43. Personal appearance
__3__ 44. Athletics
__0__ 45. Cultural activities/college events

__0__ 46. Knowledge of college policies/procedures
__0__ 47. Knowledge of college resources
__3__ 48. Multiple roles and multiple responsibilities
__0__ 49. Physical/learning disability
__2__ 50. Uncertainty about the future

Total your score to determine whether you have a high (100–150), medium (50–100), or low (less than 50) stress level.

CHAPTER 13
Managing Your Finances

The Buck Stops Here

Among the many lessons you can learn in college, one of the most important may be managing your finances. Financial planning consists of more than merely managing and investing money. It includes making all the pieces of your financial life fit together.

One of the major reasons students cite for going to college is to improve their economic standard. Students believe that getting a college degree will make them more competitive in the job market (i.e., a high-paying job), resulting in improved socioeconomic conditions for themselves and their families. Potential income and status are further enhanced as additional degrees, particularly professional degrees, are earned.

College students are often on their own for the first time in their lives and are faced with the daunting task of managing their finances, developing and keeping a budget, and balancing a checkbook. Budgeting your financial resources is important in maintaining a reasonable standard of living. If you never have enough money, it can be quite frustrating. This is a good time to learn to develop a budget that shows your income and expenses so that you don't find yourself short of cash, in debt, and unable to pay your bills. You also need to develop a plan for financing your education so that you don't encounter unexpected financial problems which may cause you to withdraw from the university.

Many people with responsible jobs live paycheck-to-paycheck and rarely save any money. To avoid this situation, sound financial planning is advised. Why not start now? Learning to manage your finances is important so that when you graduate, you will already know how to budget properly and will be a step ahead of many other new professionals entering the work force.

Developing a Budget

The best place to start is preparing a budget plan which you can follow for a month. Know how much money you have coming in from all sources (income) for a month, and be familiar with your fixed and anticipated expenses. Fixed expenses are items such as rent, your car payment, insurance, food, and gasoline for commuting to campus. Anticipated expenses include entertainment, new clothing, and purchases like a beeper or a cellular phone.

From *The Freshman Year: Making the Most of College* by Glenda A. Belote and Larry W. Lunsford. © 1998 by Kendall/Hunt Publishing Company. Used by permission.

A good budget plan will include allocating some money to open a savings account or to invest. A "nest egg" could come in handy in an emergency situation when unexpected and unavoidable expenses arise. In these situations, you can use your savings to make payments instead of drawing from money needed for your ongoing monthly expenses.

A key item in developing a budget is accepting that you will have to monitor and probably reduce your spending. Monthly budgets which end in the "red" aren't allowed! If you don't want to decrease your level of spending, then you must find ways to increase your income.

Learning to manage your money and get more out of it is not only easy, it is fun as well. Items to consider in developing an understanding of your financial circumstances and financial management needs include knowledge of checking accounts and credit cards, paying bills on time, employment, savings and investments, and buying wisely.

Complete Exercise 1: Developing a Budget for an indepth look at how your expenses add up.

Checking Accounts

Items to Consider When You Compare Banks:

- *Do they offer free checking?*
- *Are there monthly service fees?*
- *Do they cover your account when you overdraw, and if so, what fee do they charge?*
- *Do they offer an ATM card, and if so, is there a monthly service fee?*
- *If they provide an ATM card, are you charged a fee each time you use the card (not only at the bank that issued the card but at other ATM machines as well)?*
- *Do you have to maintain a monthly minimum balance, and if you don't, what is the penalty fee?*
- *What are the hidden fees the bank may charge for the "privilege" of having your business?*

Banks are as different as their names and have different ways of serving their customers. When you open a checking account, shop around for the best deal. Don't forget to check on the services offered at other financial institutions, including credit unions and savings and loan organizations. Financial companies are very competitive and offer varying deals to attract customers.

Once you have selected a bank and opened a checking account, set up your checkbook. Be sure to keep your checkbook balanced by adding all deposits and subtracting expenses as you write checks. Don't wait until your monthly bank statement arrives to learn that your account balance has dwindled to little or nothing!

Does your bank cover overdrawn checks? Most banks do not, unless you have savings to cover the amount in question. "Bounced checks" are likely to result in charges from both your bank and the business that accepted your check. The business may turn you over to a collection agency to recover their money if the amount of the check is large. Bouncing checks can also affect your credit rating. When you attempt to make a major purchase such as a car or house, or even apply for a credit card, a bad credit rating could result in your not getting approved.

Once your monthly bank statement arrives, be sure to reconcile your account to the proper balance. This means reviewing every item on the bank statement and matching it against every item in your checkbook. Even if you're a penny off, accept the challenge of locating the mistake and correcting it. You'll actually feel good about it once you're done, although the exercise may sometimes be frustrating and time-consuming.

Credit Cards

> **Items to Consider in Choosing a Credit Card:**
>
> - *Shop around for the best deal, including the lowest interest charged. Some cards have an annual fee and some do not.*
>
> - *Why pay an annual fee if you don't have to? The credit card companies are competitive, and you can often negotiate better deals with banks or credit unions than those used in their advertisements.*
>
> - *Consider getting a credit card that is also an ATM or a debit card; your purchases will be automatically deducted from your checking or savings account. (Be sure to write these cash charges down and keep your balances current and accurate.)*

Credit card debt is at the highest level it has ever been in this country. The average debt on major credit cards among consumers between the ages of 20 and 30 years old has nearly tripled since 1990. If you don't want to become part of that statistic, be wary of credit cards. College students are easy targets for companies that use promotional gimmicks to get you to apply for their cards.

Cards are easy to obtain and you get a "free" t-shirt or a coffee mug besides! Did you ever ask yourself why credit card companies are so anxious to have your business? The answer is simple: college students are more likely than many other segments of the population to **use** their credit cards. College students, you included, frequently have limited financial resources coupled with a strong consumer instinct. Students like to buy things. Without cash, the easiest way to make a purchase is with a credit card!

There are good and bad reasons for having credit cards. Two good reasons are that they are safer to carry than huge amounts of cash when making purchases, and they enable you to establish a credit history. On the flip side, however, credit cards are easy to use, and you may find that you've made too many purchases, resulting in large balances and heavy debt. Once your balances grow too large, meeting the minimum payments becomes difficult. At this point, many students begin working extra hours and cutting classes; they may even drop out of school or find they are dismissed because of poor grades.

A word to the wise: if you can't live without one, have one major credit card and pay off your balance each time you receive your bill. The average balance for a college student's credit card is $2,400! The interest rate on some cards is higher than the minimum payment. Some people find it impossible to pay off their balances because interest rates are so high. Remember that interest starts accumulating immediately for new purchases when you carry forward a previous balance. It is also important that you become familiar with the grace period that your credit card company allows for payments.

If you find that you are in credit card debt, discuss the situation with your financial institution and arrange payments that meet your budget. The company may not be pleased with this course of action, but they'd rather have some payment than none at all, and they certainly don't want you to file for bankruptcy.

Bankruptcy should be the last resort for anyone to take, particularly for a college student. In 1996, approximately one million people filed for personal bankruptcy in the United States. For the rest of your life, filing for bankruptcy could return to haunt you when you attempt to make major purchases or receive credit. Seek credit counseling before you take this drastic step!

If you believe that you absolutely need a credit card, go ahead and get one, but be honest with yourself about why you want that little piece of plastic. If you manage well with paying cash or writing checks for your purchases, stay away from credit cards for the present.

Pay Bills on Time

College students accumulate many types of bills, including credit card charges, college tuition and book costs, cellular phones and beepers, car loans, and (if you live in an apartment instead of home) rent, utility, and phone payments. Be sure to include all of your monthly expenses in the budget that you develop.

Most monthly bills list the minimum payment due as well as the payment due date. If you miss the payment deadline, late charges are applied. You'll also be penalized if you don't make the minimum payment. Always try to pay the full balance of each bill or pay more than the minimum amount due (if you can't pay the balance). This will help you avoid those late charges or interest payments.

Be aware that late payments may also affect your credit rating. Credit card companies and banks where you have loans often report consistent late payments or other payment problems to their credit agencies. This is why it is important to make payments on time or discuss your payment problems with your financial institution.

Increasing Your Income

There are various ways for you to increase your income to assist you in meeting ongoing expenses and avoiding debt. Foremost among the recommendations is a part-time job. Before you commit to a job, make sure that you weigh carefully the demands of working. Be sure it doesn't interfere with your real reason for being here: academics. Many students find it necessary to work in order to attend college. Successful students recognize that the emphasis must remain on attending classes and allowing adequate study time.

Many students find it more beneficial and enjoyable to work on campus rather than in the community. Various jobs are available throughout campus. These positions can be found through personal contacts or through postings at Career Services. Some students are eligible for College Work Study positions. These positions are part of financial aid award through the Financial Aid Office.

For positions off campus, students can use personal contacts (family, family friends, and former employers), apply in person at various businesses, or visit the university's Career Services Office to peruse listings for part-time employment.

Remember that the purpose of working part-time is to earn money while you're getting an education. A part-time job should **never** interfere with your education.

Another way to increase your income is borrowing money; however, this raises your debt and requires repayment. A large purchase, a car for example, may require that you borrow money. The monthly payment for the loan must be added to your budget expenses.

Investments or interest on savings or other accounts represent an additional source of income. If your financial situation allows you to begin making personal investments in stocks, mutual funds, or long-term savings plans, be sure to get

> ### Key Items to Remember:
> - *Pay bills on time!*
> - *Pay the full balance if possible, and if not, pay the minimum amount due.*
> - *If you have trouble making payments, discuss your situation with your financial institution.*
> - *Seek credit counseling.*

good advice and become an educated consumer. This will enable you to begin making sound investments now and hopefully receive a good return on your money for years to come.

Additional monies may also be available through financial aid, scholarships, or other grants if you are eligible. Applications as well as information for various forms of aid and assistance are available in the Financial Aid Office. You can also check with the librarian at the Reference Desk in the library, who can direct you to more information regarding various scholarships and grants. Other forms of aid are available through scholarships awarded by community or social agencies. Information can be located through a web search or Financial Aid. Be careful to read all eligibility and other documentation carefully and meet application deadlines.

Shop Wisely

Comparison shopping is another way to save your money. Don't you visit several car dealerships if you are going to buy a new car, so that you can get the best deal and save money? You should do the same with smaller purchases. Look for bargains and wait for sales. Some businesses will even negotiate the price of high-ticket items such as audio equipment, phones, and clothing because these items typically have a high price mark-up.

Sometimes it is better to pay a little more for a better quality item than to save some money on something that will not last as long. In the long run, you can save money by purchasing a better product because the cheaper item is more likely to require repairs or need replacement sooner.

Key Items to Remember:

- *Consider a part-time job to increase your income, but make sure your part-time job doesn't interfere with academics.*
- *Look for a part-time job on campus.*
- *Check your eligibility for the College Work Study Program in the Financial Aid Office.*
- *Apply for financial aid, scholarships, or grants to increase your income.*
- *If your finances permit, consider investments and other savings programs.*

It is a good practice to pay cash for your purchases. If you charge small items and don't pay the balance when you receive your bill, you will probably make interest and finance payments. That means you will pay more for the charged merchandise. Keep the receipts for your purchases in case there is a question about your bill or you need to return them. Some stores will not allow exchanges or refunds without a receipt.

Another way to save on purchases is to use coupons or take advantage of store promotions. If you plan to make a major purchase, ask the store management when the item may go on sale. If you can wait until the sale, you will save money. When making large purchases, examine your budget first and determine whether or not you can afford the purchase. If the expenditure puts you in a situation where your expenses exceed your income, delay the purchase. You could even begin a small weekly or monthly savings plan to cover expenses associated with a large purchase.

Getting Out of Debt

You say that you've tried everything and you still can't get out of debt? There is always a solution! Here are a few recommendations frequently suggested by the "experts" on money and debt management:

- Use savings or cash to reduce or eliminate debt, but do not exhaust your entire savings in case you have a severe emergency and need immediate cash.
- Comparison shop for banks that offer better checking and ATM options and switch your account.
- Locate a better credit card deal and transfer your balances to the lower-interest card.
- Cut up and discard the credit cards once the balances are transferred to the new card.
- Carry only one credit card and don't use it unless absolutely necessary!
- Seek credit counseling. Various resources are available in the community which offer advice on managing finances and debt.
- Check the Yellow Pages or contact the State Consumer Protection Agency or local Chamber of Commerce for consumer counseling recommendations. At the university, you can check with the Financial Aid Office or Counseling and Psychological Services for community referrals.

Filing for bankruptcy should be your last re-sort. Remember that this course of action re-mains a part of your credit history forever and may have a negative impact on your future financial transactions.

> **Key Items to Remember:**
> - *Comparison shop, look for bargains, and negotiate.*
> - *Pay cash for purchases.*
> - *Keep receipts for purchases.*
> - *Wait for sales.*
> - *Use coupons and other promotions.*
> - *Buy quality items.*

Summary

Most individuals work about 40 years in the course of their lifetime. At an annual average salary of $30,000, that means the "average" person will make more than $1,000,000 in his or her career. How will you spend all of that money?

Efficient and proper financial planning and management reduces stress and enables individuals to enjoy a better quality of life. Developing and following a budget, being knowledgeable about sound financial management, and learning and understanding the technicalities of finances can be invaluable for you in college and for the rest of your life.

Reflect and Apply

Create a budget for your friend Sean by completing Exercise 2. Consider whether Sean has realistic expectations by comparing his expenses to his income. Use what you learned in this chapter to give Sean helpful detailed advice.

Name: _____ Date: _____

■ Exercise 1: Developing a Budget

Category	$
Food: groceries	_____
Food: eating out, vending machines	_____
Non-food groceries (e.g., cleaning supplies, laundry detergent, etc.)	_____
Residence (dorm, apartment, etc.)	
Rent	_____
Clothing and shoes	_____
Utilities (electric, water, gas)	_____
Telephone	_____
Garbage pickup	_____
Dry cleaning/laundromat	_____
Transportation (e.g., bus pass, car, auto insurance, gasoline, auto repair, parking costs, oil change and maintenance, tag)	_____
Personal care (e.g., hair salons)	_____
Health-related (e.g., medicine, membership at a physical fitness center, doctor and dentist visits, glasses/contacts, etc.)	
Newspaper/magazines	_____
Dues	_____
Postage	_____
Household "stuff" (e.g., furniture, cookware, repairs needed for residence, decorations, etc.)	
Entertainment (getting together where you live or going somewhere else, movie rental, purchasing CDs, etc.)	_____
OTHER	
Tuition, books, etc.	_____
Child care	_____
Insurance (other than car)	_____
Taxes	_____
List "other" items not mentioned	
1. _____	_____
2. _____	_____
3. _____	_____
4. _____	_____
Total for **OTHER**	
GRAND TOTAL	_____

Name: _____ Date: _____

Exercise 2: Developing a Budget

Your task in this exercise is to develop a budget for Sean, one of your classmates. This exercise can be done individually or in small groups. Each group should select a spokesperson to present the group's budget to the class. The time limit is twenty minutes.

The following are Sean's financial conditions for each month:

- A place to live. He doesn't like roommates.
- Three meals a day.
- He has an old car that is paid for and gets 12 miles per gallon.
- His car insurance is $80 per month.
- He works 25 hours per week at $6.00 per hour. He gets paid every Friday.
- He has a school loan payment of $50 per month.
- He likes to party.
- He belongs to a health club. Dues are $50 per month.
- He goes out to eat at least three times per week.
- His girlfriend goes to school 500 miles away. He calls her twice a week.
- His job is 10 miles from school. He lives midway between school and work.
- His mom and dad give him money about every three months, usually $150 to $200.
- He has two credit cards with a combined balance of $300.
- He goes to a sporting event or a movie about once every two weeks.

CHAPTER 14
Planning for a Career

Making Career Decisions[1]

Making career decisions is a lifelong task. You have already begun the process by deciding to go to college. The courses you take, your choice of major, the work experience you accumulate, the clubs and groups you join, and the people you meet may influence the career decisions you make in your lifetime.

Chances are you are already thinking about your choice of major and related career options. Don't be alarmed if you feel uncertain or have no ideas about your career plans. Now is the time to question, explore, and wonder. It can be reassuring to know that many sources of career information and systems of career decision-making already exist to help you in this task.

Before we get into a discussion of what goes into career decision-making, let's explore some popular myths that might sabotage your efforts to make informed decisions.

Career Myths

1. "I don't need to think about my career now; I'm just starting college."
   Graduation may be years away—but the process of career-planning has already begun. Knowing who you are and what you are looking for will better enable you to find satisfying career options. And self-assessment takes time!

2. "I want to take **THAT TEST** that will tell me what I should be."
   There is **NO** test that will tell you what you should be or what career you should follow. Different types of career assessments can be useful in gathering information about you and relating it to career clusters. Test results often help you to put information in order so you can verify or challenge your ideas. These assessments are tools; the decision is yours.

3. "I'll pursue whatever career is in demand."
   Knowing what's "hot" in the job market is important information, but not the only information you need to make a decision. Without knowing about your own interests and skills, you may choose a career that's available, but later you may find you are not suited for it.

---

[1]From *The Freshman Year: Making the Most of College* by Glenda A. Belote and Larry W. Lunsford © 1998 by Kendall/Hunt Publishing Company. Used by permission.

4. "I need to find the perfect career."
   There is no "perfect" career. What you will discover is that there are several ways you can find a meaningful career. No one gets 100 percent of what she wants. There is usually compromise. Your task is to identify what you want and need from your career, put these features into priority, and use this information as a guide in making your career decisions.

5. "If I make the wrong decision, I'll be stuck forever."
   Fear of making the wrong decision can prevent you from making *any* decision. When making career decisions, you'll find that nothing is written in stone. Few people head into one career and stay there for their whole working lives. The U.S. Bureau of Labor Statistics estimates that the average worker will change careers five times during a work life.

6. "Everyone knows what major/career they want but me."
   It may seem like everyone is decided but you. However, statistics show that most students change majors (and career plans) several times while in college. It is better to recognize that you are undecided, and go about finding the necessary information to make your decisions, than to assume you have it all figured out and never evaluate your plan.

Career/Life Planning Process

How do you get started with career planning? Let's begin with a definition of the Career/Life Planning Process, which involves three components:

Career/Life

Your career decisions will include more than which job to take upon graduation. Your career is the sum of all the work experiences you will have. The work you choose to pursue will have a direct impact on the way you live your life. Your career decisions cannot be made in a vacuum, but should be made within the context of your lifestyle preferences.

Planning

Webster defines planning as "formulating a program to accomplish or attain something." It is purposeful and done ahead of time. Therefore, career/life planning implies setting short- and long-range goals about your work and lifestyle with specific objectives that will help you meet them.

Process

Your career plan will not be the result of one decision you make, but rather a series of decisions throughout your lifetime. You will go through the steps in career planning several times because as you continue to grow and develop as a person, your interests, skills, and values will also change. The job market definitely changes, sometimes beyond your control. So "process" implies a dynamic aspect of developing satisfying and successful career and life plans.

The whole process might seem overwhelming, but the career/life planning process can be broken down into three basic steps with specific tasks to accomplish. The following diagram is a picture of this process:

Step One: Understanding Yourself Requires Self-Assessment

Knowing about yourself is the basis of career decision-making. This includes identifying your interests—what you like and dislike; your skills—what you do well; your values—what is important to you about your work; and your personality traits or characteristics—how you behave as a person.

The exercises at the end of the chapter help you to start the self-assessment process.

1. Identify Your Interests and Accomplishments

Begin by identifying your interests. If you find a career that falls within your interests you are more likely to enjoy your work. Turn to Exercise 1 and complete the questions to identify your interests. A good method for analyzing what you have already done is to consider your accomplishments. These experiences do not have to be grand, such as a cure for cancer or the answer to world peace, or fit anyone else's definition of accomplishment. The accomplishments should be something you feel good about from your life (college, work, leisure, relationships). Complete the self assessment Exercise 2 to identify your accomplishments. These are usually experiences that presented a challenge and satisfaction in achieving, such as:

- passing chemistry
- running a 10K race
- volunteering in a nursing home
- researching the family tree
- being elected Student Body President

2. Analyze Your Skills and Abilities

Each of your accomplishments holds within it a key to your skills and abilities. Also, what you value as accomplishments, reflects the skills and abilities you value and may like to explore further. For example, if you list one of your accomplishments as helping another person, you likely place a high value on helping others. Helping professions are widely varied, but realising that you might draw enjoyment and satisfaction out of a helping career can put you one step closer to finding a career that might suit you. Now, complete Exercise 3. Identify your Skills.

3. Define Your Values

Values identify what is important to you. Work values describe what is important about the work you do. It is useful to identify values when considering possible careers because they may tell you about work-related needs, motivators, and long-term satisfaction. Complete the values checklist in Exercise 4 to explore your values.

Do you notice a pattern or relationship among your interests, skills, values, and personality traits? What implications might these similarities have on careers that might be interesting to you? Share your insights with someone who knows you and compare notes.

Learn to evaluate all of your experiences—work, school, and hobbies—on a regular basis. This process can turn up characteristics you might find satisfying in your future career. And remember, identifying what you don't want can be as helpful as finding what you do want. Both help define what you are looking for.

4. Measure Your Personality Traits

Take a further look into your personality by completing Exercise 5: Coming Alive from 9 to 5. This informal inventory begins to connect your interests to occupations.

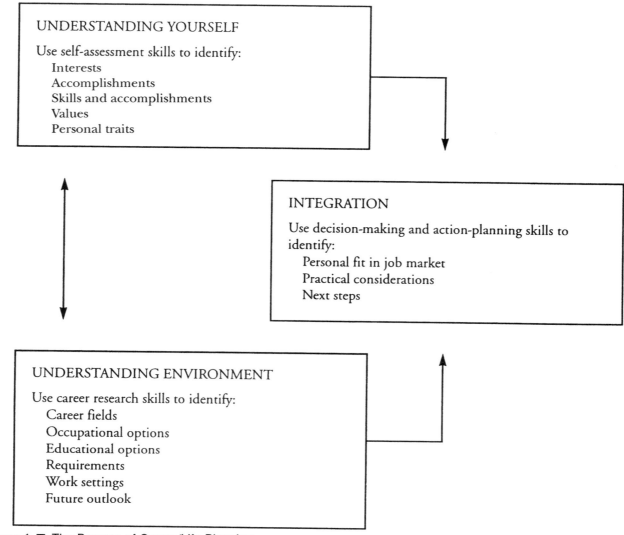

Figure 1 ■ The Process of Career/Life Planning

■ Step Two: Conducting Career Research

When considering a career option, careful research into careers and specific occupations will help you find out:

- ■ Is there a cluster of occupations for the career you are interested in?
- ■ What occupations or jobs interest or suit you from that cluster?
- ■ What are the specific duties of the job?
- ■ What pay and benefits does the job offer?
- ■ What is the employment outlook for this occupation?
- ■ What education or training is necessary to qualify for the job?

Three sources of career information include: the career services office at your college, the Internet, and personal interviews.

A. Career Services

Your campus Career Service office provides career advising, career reference materials, employer literature, and job search information. Computerized career guidance programs, such as SIGI Plus, DISCOVER, or CHOICES, are excellent tools for self-assessment and career exploration. Services might also be available for student employment, internships, resume writing, interview preparation, and Internet searches.

B. Career Resources on the Web

Internet sites are a good resource for finding up to date information on occupations, employment opportunities, and education. The resources below will only get you started. If you are interested in researching career information on the web, the resources are seemingly endless.

Human Resources Development Canada

Publishes Jobboom a website and pamphlet that includes the top 100 internet sites for learning and employment.
http://www.jobboom.com/conseils/top-100.html

Job Futures Canada

Job Futures is also a Human Resources Canada website. It provides details on the current labour market in Canada, as well as forecasts and details organized by occupation.
www.jobfutures.ca

Work Futures British Columbia Outlooks

This site is specific to British Columbia. Search by occupation to find detailed career information and income forecasts.
http://www.workfutures.bc.ca

Work Destinations

The Work Destinations site provides detailed occupational information, including work conditions, placement, and recruitment, for Canadians who want to work in another province or territory.
http://www.workdestinations.ca

EntreWorld

This site is for all of you entrepreneurs out there. It is a comprehensive guide to setting up your own business that tells both the good and the bad of working for yourself.
http://www.EntreWorld.org/

C. Informational Interviewing

Another way to get information is to talk to people about their jobs. This can be on a casual basis, such as talking with family and friends, or it can be done in a formal way by contacting experienced professionals in your field of interest and scheduling an appointment to meet with them. Either way, you are interviewing for information. This technique is an excellent way to get inside information that might not be available in written sources. It also helps you to develop your communication skills and a professional network, which you will need in your future career. Try the following exercise to gather career information and practice your interviewing skills.

Investigate careers on the web, in career services or by conducting a personal interview. As you conduct your research complete Exercise 6. Career Write-Up one and two.

Step Three: Integration Requires Decision-Making and Action Planning[2]

This is probably the most important step because integration requires taking what you know about yourself and putting it together with the reality of the work world. Complete Exercise 7 to begin matching your personal and occupational information from steps one and two. In doing so, you begin to identify and evaluate career options that are practical for you. Consider the following questions:

- What career fields am I interested in?
- What specific occupations are found in these career fields?
- What type of preparation is needed for these jobs?
- What college, university or training program offers these programs of study?
- Do I have the academic strengths to pursue that major?
- What challenges might be presented in the job market (competition, relocation)?
- Do I have the time, money, and support resources to pursue these options?
- What else do I need to know in order to identify my career objective?

Gathering and evaluating information is a critical part of choosing a major and making career plans.

Experience

After you have gathered substantial information, the next thing to do is test your ideas through some first-hand experience. Many people find they learn best by doing; this is described as experiential learning. Experiential learning programs include Cooperative Education, Internships, and career-related volunteer work. Work experience helps you get a first-hand look at your intended career field. This realworld opportunity will allow you to develop experience for your resume, meet employers, apply what you are learning in the classroom, and evaluate the fit of this career. Participation in experiential learning programs is usually competitive, and requires planning. Think about making it part of your college agenda. Contact the Career Service office at your college for more information.

Summary

As you can see, there are many career-planning tasks you can be working on during your first year. Remember the three steps in the process: Self-Assessment, Career Research, and Decision Making/Action Planning. These exercises will serve as a handy guide and reminder of career-related things to do during your college program. It also provides suggestions for making and implementing your career plans for the future. Start using it!

---

[2] From *The Freshman Year: Making the Most of College* by Glenda A. Belote and Larry W. Lunsford. © 1998 by Kendall/Hunt Publishing Company. Used by permission.

Name: _____ Date: _____

Exercise 1: Identify Your Interests

By answering the questions below you will start to highlight activities you enjoy.

1. What subjects do you like?

2. What books or magazines do you read?

3. What do you like to do for fun? What do you do in your spare time?

4. What jobs have you had? What did you like or dislike about them? (Remember to include volunteer work.)

5. Based on your responses, write a short statement about the things you like to do, and why. What types of activities are included or excluded?

Name: _____ Date: _____

Exercise 2: Accomplishments

Identify five accomplishments. Write a short description of each, including the situation, your actions, and the outcome. What challenges did you face? How did you overcome them?

1. going back to school (post secondary) started making 30k almost right out of high school was used to the money and lifestyle but knew

2.

3.

4.

5.

Name: _____ Date: _____

■ Exercise 3: Analyze Your Skills and Abilities

Now, select three of your accomplishments. Then answer the following questions regarding each accomplishment. What you will find is a window into your abilities.

- ■ What skills did you use?

- ■ How did you interact with people?

- ■ Did you work alone or with others?

- ■ Did it require you to be a leader or team member?

- ■ How did you deal with data, ideas, and/or things?

- ■ Which did you enjoy the most?

- ■ What was most difficult?

- ■ What was most rewarding?

- ■ How much structure was involved?

- ■ Summarize the skills and abilities represented in your answers above.

- What interests are represented? Art, music, sports, travel, animals, science, etc.?

- After completing the values checklist, consider what values are represented? Helping society, competition, influencing people, fame, self-expression, excitement, etc.?

Name: _____ Date: _____

Exercise 4: Values Checklist

Following is a partial list of work values, with an example of each. Read the list and examples of each value when applied to work settings. Rate each value according to the scale below.

Rate each work value: V if it is very important; S if it is somewhat important; or N if it is not important.

Adventure	S	take risks in work
Creativity	S	developing new ideas or things
Authority	S	being in charge
Altruism	V	helping others
Independence	V	plan own work schedule/work without close supervision
Travel	S	opportunities to travel on the job
Prestige	S	be recognized and respected for the work I do
Stability	S	keep a routine without surprises
Variety	V	experience change and enjoy different tasks
Family	V	have time and energy to spend with family
Teamwork	V	work as a member of a team
Learning	S	opportunity to learn new skills and apply them on the job
Challenge	V	use your skills and abilities to solve complex problems
Advancement	V	opportunity for promotion
Leisure	V	have time out of work to pursue other interests
Wealth	S	have a high income

Of course, just identifying what you want is not realistic. There is no guarantee that you will be able to satisfy all of the values that are very important to you. Compromise will be a necessity. From your list of Very Important values, choose five that you believe are most important (probably things you will not be able to live without). Now prioritize these five values on the list below.

1. FAMILY
2. LEISURE
3. INDEPENDENCE
4. ALTRUISM
5. TEAMWORK

Name: _____ Date: _____

Exercise 5: Coming Alive from Nine to Five[3]

Personality Mosaic

DIRECTIONS:
Circle the numbers of statements that clearly feel like something you might say or do or think—something that feels like you.

1. It's important for me to have a strong, agile body.
2. I need to understand things thoroughly.
3. Music, color, beauty of any kind can really affect my moods.
4. People enrich my life and give it meaning.
5. I have confidence in myself that I can make things happen.
6. I appreciate clear directions so I know exactly what to do.
7. I can usually carry/build/fix things myself.
8. I can get absorbed for hours in thinking something out.
9. I appreciate beautiful surroundings; color and design mean a lot to me.
10. I love company.
11. I enjoy competing.
12. I need to get my surroundings in order before I start a project.
13. I enjoy making things with my hands.
14. It's satisfying to explore new ideas.
15. I always seem to be looking for new ways to express my creativity.
16. I value being able to share personal concerns with people.
17. Being a key person in a group is very satisfying to me.
18. I take pride in being very careful about all the details of my work.
19. I don't mind getting my hands dirty.
20. I see education as a lifelong process of developing and sharpening my mind.
21. I love to dress in unusual ways, to try new colors and styles.
22. I can often sense when a person needs to talk to someone.
23. I enjoy getting people organized and on the move.
24. A good routine helps me get the job done.
25. I like to buy sensible things I can make or work on myself.
26. Sometimes I can sit for long periods of time and work on puzzles or read or just think about life.

Source: Adapted by UCLA Career Planning Center from *Coming Alive From Nine to Five* by B. N. Michelozzi, Mayfield Publishing Company.

[3]From *The Essential Handbook for Academic Success Skills* by California University Regents. Copyright © 1998 by Kendall/Hunt Publishing Company. Used by permission.

27. I have a great imagination.
28. It makes me feel good to take care of people.
29. I like to have people rely on me to get the job done.
30. I'm satisfied knowing that I've done an assignment carefully and completely.
31. I'd rather be on my own doing practical, hands-on activities.
32. I'm eager to read about any subject that arouses my curiosity.
33. I love to try creative new ideas.
34. If I have a problem with someone, I prefer to talk it out and resolve it.
35. To be successful, it's important to aim high.
36. I prefer being in a position where I don't have to take responsibility for decisions.
37. I don't enjoy spending a lot of time discussing things. What's right is right.
38. I need to analyze a problem pretty thoroughly before I act on it.
39. I like to rearrange my surroundings to make them unique and different.
40. When I feel down, I find a friend to talk to.
41. After I suggest a plan, I prefer to let others take care of the details.
42. I'm usually content where I am.
43. It's invigorating to do things outdoors.
44. I keep asking why.
45. I like my work to be an expression of my moods and feelings.
46. I like to find ways to help people care more for each other.
47. It's exciting to take part in important decisions.
48. I'm always glad to have someone else take charge.
49. I like my surroundings to be plain and practical.
50. I need to stay with a problem until I figure out an answer.
51. The beauty of nature touches something deep inside me.
52. Close relationships are important to me.
53. Promotion and advancement are important to me.
54. Efficiency, for me, means doing a set amount carefully each day.
55. A strong system of law and order is important to prevent chaos.
56. Thought-provoking books always broaden my perspective.
57. I look forward to seeing art shows, plays, and good films.
58. I haven't seen you for so long; I'd love to know how you're doing.
59. It's exciting to influence people.
60. When I say I'll do it, I follow through on every detail.

61. Good, hard physical work never hurt anyone.
62. I'd like to learn all there is to know about subjects that interest me.
63. I don't want to be like everyone else; I like to do things differently.
64. Tell me how I can help you.
65. I'm willing to take some risks to get ahead.
66. I like exact directions and clear rules when I start something new.
67. The first thing I look for in a car is a well-built engine.
68. Those people are intellectually stimulating.
69. When I'm creating, I tend to let everything else go.
70. I feel concerned that so many people in our society need help.
71. It's fun to get ideas across to people.
72. I hate it when they keep changing the system just when I get it down.
73. I usually know how to take care of things in an emergency.
74. Just reading about those new discoveries is exciting.
75. I like to create happenings.
76. I often go out of my way to pay attention to people who seem lonely and friendless.
77. I love to bargain.
78. I don't like to do things unless I'm sure they're approved.
79. Sports are important in building strong bodies.
80. I've always been curious about the way nature works.
81. It's fun to be in a mood to try or do something unusual.
82. I believe that people are basically good.
83. If I don't make it the first time, I usually bounce back with energy and enthusiasm.
84. I appreciate knowing exactly what people expect of me.
85. I like to take things apart to see if I can fix them.
86. Don't get excited. We can think it out and plan the right move logically.
87. It would be hard to imagine my life without beauty around me.
88. People often seem to tell me their problems.
89. I can usually connect with people who get me in touch with a network of resources.
90. I don't need much to be happy.

Name: _____ Date: _____

Exercise 6: How to Find a Major[4]

Scoring Your Answers

To score, circle the same numbers below that you circled on the exercise:

R	I	A	S	E	C
(1)	2	3	(4)	(5)	6
(7)	(8)	(9)	10	11	(12)
13	(14)	(15)	16	(17)	(18)
19	(20)	21	(22)	23	24
25	(26)	(27)	(28)	(29)	(30)
31	(32)	(33)	(34)	35	36
37	38	39	40	41	(42)
(43)	(44)	45	(46)	47	48
49	(50)	(51)	52	53	(54)
(55)	(56)	(57)	(58)	(59)	(60)
(61)	62	63	(64)	(65)	(66)
67	(68)	(69)	70	(71)	72
(73)	74	(75)	76	77	78
(79)	(80)	(81)	(82)	(83)	(84)
(85)	(86)	(87)	(88)	(89)	(90)

Now add up the number of circles in each column:

R __8__ I __12__ A __10__ S __9__ E __8__ C __9__ TOTALS

Which are your three highest scores:

1st ____I____

2nd ____A____

3rd ____S & C____

---

[4]From *The Essential Handbook for Academic Success Skills* by California University Regents. Copyright © 1998 by Kendall/Hunt Publishing Company. Used by permission.

Name: _____ Date: _____

■ Dimensional Analysis

Holland's Group	Characteristic Interests	Characteristic Personal Traits	Characteristic Occupations
Realistic (R)	Activities that involve the precise, ordered use of objects, tools, machines and animals and includes agricultural, electrical, manual, physical and mechanical things and activities. Example: Working on cars.	Present-Oriented Thing-Oriented (rather than people or data) Conforming Practical Shy	Engineering Skilled Trades Agricultural and Technical Occupations
Investigative (I)	Activities that involve the exploration and examination of physical, biological and cultural things to understand and control them: sometimes includes scientific and mathematical activities. Example: Reading fiction	Analytical and Abstract Rational Curious Intellectual Introverted	Scientific, Analytical and some Technical Occupations
Artistic (A)	Activities that involve the use of physical, verbal or human materials to create art forms or products; includes activities and things related to language, art, music, drama and writing Example: Listening to music	Creative Expressive Rely on Feelings Imagination Non-Conforming Idealistic	Musical Artistic Literary and Dramatic Occupations
Social (S)	Activities that involve interaction with other people for enjoyment or to inform, train, develop, cure and educate. Example: Entertaining guests	Sensitive to needs of others Friendly Outgoing Persuasive Tactful	Teaching Ministry Social Welfare and other "Helping People" Occupations
Enterprising (E)	Activities that involve interaction with other people to reach organizational goals or economic gain; leadership, interpersonal and persuasive activities included. Example: Working for a community action or political organization	Aggressive/Assertive Self-Confident Ambitious Sociable Persuasive	Sales Supervisory and Leadership Occupations
Conventional (C)	Activities that involve the precise, ordered use of data, e.g., keeping records, filing materials, organizing numerical and written data, clerical, computational and business. Example: Working as a treasurer for a political campaign	Practical Conforming Efficient/Accurate Orderly Set in Ways	Accounting Computational Secretarial and Clerical Occupations

Name: _____ Date: _____

■ Exercise 7: Career Write-Up A[5]

Sources used _____

Job title _____

Nature of Work

Working Conditions

Employment (Where are the jobs?)

Training, Qualifications, and Advancement

Job Outlook

Earnings

Related Occupations

---

[5]From *The Essential Handbook for Academic Success Skills* by California University Regents. Copyright © 1998 by Kendall/Hunt Publishing Company. Used by permission.

Name: _____ Date: _____

■ Exercise 7: Career Write-Up B

Sources used _____

Job title _____

Nature of Work

Working Conditions

Employment (Where are the jobs?)

Training, Qualifications, and Advancement

Job Outlook

Earnings

Related Occupations

Name: _____ Date: _____

 # Exercise 8: Matching Personal and Occupational Information[6]

DIRECTIONS: Write the titles of two occupations you've explored (A and B) at the top of the columns. Read each statement under self-awareness. If the statement is correct for either or both occupations put a check on the line under that occupation. If neither occupation matches your personal traits put a check on the line under neither.

Self-Awareness	Occupation A	Occupation B
Interests My personal interests seem to match the interest areas related to this occupation.	_____	_____
Skills/Abilities I have the abilities that this occupation requires.	_____	_____
My plans for future education or training are at least equal to the amount and type this occupation requires.	_____	_____
Values (What's important to me) The employment outlook for this occupation gives me the job security I need.	_____	_____
The chances for advancement in this occupation are good enough to satisfy me.	_____	_____
The pay range in this occupation is high enough to satisfy me.	_____	_____
Patterns My work patterns fit in with the working conditions typical of this occupation.	_____	_____
Personality My personality seems to be right for this occupation and I can be myself on the job.	_____	_____

---

[6] From *The Essential Handbook for Academic Success Skills* by California University Regents. Copyright © 1998 by Kendall/Hunt Publishing Company. Used by permission.